Jad Adams is a writer and  include *Madder Music, Stron* *Poet and Decadent* (I.B.Tauri: praise in Britain and the US/ Tony Benn and of the Nehru-Gandhi dynasty. He lives in London and on the Greek island of Leros.

'An extraordinary polymath [Adams] is a master of a classically lucid style enlivened by dashes of the colloquial and by entertaining detail . . . *Hideous Absinthe* is a model of how to convey the exhilaration of an exciting subject without getting all melodramatic . . . a most beguiling book.'   *Spectator*

'A splendidly detailed examination of the subject . . . From Adams' book it is clear that the drink was neither as inspirational, nor as exotically bad for you as writers and artists liked to claim.'   *The Times*

'In this entertaining history Jad Adams traces the emerald drink's astonishing popularity . . . a diligent social historian.'   *Observer*

'Jad Adams makes an interesting tale out of this demonised drink.'
                                                                Sunday Telegraph

'Considering myself a bit of an expert, I was expecting when I opened Jad Adams' book, to read a lot of stuff I already knew . . . how much more I had to learn. Adams is clearly the man for the job. He has a real feel for the period and there is a wealth of detail and insight here.'
                                                        Tom Hodgkinson, *Guardian*

'This book is as titillating as it is sobering.'   *New York Times*

'Well researched, often poignant, and always fascinating biography of a subject whose history, rather like the liqueur itself when added to seven parts water, has often been clouded and opaque.'   *The Lancet*

'Hideous Absinthe is a careful and considered account of a drink whose reputation has always exceeded its consumption . . . even specialists will learn something from this balanced and informative account.'
                                                New England Journal of Medicine

'Marvellously entertaining'   *New York Press*

Tauris Parke Paperbacks is an imprint of I.B.Tauris. It is dedicated to publishing books in accessible paperback editions for the serious general reader within a wide range of categories, including biography, history, travel and the ancient world. The list includes select, critically acclaimed works of top quality writing by distinguished authors that continue to challenge, to inform and to inspire. These are books that possess those subtle but intrinsic elements that mark them out as something exceptional.

The Colophon of Tauris Parke Paperbacks is a representation of the ancient Egyptian ibis, sacred to the god Thoth, who was himself often depicted in the form of this most elegant of birds. Thoth was credited in antiquity as the scribe of the ancient Egyptian gods and as the inventor of writing and was associated with many aspects of wisdom and learning.

HIDEOUS ABSINTHE

A History of the Devil in a Bottle

Jad Adams

TPP

TAURIS PARKE
PAPERBACKS

For Julie

Published in 2008 by Tauris Parke Paperbacks
an imprint of I.B.Tauris & Co Ltd
6 Salem Road, London W2 4BU
175 Fifth Avenue, New York NY 10010
www.ibtauris.com

First published in 2004 by I.B.Tauris & Co Ltd
Copyright © 2004, Jad Adams

Cover image: Nineteenth-century advertising poster,
Collection Marie-Claude Delahaye

ISBN: 978 1 84511 684 2

A full CIP record for this book is available from the British Library

Typeset in Zapf Calligraphic by Dexter Haven Associates Ltd, London
Printed and bound in India by Replika Press Pvt. Ltd

Contents

Illustrations   vii

Acknowledgements   ix

Introduction: The Devil Made Liquid   1

1 Bitter Beginnings   15

2 The Green Hour and the New Art   24

3 Absinthe for the People   46

4 Poets Breaking the Rules   65

5 Madmen of Art   87

6 The Absinthe Binge   123

7 English Decadence and French Morals   138

8 Anglo-Saxon Attitudes   159

9 Absinthe Paranoia   177

10 Twilight of the *Fée Verte*   196

11 Green in the USA   216

12 Pop Goes the Fairy   236

Appendix: 'Lendemain'   251

Notes on the Text   253

Select Bibliography   275

Index   283

Illustrations

Black-and-white plates

Absinthe drinkers, a curious form of continental life, in the London magazine *The Graphic* in 1872.

'There's nothing like an absinthe to set you up', by Honoré Daumier.

The picturesque poverty of the social outcasts, *Les Déclassés*, by Jean-François Raffaëlli in 1881.

A woman sends her child out for a small amount of bread and a large amount of absinthe: 'Six sous d'absinthe et un sou de pain'.

A courting couple get in the mood with an outdoor absinthe.

A good-time girl explains that absinthe is one of her minor sins.

La Buveuse d'Absinthe, by Félicien Rops – a vamp hanging around the dance-halls.

A tree nourished by absinthe and alcohol produces the fruits of prostitution, madness and the death of the race.

'Alcohol is the enemy' – but the enmity omits such 'patriotic' alcoholic drinks as wine, beer and cider ('fine champagne' is a brandy made from champagne).

The Old Absinthe House in New Orleans – keeping the name of absinthe alive in the US.

How to make an absinthe – the old techniques have to be relearned in a turn-of-the-(twentieth) century card for customers.

Colour plates

Edgar Degas's *Au Café*, or *L'Absinthe* as it came to be called, 1876.

Vincent van Gogh with Absinthe, by his friend Henri de Toulouse-Lautrec.

The Absinthe Drinker, by Edouard Manet, 1859.

The All Night Café, by Vincent van Gogh, 'a place where one can ruin oneself…'

The same all-night café, painted by Paul Gauguin – Mme Ginoux drinks her absinthe while behind her the postman sits with three prostitutes.

The Green Muse, by Albert Maignan: the writer is seized with an absinthe inspiration.

A. Bertrand's *Absinthe Drinker* of 1896 is closer to the reality than are the jolly girls in the posters.

M. Boileau dans un café, by Toulouse-Lautrec.

The Absinthe Drinker, by Picasso, 1901.

The young cousin holds out the promise of fun and absinthe.

An advertising poster at the end of the nineteenth century becomes an art poster at the end of the twentieth.

The absinthe lobby protests the ban: the great days of the founding of the Swiss Confederation are contrasted with the murder of the green fairy by a ghoulish puritan.

Louche twenty-first-century absinthe drinkers on the green promotional bus with the destination sign 'Oblivion'.

Acknowledgements

An Authors' Foundation grant was gratefully received, allowing me to travel for research to Auvers-sur-Oise and to Pontarlier. Julie Peakman from the Wellcome Institute kept me company here as she did in Greece, on Artemis's island of Leros, an appropriate place to be writing about Artemisia, where she gave the work its first criticism.

Marie-Claude Delahaye, whose extensive publications and labours in the field of absinthe over 20 years are documented elsewhere in this book, was so generous with her time as to read the manuscript and save me from many errors. Similarly Matthew Sturgis, historian of the English decadence, kindly read key chapters.

Other individuals who have patiently answered my queries and helped my research in other ways have included: Leslie Choquette from Assumption College, Massachusetts; Natalia Gerodetti from the University of Leeds; Roddy Morrison from the Royal Pharmaceutical Society; Christopher Riopelle, Curator of Nineteenth Century Paintings at the National Gallery; Jo Barnes and Jo Castle from the University of London's School of Pharmacy; Patricia Allderidge, Archivist and Curator at the Bethlem Royal Hospital; Laurel Brake of Birkbeck College, University of London; Harriet Jones from the Institute of Contemporary British History; Ewa Kwasniewski from the *Polish Daily*; Jean Bloch, Pam Pilbeam and Tim Unwin of Royal Holloway College, University of London; Rebecca Spang of University College London; Martin Cutbill of BBH Spirits; Christine Angiel, Jean-Paul Partensky and Claude Bonnaud.

I have benefited from the expertise of staff at the British Library, the London Library, Wellcome Library, Senate House Library, National Art Library at the Victoria and Albert Museum and the Institut Français, and also at the Absinthe Museum and the Pontarlier town museum.

Introduction:
The Devil Made Liquid

C'est le diable fait liquide

Raoul Ponchon

ONE SATURDAY MORNING IN THE SMART new rooms of a London art dealer in a street leading to the flower market in Covent Garden, a sale is in progress. It is a cold February day in 1893, but the auction room of Christie's is comfortably heated, so the well-dressed art lovers have left their silk hats and coats at the door. One picture among the landscapes, still lifes and stories of classical myth or Victorian home life inspires disgust. Bizarrely, in the place of quiet disapproval or disdain, a painting is hissed by the elegant buyers. Its later exhibition leads to weeks of disapprobation, with calls for this abomination to be banned and never again shown in Britain, and it is, in fact, shipped overseas.

The picture which was numbered Lot 209 that day shows a man and a woman in a Paris café. The downcast woman has a weary face denoting a lifetime of grinding toil. Her companion, with whom she has no apparent connection except that they are sitting next to each other, holds a pipe in his mouth with an expression of quiet intensity. In front of the woman is a green drink.

What was happening when a group of well-off English art lovers jeered a painting of a couple of working-class people in a Paris café?

How did this picture, now universally known as *L'Absinthe* and considered a great masterpiece, come to arouse such negative emotions over such a short period? Why did absinthe, venerated as a healing draught by the ancients and treated as such at the beginning of the nineteenth century, become so cursed at its end? Within 21 years of the scene at Christie's, absinthe would be banned all over the world.

Hideous Absinthe is an attempt to understand the preoccupations and fears of a century through the myths that were created around absinthe, and the way in which art, science and politics were marshalled into service in the battles over it. Absinthe deserves analysis because of the claims that it took part in a change in the course of Western art; because of its supposed role in racial degeneration (one of the preoccupations of the late nineteenth century); and because bans on absinthe presaged a drive towards widespread alcohol prohibition in the first quarter of the twentieth century.

Over mere decades absinthe was transformed from the green fairy, muse of artists, hymned by poets, aperitif of the middle class, to the poison of the haggard working class, responsible for all the ills of industrialisation. A bitter green liqueur had become 'the scourge', 'the plague', 'the enemy', 'the queen of poisons', blamed for the near collapse of France in the first weeks of the Great War and for the decadence threatening the British Empire.[1]

Absinthe was accused of filling the asylums, of the murder of whole families, of leading to spontaneous human combustion in habitual users. Crimes in which the perpetrator drank the aperitif occasionally were described as absinthe atrocities. At its most extreme, the paranoia over absinthe in France found the promotion of the drink to be part of a Jewish plot to undermine the moral and racial integrity of the nation.

Yet it has also been invoked by poets and depicted by artists from Manet to Picasso. Many, such as van Gogh and Toulouse-Lautrec, used it to excess. Its story is of such people as Baudelaire, who died thinking his life had been a failure but who created the intellectual underpinning of painting and poetry for the next 50 years.

What was Absinthe?

From antiquity absinthe potions were used as a vermicide, for venereal disease, as a remedy for indigestion and even a cure for drunkenness. Absinthe drinks were well known in the time of Shakespeare and Pepys. It was not considered, for most of its long existence, a magical elixir for poets, and its presence was not a signpost to the madhouse until the nineteenth century.

The basic facts about absinthe do not mark it out for greatness. As drunk in the nineteenth century it was a liqueur with alcohol, wormwood (in Greek *apsinthion*) and anise as essential ingredients. The anise gave an aniseed smell and taste to the mixture, the wormwood gave it a bitter taste. An alcohol level of up to 75 per cent by volume meant the drink was highly alcoholic, so much so that on first appearance it was an emerald liquid, as the essential oils of the plants which provided its taste were suspended in alcohol. The addition of water freed the oils and made it a cloudy pale green drink, an effect known as 'louching'. Many dreamy hours were spent in observing this magical process taking place in a glass, to which sugar might also be added to counter the bitterness of the wormwood.

Absinthe was claimed to give its drinkers a different view of the world. Its high alcoholic content certainly changed the world view of those whose previous experience of alcohol was table wine. Absinthe was also claimed to produce new and different sensations because of the chemical thujone found in wormwood. Research in the 1970s and 1990s has to some extent validated the claim that absinthe's appeal was greater than its alcoholic content, that thujone does have a peculiarly stimulating effect on the brain chemistry. The amount of thujone in a bottle of absinthe, however, varied widely depending on the manufacturer.

Absinthe Conquers France

Absinthe played its part in the creation of the French overseas empire in North Africa and Indo-China when it was used as a disinfectant and anti-malarial by the troops, thus becoming associated with national pride and military success. The military brought a taste for absinthe back from their campaigns and into the cafés and boulevards of Paris. There the rising middle class enjoyed the symbolic sharing of glory demonstrated by enjoying the drink characteristic of those who had fought with the Bataillon d'Afrique. Absinthe therefore emerged as a tonic that was patriotic, associated with vigour, the army and the overseas empire. It was largely restricted to the middle class, which could afford the comparatively high price and, unlike the poor, felt the need to stimulate their appetites with an aperitif.

While bourgeois financial speculation was creating one part of the new culture of France under the rule of Louis Napoleon after 1848, artists were speculating with theories and their lives to create another. The lives of these impoverished writers and painters who flocked to Paris were chronicled in Henri Murger's *Scènes de la vie de Bohème*. In this earliest definition of the bohemian lifestyle, absinthe features not at all, making it possible to date absinthe's association with artists as taking place soon after the middle of the nineteenth century.

Artists carved out parts of Paris as their own, first the Latin Quarter, then the north bank and later Montmartre in a life of cafés and the interchange of ideas powered by alcohol, often absinthe. The often eccentric behaviour of such characters tended towards the creation of a new myth: to be an artist it was necessary to frequent cafés, drink absinthe and behave unconventionally. Countless hopefuls of limited talent swelled the ranks of the bohemians, giving rise to jocularities about artists whose inspiration came only after eight absinthes but were too poor to afford more than seven.

Some absinthe-inspired art required no drinking on the part of the artist. Edouard Manet's first major work, *The Absinthe Drinker*, depicted an impoverished absinthe drinker. Its rejection by the Salon was an important staging post in the denunciation of the conservative Institute by French art and the creation of the movement which came to be called impressionism.

In the 1850s and 1860s the poor were not drinking the same absinthe as the rich: small operators were producing cheap copies of absinthe, often made with adulterated ingredients but always highly alcoholic. A book published in 1860 pictures, probably for the first time, the *absintheur*: 'Dull, brow-beaten, eyes lifeless, hollow cheeked, he stays for whole days with elbows on the table, staring with a sombre mien at his empty glass and extinguished pipe'.[2]

The fear and horror of absinthe's unrestrained use is apparent through this temperance tract: absinthe had been the drink of men, of the military, the bourgeois, the artist. Then it became seen as a drink also of women of the demi-monde. Now absinthe was becoming a drink of whole families, with absinthe-drinking parents dosing children with the liqueur.

Such activity was known, but it was not considered a widespread social evil until the 1870s, when the vine-pest devastated French crops and put wine, their usual drink, out of the financial reach of the poor. Now absinthe became the standard drink, a product with many times the alcoholic strength of wine.

France's defeat in the Franco–Prussian War and the debauches of the Commune left the country in the 1870s and 1880s a chastened nation. It was in this atmosphere of crisis and upheaval, a failure of the old order, that the first impressionist exhibition took place in 1874. The doom was intensified for Degas by family death, bankruptcy and his fear of blindness, and it was in this atmosphere that he painted the picture, simply called *Dans un Café* or *Au Café*, which was later jeered in Christie's showroom.

Absinthe and Medicine

As its use widened, absinthe increasingly attracted medical attention. The term 'alcoholism' had been used since the 1850s, when it was thought to be a form of poisoning caused by distilled spirits – wine and beer were not considered responsible. An unchallenged assumption was that, however culpable alcohol might be, absinthe was worse, responsible for a range of somatic conditions as well as mental derangement, sterility and impotence.

The first examinations of insanity in 'absinthistes' were taking place in 1859. The 1870s saw the establishment of a relationship between absinthe and madness in lay and medical opinion. Researchers continued to seek proof of a distinct condition called 'absinthism' that was described in medical dictionaries as a 'variety of alcoholism'. It was believed not only that alcohol had a role in madness but that alcohol led to mental disturbance.

As the century wore on absinthe drinking was presented not only as an individual malady but a cause of degeneracy in the entire French race. A belief in the acquired characteristics of absinthe damage being passed on down the generations fitted in with contemporary notions of eugenics and fears for the quality of the national stock.

Suggestions of an addictive element to absinthe came only late in the second half of the nineteenth century, while developments in the theory of addiction were transferring culpability for addiction from the moral failings of the addict to the addictive qualities of the substance being used.

Absinthe and the Arts

Bohemians such as Verlaine and Rimbaud defined themselves by uncontrolled drinking and deliberate disorder, a rejection of the nice rules of society. They were careless of appearance to the point of dirtiness; spent Verlaine's inheritance freely then sponged from friends; openly exercised sexual licence; went to the bars of the lower classes and had sex with those who drank there. Absinthe was the lubricant for this behaviour, but did it cause it? Verlaine wrote 'J'aime l'absinthe bicolore [I love two-coloured absinthe]' but he also drank to excess in general.

By the late 1880s, Paris had become an absinthe-fuelled bonanza of disparate literary groups, performances and small magazines, including the *Décadent*, a literary magazine that owed its philosophy to Verlaine and set the tone for much of the bohemian life that followed. Verlaine was a local monument in the last years of his life, a character for literary adventurers to see and admire so they could tell friends back home that they had bought a drink for the legendary poet, the genius devastated by absinthe. Verlaine and his followers gave the outward impression that poetry and absinthe were inter-linked, but instead of breeding a race of poets, the pursuit of absinthe spawned a crop of tiresomely drunk, talentless poseurs.

How many of the artists who are always associated with absinthe were actually *influenced* by it to any degree? Vincent van Gogh is often claimed to have been out of control in his absinthe use. Was van Gogh addicted to alcohol, to absinthe or to some other substance, for there is evidence for all of these? His is also a testing case for the artistic potential of absinthe, as the most creative period of his life was the last three years, when he was drinking it heavily.

Absinthe formed a part of Gauguin's life in France and in the south seas, and the life of the Scandinavian and Berlin bohemian world in which others such as Munch and Strindberg worked, though in all these cases it is questionable whether its role was anything more than mere scene-setting.

There was a 15-fold increase in absinthe consumption in France between 1875 and 1913. Between 1885 and 1892 alone the consumption of absinthe in Paris increased by more than 100 per cent.[3] This atmosphere of increased drinking was pictured by Jean-François Raffaëlli, who painted the poor drinking absinthe, and Henri de Toulouse-Lautrec, who painted the rich. Others, such as Alfred Jarry, claimed absinthe was a route to higher artistic understanding.

Absinthe and the English

Absinthe was long protected from condemnation in French society by its association with the military and the bourgeoisie. For the conservative English, however, absinthe symbolised the dissolute, sexually depraved world of the French. For English writers and artists of the 1880s and 1890s, France represented everything new and challenging in art, all symbolised by the diabolical green drink. Artists became not only pro-French but anti-English.

In painting, the battle for the acceptance of French ideas was promoted by the New English Art Club, comprising such leading figures of the 1890s as Aubrey Beardsley and Walter Sickert. Critics feared French influence, however, nervously noting that 'the influx of French art into this country creates a difficulty', and presenting the rule that what was permissible in art was what was permissible in the Victorian drawing-room, a notion that transgressed every principle of artistic integrity the New English Art Club was promoting.[4]

The infection from French art was, however, only the cultural manifestation of a fear and abhorrence of a country which was suspected of having designs on British overseas possessions, and to be contemplating an invasion of Britain. Absinthe was a visible, poisonous symbol of this French encroachment on British art, morality and territory. Disgust for it found best expression in Marie Corelli's immensely successful book *Wormwood: A Drama of Paris*. Into it Corelli pours every cliché of the English attitude to the French: the wretched artist-genius; the lascivious, inveigling priest; the easily seduced French girl; vile tenements inhabited by backward children born to *absintheurs*; and absinthe mania haunting the depraved narrator.

The attitude of disgust for the decadents and for their diabolical drink permeated even the medical press. While attempts had been made in France to define the difference between alcoholism and absinthism, English medical journals reported such work with disdain, as all the signs supposedly unique to absinthe were also seen in alcoholics in England, where absinthe was not a factor. The very beginning of the twentieth century, however, now found the *Lancet* (on no better evidence than it had previously) supporting the notion of 'absinthism'. Soon absinthe was hardly drunk in Britain, and it was not thought necessary to ban it.

Absinthe Prohibition

In France an anti-absinthe movement was seeking to blame the liqueur for all the social ills which had developed over the second half of the nineteenth century; from social unrest to sexual deviance, absinthe was the culprit.

It was widely believed that the problem with alcohol was not the quantity consumed but the quality. The very terminology in use by all levels of society was against an understanding of the relationship between illness and alcohol, as in France *alcool* did not mean alcohol, but spirits. A hardening of attitudes, actively promoted by the producers of these drinks, ensured that wine and beer were not only considered harmless but healthy, even to be prescribed as a treatment for alcoholism. Temperance organisations maintained that a litre of wine a day was a reasonable dose for a healthy man. Drunks were referred to as *absintheurs* as a general term, even if they did not drink absinthe. Major absinthe producers acknowledged the problems of excessive use but claimed that these were caused by the adulterated mixes of small producers, not their own product.

A national obsession with low population growth, compared to that of Germany, increased the absinthe paranoia, with the drink being blamed for the poor quality of recruits to the French army. The state of the national stock was also ascribed to women absinthe drinkers, who showed such signs of degeneracy as a reluctance to marry and have children, a hankering after traditionally male roles and lesbianism.

The absinthe prohibition crusade in France was a paradoxical campaign in which the wine-producers, suppliers of the vast majority of alcoholic drinks consumed, backed the temperance movement, and in which a restriction in the sale of low-alcohol absinthe was hailed as a victory for abstinence. By the end of the nineteenth century, as an observer noted, 'temperance groups had ably demonstrated their energy, good intentions and total lack of success'. France was the largest consumer of alcohol per head of population in the world.[5]

The murder of his wife and two children by a Swiss peasant in 1905 led to a successful referendum on the banning of absinthe in Switzerland. Belgium banned absinthe soon after, and the temperance movement in France was galvanised with a petition arguing that absinthe renders its drinkers mad and bad, and endangers the future of the nation. Temperance campaigners had determined to attack absinthe as a soft target, with the expectation of later making an assault on alcohol in general. The legislation allowing for a ban was enacted after the outbreak of the First World War amid stories of soldiers going mad from absinthe while in the act of defending the country from the invading Germans.

The Twentieth Century and Beyond

Lurid warnings about absinthe were imported wholesale from France into America as news and as fiction, where they found fertile soil in the prohibitionist movement.

There was scant evidence of widespread absinthe use, but it attracted the attention of the Department of Agriculture, which banned it as 'one of the worst enemies of man' in 1912. This was in line with bans by other countries, but also with the trend towards the general control of drugs. General alcohol prohibition followed in many countries, most disastrously in the US, and any arguments over absinthe were subsumed in the melee.

It was the North American adventurers and travellers who now drank absinthe in foreign countries where it was still legal. By the 1930s only the European cocktail set were using absinthe, though with the revival of interest in illicit substances in the 1970s absinthe was again discussed. It was the fall of the Berlin Wall in 1989, leading to US tourism to Eastern Europe, which rekindled widespread interest in absinthe. Travellers were disappointed, however, that the experiences they had in Prague did not match up to the nineteenth-century description of absinthe use: it was neither a palatable drink nor an enjoyable experience.

In the late twentieth and early twenty-first century a new generation of bohemians, this time magazine writers and popular musicians, made the discovery of absinthe in Czechoslovakia, and began to import it to Britain in time for the millennium celebrations. Websites sprang up discussing absinthe and absinthe experiences, including sometimes dangerous do-it-yourself absinthe concoctions.

In Britain, absinthe became a fashionable drink, but was criticised for its failure to behave like the absinthe of nineteenth-century literature. When it was realised that Czech absinthe was not the absinthe of the boulevards of Paris, new absinthes were produced according to French recipes. Now they looked and smelled like those of the past, but still did not have the same effect, perhaps because the thujone content of modern absinthe is too low.

Absinthe in the twenty-first century finds its way into the cocktail cabinet of similar drinks, safe enough if used sensibly, dangerous in the hands of those who tend to misuse substances, as has always been the case. Now a glamorous drink of the affluent young, it continues to fill the role required of it, regardless of its physical properties.

Hideous Absinthe

The first chapter of *Hideous Absinthe* covers the history of absinthe from antiquity to the nineteenth century. The second demonstrates how the smell and sight of absinthe became the characteristic cultural event of the boulevards of Paris, the so-called 'green hour' which often stretched into several hours as the newly rich paraded their wealth and the bohemians developed new artistic ideas. Chapter 3 examines the way absinthe permeated through the poorer levels of society. The effect of the widespread use of absinthe on both the bourgeoisie and on the bohemians is examined in chapter 4, while chapter 5 asks whether absinthe made a genuine contribution to artistic ideas. The absinthe binge in 1890s France is the subject of chapter 6; chapter 7 demonstrates how the liqueur was held in suspicion in England, where only the artists, and only a minority of them, used it. It was in this atmosphere of suspicion of France and disgust with its national drink that, as chapter 8 describes, Degas's *L'Absinthe* was presented to the English public. In France, as described in chapter 9, absinthe was being considered responsible for the ills of society which had accompanied industrialisation and urbanisation. With absinthe being blamed for putting race and nation in danger, the scene was set for a major prohibition movement, as described in chapter 10. Chapter 11 covers absinthe in the USA, where, particularly in French-influenced Louisiana, an absinthe sub-culture grew up. The phenomenon of the return of absinthe at the end of the twentieth century is the subject of chapter 12.

Absinthe Research

The study of absinthe as a social phenomenon suffers from the repeated quotation of anecdotal or even openly fictional events as historical fact. It is not uncommon for writers on absinthe to quote Marie Corelli's description of an absinthe reverie from her novel *Wormwood* as if the first-person narrator were a real person and the experience a real one.

Of the serious writers, everyone interested in the subject owes a great debt to Marie-Claude Delahaye, who over 20 years has brought together disparate material to make further investigation possible. Her publications include a history of absinthe in 1983; an anthology of artists influenced by absinthe in 1999; of poets similarly influenced in 2000; and an improved version of her absinthe history in 2001. She has also written on absinthe, art and history, absinthe spoons and absinthe posters.[6] Delahaye has also set up a museum of absinthe in Auvers-sur-Oise, and has assisted with the re-creation of twenty-first-century absinthe based on nineteenth-century recipes.

The best historical work on the absinthe ban in France is Patricia Prestwich's article in Canada's *Historical Reflections*, an analysis of the campaign against absinthe with the conclusion 'Absinth [*sic*] was less a villain than a convenient victim and its prohibition provided the satisfaction of resolute action without entailing grave economic dislocation or real personal sacrifice'.[7] This argument finds the agreement of Jean-Charles Sournia in his *History of Alcoholism*, who says, 'It is now evident that the twenty-year-long anti-absinthe campaign, which culminated in prohibition in numerous countries, had no scientific basis'.[8]

Another specialist, biochemistry professor Wilfred Niels Arnold, started writing about the pharmacology of absinthe, and has produced a number of valuable articles and one excellent book on Vincent van Gogh's problems, with a great deal of scientific detail, particularly on the chemical composition of absinthe.[9]

The title of Doris Lanier's book *Absinthe: The Cocaine of the Nineteenth Century* suggests its approach, which is that 'for several decades, the drink caused social problems of great magnitude – similar to the cocaine problems of this [the twentieth] century'.[10] Though this is a comparison of no great profundity, Lanier does a service in collecting a number of referenced sources to tell the absinthe story chronologically. Her original research on absinthe in America has been particularly helpful. She is not so concerned to analyse the research, however, and agrees with Arnold on the banning of absinthe to such an extent that in lieu of her own, she quotes his conclusion, 'Absinthe tippling…was judged to be negative and destructive, and, in retrospect, the interdiction was tardy but surely justified'.[11]

Barnaby Conrad considers absinthe 'a skeleton key to the fin de siècle's secrets'[12] in his well-illustrated, anecdotal history, though, to continue the metaphor, he does not fit the key into the lock and turn it: he is content to allow the colourful history of absinthe to speak for itself. Phil Baker is equally enthusiastic about absinthe, which he once memorably refers to as 'bottled doom' in his well-researched *Dedalus Book of Absinthe*. He includes a section on available brands which he has product-tested, giving each a 'Dowson rating' out of five. Much of Baker's book is focused on individual experience of absinthe, with a conclusion very much rooted in the personal. 'People *want* [my emphasis] absinthe to be fearful stuff, with the distinctive form of pleasure that fearful things bring.'[13] It is the projection onto absinthe of personal and political desires that forms the starting point of my understanding of the drink's history.

1 Bitter Beginnings

WORMWOOD FELL AS A STAR FROM THE SKY, flaming like a torch to poison the rivers and springs, 'and men in great numbers died from its bitterness'. The description from Revelation gives some idea of the power attributed to the basic constituent of absinthe.[1]

The righteous are further warned to beware the adulteress, as the writers of Proverbs testify, for though her lips drip honey and her tongue is smoother than oil, ultimately she is more bitter than wormwood and sharp as a two-edged sword.[2] The judgement of God for apostasy is like being fed with the plant; only such terrible experiences as the loss of Jerusalem can be described by this awful bitterness: to be fed on ashes, racked with pain, 'drunk with wormwood'.[3]

Wormwood, therefore, has long had what would come to be called a bad press, but it had its many uses, as the frequent references to it in ancient times attest. The Ebers papyrus, an Egyptian compilation of seven hundred medical texts dating from around 1550 BC, includes advice on the use of wormwood as an antiseptic and as valuable against worms, fevers and period pains.

The Biblical wormwood (*Artemisia judaica*) was one form of the sage known as *Artemisia absinthium*. The term absinthe derives from the Greek word 'apsinthion', meaning unusable (that is inedible as a food plant). Wormwoods are different species of the genus *Artemisia*, perhaps called after Artemis, the goddess associated with the hunt and the moon, and called Diana by the Romans. In legend she was said to have given the plant to Chiron the physician Centaur to form part of his healing pharmacopoeia.

It has also been suggested that the name of the genus came from Queen Artemisia, builder of the Mausoleum, one of the seven wonders of the ancient world, for her husband (also her brother) Mausolus, in the fourth century BC. Artemisia, who ruled alone after the death of her husband, was a renowned and resourceful healer with extensive knowledge of plants. Certainly wormwood's properties were well known to the ancients: Pythagoras advised wormwood steeped in wine to ease labour, and it is recommended in works by Hippocrates and Galen. The mediaeval physician and alchemist Paracelsus was the first to treat fever, especially malaria, with wormwood.

Pliny in the first century AD, in *Historia Naturalis,* recommends extracts of wormwood for stomach complaints, for intestinal worms and as an insect repellent; and for the first time there is mention of a wine known as absinthites made with extract of wormwood. Infusion of wormwood in water is described as 'in great request, and a common drinke'. Philemon Holland's 1601 translation has Pliny remarking on wormwood as 'an herbe as common as any, and most readie at hand, howbeit, few or none so good and whole-some'. He records the custom of the Romans at chariot races on the Latinae festivals, where 'he that first attaineth the goale and winneth the prize, hath a draft of Wormwood presented unto him…our forefathers and ancestors devised this honourable reward, for the good health of the victorious charioteer, as judging him worthie to live still'.[4]

In Christian folklore wormwood was said to have sprung up in the track of the serpent as it writhed along the ground when driven out of paradise. The drink offered to Jesus while he was being crucified is said to have been wormwood and vinegar.

St Luke's Day, 18 October, was said to be a lucky day to choose a husband with the aid of wormwood. In order to see a dream of her future husband a girl was told, 'before going to bed on St Luke's night, anoint your stomach, breast and lips with a powder of dried marigold flowers, marjoram, thyme and wormwood, simmered in virgin honey and white vinegar'. She should then repeat three times 'St Luke, St Luke, be kind to me/ In dreams let me my true love see'. A vision of her future husband will then appear, with some guide as to his conduct: if he is going to be a loving partner, he will smile, but he will be rude to the dreamer if he is destined to 'forsake thy bed to wander after strange women'.[5] The fires of Midsummer Eve were fuelled with wormwood to ward off evil, and it was worn at the waist to protect from witchcraft (that is to protect the genitals from malevolence) and to ensure no one could cast an evil spell.

Nicholas Culpeper in *The Complete Herbal* in the seventeenth century recommends wormwood for venereal disease, saying it 'helps the evils Venus and the wanton Boy [Cupid] produce'. He also suggests it as a treatment for intestinal worms and a cure for drunkenness.[6] It is notable how many of the folk myths surrounding wormwood relate to sex or the reproductive organs; until quite recently in the French countryside newlyweds would find the marriage bed garnished with branches of wormwood, the belief being that its mere presence bestowed sexual prowess.[7]

The English word for the plant is not connected with worms, but is from the Anglo-Saxon 'ver mod' meaning man-inspiriting, for its tonic properties. One of its uses was in child-rearing: a nursing mother or wet-nurse would put wormwood on her nipple to wean a baby off breast milk, as Juliet's nurse did, remembering, 'When it did taste the wormwood on the nipple of my dug and felt it bitter,' at which she would 'see it tetchy and fall out with the dug!'[8]

The French aphorist Martin, in a medical handbook of the seventeenth century, notes, 'L'absinthe confort les ners/ Est bon aussi pour les vers [Wormwood calms the nerves, and is also good for worms]', perhaps the first mention of the nervous-system effect which was to become so significant in the nineteenth century. An Italian book of aphorisms in the eighteenth century (though its observations are much more ancient than that) also advises absinthe for 'Conforte l'estomac et les nerfs [Settling the stomach and the nerves]'.[9]

The Marquise de Sévigné in the1660s helped to spread the word when a doctor in Switzerland gave her absinthe for her stomach, after which she remarked, 'Ma petite absinthe, est le remède à tous maux [My little wormwood is the remedy for all ills]'.[10]

Common wormwood (*Artemisia absinthium*) was so frequently seen in England that Culpeper in the seventeenth century thought it unnecessary to describe it, 'for every boy that can eat an egg knows it'. The *Encyclopaedia Britannica* for 1771 noted there were 23 species, of which four were native to Britain, including the 'absynthium or common wormwood'. The herbs and shrubs of the *Artemesia* genus all go by the general name 'wormwood' in English, they have numerous small, greenish-yellow flower heads normally grouped in clusters, the leaves are divided and alternate down the stem. The other common forms of wormwood in the world are common mugwort (*Artemisia vulgaris*); field southernwood (*Artemisia campestris*); bluish mugwort (*Artemisia caerulescens*) and sea wormwood (*Artemisia maritima*). They are found on waste ground, rocky slopes and footpaths in Europe, Asia and North Africa. In the British Isles they are a native species found mainly in England and Wales.[11]

The means of producing oil of wormwood from the leaves, flower and stem of the Artemisia family were standard from antiquity to the Enlightenment: decoctions were made by boiling down mixtures of the herb with water. The development of steam distillation in the sixteenth century (described in books published by Hieronymus Brunschwig in 1500 and 1512) exponentially increased the ability of alchemy to take extracts from plants. Weak decoctions of wormwood were replaced in the sixteenth century by powerful essences.

Artemisia absinthium was used to flavour an ale called purl or wormwood beer at least from the seventeenth century. Samuel Pepys remarks in February 1660, 'forth to Mr Harpers to drink a draught of purle'; and *Poor Robin's Almanac* in 1718 notes, 'Scurvy-grass Ale, clarified Whey and Wormwood Beer are good'.[12] Purl, a weak infusion of wormwood in ale, was probably not dissimilar from the beer which came to be universally sold as 'bitter'. Purl seems to have died out by the end of the nineteenth century, and there is virtually no mention of it in the twentieth, presumably because ale was overtaken as the national drink by the more stable beer.

Another absinthe drink, called purl-royal or wormwood wine, was made by infusing wormwood in wine, and again Pepys remarks on drinking it on 24 November 1660 when he and five other gentlemen went 'to the Renish wine-house, and there I did give them two quarts of wormwood wine'.

Wormwood drinks went so far out of fashion in Britain, however, that in the middle of the nineteenth century the magazine *Notes and Queries* was responding to the question 'whether wormwood could be an ingredient in any palatable drink' with the reply 'that crème d'absinthe ordinarily appears with noyau & c. in a Parisian restaurateur's list of luxurious cordials'.[13]

Clearly until a point in the nineteenth century wormwood drinks were among a number of alcoholic beverages, and were considered in no way remarkable; wormwood was merely one of a number of available flavourings, the substance was interesting and valuable but no boon to poets or originator of madness.

Wormwood, or absinthe to give it the French name by which it became notorious, developed its diabolical glamour directly from its medical use as a vermicide and anti-malarial. Absinthe retained a standard role as part of the herbal pharmacopoeia until after the French Revolution, when the restored Bourbon monarchy needed to enhance its prestige in its short reign, and this took the form of colonial expeditions. One of these, in 1830, was against Algeria, and achieved complete success in three weeks, laying the foundation for the French North African Empire.

Initial conquests of Algiers, Oran and Bône led to a gradual extension of French territory, until in 1839 an Arab chief, Abd-el-Kader, led resistance against them. It took an army of 88,000 years of campaigning in a barbarous war before Abd-el-Kader was defeated and captured in 1847.

French soldiers, unaccustomed to fighting in African conditions, suffered from all the ills the continent had to offer. 'Fever made grievous havoc in the ranks of the army,' and doctors recommended absinthe in place of quinine, which was too costly to be generally distributed.[14] Absinthe had long been used as an insecticide, to be rubbed on the skin or placed in stored clothes to guard against insects. To ward off dysentery, African Battalion soldiers were issued with absinthe to put in their unhealthy drinking water, which probably had something of the desired effect, as it causes round-worms to loosen their grip, allowing them to be defecated from the body.[15]

Bitter water, however supposedly hygienic, was not palatable, and the soldiers took to spiking their wine with absinthe (facilitated by the large amounts of wild wormwood growing in Algeria), thus creating a more strongly alcoholic drink. Absinthe then went with the French on all their foreign campaigns, to such insalubrious climes as Madagascar and Indo-China. When they returned home, they took this acquired taste for bitter-flavoured alcohol back to the cafés of France, calling for 'une verte', in reference to the drink's green colour before water is added.

The habit started in Marseilles and advanced through France. The fact that the army had been successful and France was enjoying pride in a developing empire, meant that others wished to share the experience, as if by drinking the same exotic drink they became one with the victorious soldiers who were enjoying France's first victories since the early years of the Napoleonic wars.

This taste for absinthe drinks was said to have been supplied by a refugee from the French Revolution, Pierre Ordinaire, who settled in the canton of Neuchâtel, Switzerland, where he practised his skills as a physician to make medicines. These included a successful tonic against fever and bad digestion using extract of wormwood, which he first made in 1792. The common story features an old wise woman of the region, Mère Henriod, said to be Ordinaire's housekeeper, and also his lover. She was bequeathed the recipe for absinthe by Ordinaire, who died in 1793.

In fact this frequently told tale is false. It is a concoction, like many tales about absinthe, of the late nineteenth century, when French local historians of the Doubs region wished to create an acceptable historical background to the immensely successful drink that absinthe had become.[16] There was a Dr Ordinaire who was a political refugee in Switzerland, where he practised his profession, but he had nothing to do with the creation of absinthe.

What was called *l'elixir absynthe* long predated Ordinaire's stay in Neuchâtel. Henriette Henriod of the town of Couvet had been making an advanced form of the common infusion of absinthe plants in water. She would not have been the first to distil this decoction, making a weak drink into a strong one (some long-forgotten alchemist will have done that), but she can reasonably be credited with the realisation that infusing in alcohol, rather than water, exponentially increased the power of the drink. Her elixir was sold widely with a label, one of which has survived, showing an alembic and the inscription 'superior quality absinthe extract from a unique recipe of Mademoiselle Henriod of Couvet'.[17]

Several cultural functions were served when Ordinaire and not Henriod was seen as the originator of modern absinthe: it meant the drink was a product of science rather than folk medicine; it became the creation of a man, not a woman; and if it had been made by a Frenchman only staying in Switzerland then it could be claimed as French, not Swiss. This creation of a culturally acceptable myth was characteristic of the whole long history of absinthe, in which the green fluid accepted whatever desires were projected onto it and combined with them in an opaque, cloudy mix.

One of Henriod's customers was a Major Daniel-Henri Dubied, a Frenchman who rejoiced in the use of absinthe for indigestion and fevers, and took to drinking one each day before dinner and one as a nightcap. It is said that he found himself stimulated erotically by this regime, perhaps because absinthe gives rise to unexpected ideas (no one has ever maintained that it stimulates the genitals, but an aphrodisiac effect has often been claimed).[18]

Dubied bought the formula from Henriod in 1797 and set up the first commercial absinthe distillery in Couvet the following year. He was helped by his sons and son-in-law, but it was the latter, Henri-Louis Pernod, who made the drink successful. In 1805 he established a factory close to the Swiss border at Pontarlier in the Doubs region of France, siting it there in order to avoid duties on importing the drink; and he became the first to manufacture absinthe on a large scale. In 1826 there were four distilleries at Pontarlier making 100,000 litres of absinthe; by 1849 there were 25 distilleries in and around Pontarlier producing ten million litres.[19]

There were as many recipes for absinthe as there were producers of it, and successful formulae were jealously protected, but the principal ingredients were distilled wine alcohol, plants of the Artemisia species for bitterness, with an addition of anise and fennel to give a liquorice taste. The only universal ingredients were wormwood and high-strength alcohol, usually between 65 and 72 degrees proof. One function of the alcohol was to keep the oil constituents in solution, from which they were released by the addition of water to turn a bright green drink into a turbid, cloudy green one, the so-called louche effect.[20] The green colour was produced by the chlorophyll from the leaves of plants other than wormwood. The distinctive aniseed smell which was so often to be remarked on as redolent of the boulevards of Paris in the *belle époque* was conferred by the anise.

A classical procedure for production which has survived said that dried wormwood, anise and fennel were steeped in a high concentration of ethyl alcohol (that is 'drinking alcohol'). After a day, water was added and the concoction boiled with the distillate collected. The process was completed with a further extraction of wormwood and hyssop and lemon balm, which was filtered to give a clear, green liquid. Other ingredients which were used were tansy, angelica, dittany of Crete, juniper, star anise, mint, coriander and veronica. A surviving recipe calls for 3.5 kg of 'Grande Absinthe' (*Artemisia absinthium*), 4 kg of green anise, 4 kg of fennel, 675 g of star anise, 1 kg of lemon balm and 1.5 kg of hyssop.[21]

Absinthe's origins as a medicine meant it began its commercial life with a revivifying image, the exact opposite of its situation just over a century later, when it was excoriated and banned. In a nation known for its range of aperitifs, absinthe was ideal: it was startlingly different in taste, had an intriguing colour change when water was added, and was reassuringly expensive. Its complex production meant absinthe was relatively costly, and at a time of urbanisation when many could scarcely afford to feed themselves the price of a drink taken as a stimulant to appetite restricted it to the middle class.

Absinthe might have remained an occasional addition to France's hundreds of aperitifs, were it not for the delight which poets and artists found in it. They became in art and literature the advertisers and propagandists of what came to be called the green fairy.

2 The Green Hour and the New Art

THE BOURGEOISIE AND THE MILITARY were creating a new France in the middle of the nineteenth century, a France which was confident and eager for novel sensation, in which absinthe was to play its part to the full. The revolution of 1848 had led to the election of Louis Napoleon (nephew of Napoleon Bonaparte) as president with an overwhelming majority, followed in 1851 by his coup d'etat and the inauguration of the Second Empire. From the position of president, Louis Napoleon took the step in 1852 of declaring himself Emperor Napoleon III, and putting his popularity to the test in a referendum, winning the popular vote by almost eight million to a quarter of a million.

The return to a sense of imperial destiny was the boost to confidence the middle classes needed to unleash their creative greed. Share prices rose rapidly, and the Bank of France reduced its interest rate to 3 per cent, making it easier to borrow money to invest. If revolutions were the festivals of the oppressed, the decades of speculation following Napoleon III's assumption of power were a long bourgeois party where ostentatious expenditure and display took the place of value. The Goncourt brothers' cousin used to pray each night for God to, 'Let the Emperor stay in power so that my dividends may increase'.[1] France under the Second Empire resembled a vast casino, and one in which everyone seemed prepared to take a chance, the middle classes with their money, the artists with their work and their lives.

It was the time of the *fête impériale*, when theatres, indoor circuses, the ballet, dance-halls and opera houses were crowded out with people seeking 'du plaisir a perdre haleine', 'pleasure to the point of breathlessness'. The burgeoning cafés along the *grands boulevards*, with their tables and chairs on the pavements, became the environment of officers, bourgeoisie, artists and *femmes du demi-monde*, not quite prostitutes but of a doubtful reputation. There were obvious preferences: the military tended to congregate in the Boulevard des Italiens, and each group had a favoured café, but they all partook of *l'heure de l'absinthe* or *l'heure verte*.

The distinctive scent of absinthe floated through the Paris air between six and seven, though the green hour was archly said to be remarkable for its ability to last two hours or three. A poem by Maurice Millot describes the scene:

> When pale twilight falls on the great city of Paris, the gas lamps
> of the boulevard illuminate the well-dressed at their pleasures. It
> is the sainted hour when, on the café tables, each one takes their
> absinthe … The drinker, no more a dreamer, nose in the air he
> follows the path: a carafe of water slowly poured drop by drop
> with a knowing familiarity. He contemplates gravely the opaline
> tint: the man has made his absinthe.[2]

A writer for the popular English magazine *Once a Week* in 1868 described the scene as observed by a tourist, incidentally indicating the level of knowledge of French a non-specialist audience might be expected to have:

> The poet and the artist may be seen descending Montmartre, the
> *cocotte* [tart] the Rue Blanche, the *crevé* [flashy young man] turns
> out of the rue Laffitte, and the *boursier* [stock exchange speculator]
> out of the Rue Vivienne. Actors install themselves at the Café de
> Suède, military men at the Helder, financiers at the Café Cardinal,
> journalists at Brébant of Mulhouse, dandies at the Café Riche or
> Tortoni's, and at the *boulevardier* [promenader] for whom Paris
> commences at the corner of the Rue Scribe and ends at the

Faubourg Montmartre, goes gossiping from café to café. What is called the hour of absinthe is as necessary to a Parisian as his wine or his cigar.[3]

Henri Balesta, a playwright and short-story writer, described in 1860 how young people admired a veteran of the art of 'making absinthe in society':

As soon as he grasps the carafe, conversations are suspended, pipes go out, all eyes are on the absinthe maker, following all the details of the operation without missing a thing…He, sensing himself at the centre of their attention, rejoices secretly in the admiration he inspires and strives to merit it. He holds the carafe with a detached air, tilts it with a haughty look, making an elegant circle with his arm, then lets the water fall drop by drop in the glasses with the gradualness of wisdom, to make the combination of these liquids. That's the shibboleth of the absinthe drinker: the *chic* manner in which he carries out this delicate operation.

Balesta quotes the juvenile taunt, 'What a simpleton! He doesn't even know how to make an absinthe.'[4]

For a long time no absinthe paraphernalia was deemed necessary, just a receptacle for water, one for the absinthe and one in which to mix the drink. As late as 1881 *Le Monde Plaisant* has a man enjoying mixing an absinthe with a glass of water and a jug with no spoon or sugar cube.[5] The drollery in the case of this cartoon, depicting a poem by Henri Bourette, concerns the concentrated patience with which the character contemplates and pours his absinthe, which, his satisfaction having been achieved by this act alone, he then throws out of the window.

Writers and painters were taking an active part in this creation of a new French identity. While such artists as Baudelaire might excoriate the bourgeoisie, they were unknowingly all part of a common purpose to revolutionise the culture of French society. As they had more than a little in common (and were sometimes the same people), it is unsurprising that the middle class and the artists became associated with absinthe, the varied use of which came to represent the culture of both. Absinthe was chic for its distinctive appearance and daring for its exotic origins, its fascinating colour changes, its extreme, almost unbearable bitterness, and the suggestion that it acted on the consciousness to produce ideas not otherwise accessible. As an official report of the following century remarked, writers and painters in artistic circles in Paris 'gave themselves to "the green" with passion, seeking to make their thoughts faster and more original, trying to promote newer and more exquisite ideas'.[6]

The legend of the bohemian lifestyle developed in the cafés of the Latin Quarter of Paris, so called because, as the university area, Latin had once been the common language between students who arrived from all over Europe to study there. Henri Murger, living a precarious existence as a writer in the late 1840s, described his circles in *Scènes de la vie de Bohème*, which was first published as a series of sketches in the review *Le Corsair* in 1848. Celebrity came with their dramatisation in the Théâtre des Variétés in 1849 and publication in book form in 1851, long before 1896, when the work became the basis of Puccini's opera *La Bohème*.

Murger was the son of a tailor and an apartment-block caretaker who determined on a career in literature and kept himself by writing for trade magazines and any periodical which would accept his work. His painters and poets were depicted having affairs with *grisettes* (working-class girls so called because of the grey dresses they wore), evading their landlords and struggling for commissions for their work. The bohemian group was centred on the Café Momus in Saint-Germain-L'Auxerrois, where the artists and poets and their girlfriends would meet, though Murger's description of their lives is much sentimentalised – Murger later recalled entire days of hunger and the times when he was so ragged he felt too indecent to go out in the daytime.

Murger is notable in the absinthe story because of the absence of the drink from *Scènes de la vie de Bohème*, in which there is a good deal of drinking and even reference to 'liqueurs' but absinthe is never singled out as an artistic drink as it would be in later decades. Indeed Murger in 1853 was to define bohemians as 'water drinkers' in his book *Les Buveurs de l'eau*, meaning that they were too poor through their dedication to their work to afford alcohol. The association of absinthe with artists can be dated therefore to the 1850s, after Murger had published *Scènes de la vie de Bohème* and when young people began to flock to Paris to live the legend that he had created.

A key character in the creation of the bohemian persona was Murger's friend Alfred de Musset, whom he would meet at the Académie café on the Rue Saint-Jacques. De Musset, 12 years Murger's senior, was one of the four great figures of the romantic movement (along with Hugo, Lamartine and Vigny), a poet, dramatist and novelist by the time he knew Murger. His first published book was a translation of Thomas De Quincey's *Confessions of an English Opium Eater*. In 1830 he published his first collection of poems, somewhat reminiscent of Byron, and continued to write dramatic verse and drama, often for armchair consumption after the failure of his stage play *A Venetian Night*.

His life was one of hectic sexual exploits and heavy drinking, though absinthe is not mentioned as a prominent factor. He fell in love with the novelist George Sand (Lucile-Aurore Dupin), who wrote of passion and the right of the individual to follow their heart. They ran off to Italy together and both fell ill at different times, whereupon Sand had an affair with the doctor treating de Musset, and the poet returned to Paris alone, broken in spirit.

In the 10 years following his return to Paris in 1834 he produced some of his finest work, including *Les Nuits*, lyrics on the theme of disappointed love. It was probably in this period that he started serious absinthe drinking. By 1852, when he was elected to the Académie française, he had virtually stopped literary work and his life of sexual and alcoholic dissipation had ruined his health. At the Académie he was part of a committee working on a dictionary; when it was remarked that de Musset absented himself rather frequently from his work, the Académie secretary said, 'You should say he absinthes himself too often,' probably the first example of an artist being defined by an absinthe habit. De Musset felt that, like the troops who were refreshed before battle by 'brandeviniers', a slug of brandy, artists should be fortified with absinthe.[7] He was more than liberally fortified. Edmond de Goncourt describes a scene related to him of 'Musset taking his absinthe at the Café de la Régence, an absinthe that looked like a thick soup. After which the waiter gave him his arm, or rather half carried him, to the carriage waiting at the door.'[8]

Murger crafted the bohemian myth in a form which was accessible to others, but de Musset was a far more important writer in literary terms. De Musset's natural home was in the café in front of an absinthe, but this was hardly enough to qualify him as an artist (not that every artist *manqué* was to grasp this fact). He also wrote a corpus of work, was a serious scholar, and enjoyed a sexual life uninhibited by bourgeois morals, a side of his life which he set down in his autobiographical novel *Confessions of a Child of the Century*, published when he was 26. He was dead at 47, but his poetic work was finished by 31. It was commonly reported that absinthe killed him.[9] Alexandre Dumas certainly held to this view, commenting it was 'De Musset's fatal passion for absinthe which may have given some of his verses their bitter flavour'. He remarked that

> Among our Bohemian poets absinthe has been called 'the green muse'. Several, and unfortunately not the poorest, have died from its poisoned embraces. Hégésippe Moreau, Amédée Roland, Alfred de Musset, our greatest poet after Hugo and Lamartine – all succumbed to its disastrous effects.[10]

De Musset did not himself write verses about absinthe, though in 1905 the French newspaper *Le Gaulois du Dimanche* published an ode to absinthe attributed to him, with such lines as 'Salut verte liqueur, Némésis de l'orgie! [Hail green liqueur, vengeance of the orgy]'. It was suspicious that 50 years after his death, at a time when absinthe was threatened with prohibition, verses praising it should be found penned by one of France's greatest poets and, indeed, it was a wrongful attribution of a poem by Valéry Vernier, a young contemporary of de Musset.

A minor poet, Edmond Bourgeois reflected de Musset's philosophy in a poem in homage, including the lines, 'I write, I write, saying: absinthe is holy, and the muse with green eyes reigns forever'. The poem tells of how the poet drinks for inspiration, but takes a glass too many and his brain empties of brilliance: 'It needed only one glass and I drank two'.[11] De Musset linked the younger generation of writers with the great romantics such as Hugo and formed part of the bridge by which romanticism developed into realism, but this was not solely a literary movement – painters and writers developed their theories concurrently, and the crucible of that development was the café.

Before 1860, writers generally had their home in the Latin Quarter while the artists were on the north of the Seine. De Musset was an early migrant north of the river in 1850 when he established himself at the Café de la Régence on the north bank (near the Palais Royale). Around 1860 the rest of the artists who made up bohemia abandoned the Latin Quarter to the students and began to gravitate towards the cafés in the boulevards. These boulevards were the embodiment of progress in France, being built by Baron Haussmann, Prefect of the Seine, who was commissioned by Napoleon III with the construction of an imperial city.

A lithograph by Honoré Daumier of 1863, *The first glass … the sixth glass …* shows a scene in such a café. An obviously bourgeois man is in an animated state with his first glass, while his companion is in an open-mouthed, open-eyed reverie after the sixth. Daumier, born in 1808, made his living principally as a cartoonist, producing lithographs of bitter political and social satire – one of his cartoons of King Louis Philippe had him imprisoned in 1832. His unflinching realism and disregard for any concepts of picturesque poverty made him a favourite of early impressionists, including Degas, who owned 1800 Daumier lithographs.[12] One of his lithographs shows a haggard wretch in front of a glass saying, 'There's nothing like absinthe to set a man up'. Daumier frequented The Hashish Club in the Hôtel de Pimodan de l'île Saint-Louis, also used by Charles Baudelaire, Eugène Delacroix and Gérard de Nerval.

Drinking circles were not necessarily artistic. A contemptuous English correspondent remarked on the clubs of absinthe drinkers, 'the members of which are pledged to intoxicate themselves with no other stimulant, and even to drink no other fluid – the only pledges, it is believed, which they do not violate'. In an early reference to the supposedly maddening qualities of absinthe, the journalist, writing in 1864, reports, 'They assemble daily at some appointed place of rendezvous at a certain hour, and proceed to dissipate their energies and their centimes in draughts of that fatal poison which fills the public and private madhouses of Paris'.[13]

Henri Murger would entertain in the Brasserie des Martyrs, though its veneer of respectability was thin, and after 11 pm was said more to resemble a robbers' den than a poets' circle. The artists would meet and plan under the eye of a patron who was often literally a patron of the arts, willing to help his favourites with a glass or a meal. The Café Brébant, on the Boulevard Poisonnière, had a patron who was fond of artists and actors, who were said often to get by with paying nothing but a compliment. La Taverne Montmartre was another favourite café where the evenings presided over by the patron Fernand Pousset resembled parties for his literary friends, who could often receive a free beer or absinthe. Here writers would read works in progress to each other, though by as early as the 1860s the artists were already becoming a 'sight' for the curious, who would frequent their cafés in the hope of spotting some of this exotic species of metropolitan life.

The changing nature of French society was reflected in new artistic movements: romanticism, emphasising personal emotions and enthusiasms, gave way under the pressure of urbanisation, the development of industry and discoveries of science to a form of artistic expression which could reflect this altered society. Realism, which flourished between 1850 and 1865, owed a principal debt in literature to Balzac and in art to Courbet, who had declared in 1848 his intention of painting only the modern and the vulgar. While the romantics (including Alfred de Musset) had desired artistic freedom to pursue their personal goals, the realists insisted on sincerity in art – art was to tell the truth about life, however sordid or ugly.

The creation of new artistic forms led the Bohemians into a world where they could equally experiment with their own lives. Some became known for their eccentric behaviour, such as Murger and de Musset's friend Gérard de Nerval, bizarre to the point of madness, remembered more for walking his pet lobster around the Palais Royale on a blue ribbon than for his verse. Another eccentric was the flamboyant critic Théodore Pelloquet. Pelloquet, art critic of the *Gazette de Paris*, was always to be found in the Brasserie des Martyrs, the Café des Variétés or the Café Brébant, an unmistakeable figure with his fantastic hats, strange coats and enormous white cravat. Garrulous and influential, he was never without a pipe and an absinthe until he died at the age of 48, half paralysed and able to say only 'abs…' His friend Raoul Ponchon wrote a comic poem about the death-bed scene where Pelloquet's final attempts at utterance were interpreted by his grieving friends: was he trying to speak of an abs-ence? of the abs-urdity of existence? Was he calling for abs-olution? Of course, Pelloquet's final syllable was an attempt to call for just one last abs-inthe.[14]

The Goncourt brothers, in their diary, defined the bohemian life in 1861 as

the orgies of work at night, the periods of poverty followed by periods of junketing, the neglected cases of pox, the ups and downs of an existence without a home, the suppers instead of dinners, the glasses of absinthe bringing consolation after a visit to the pawnshop; everything which wears a man out, burns him up, and finally kills him; a life opposed to all the principles of physical and spiritual hygiene, which results in a man dying in shreds at the age of forty-two, without enough strength left in him to suffer, and complaining of only one thing, the smell of rotten meat in his bedroom – the smell of his own body.[15]

Among the younger generation active in the circles of de Musset and Murger was Charles Baudelaire, the first to connect poetry with a life of depravity and vice. Christopher Marlowe and Lord

Byron had led dissolute lives and were also great writers, but for Baudelaire the life was the art, an unapologetic crusade with verse written on the banners of a decadent army. Baudelaire was the harbinger and absinthe was the fuel for a caravan of creative individuals who made France the undisputed centre of world artistic life in the nineteenth century.

Baudelaire was born into a bourgeois family in 1821 to a 26-year-old mother and a 60-year-old father who was a civil servant and also a painter. He died when Baudelaire was six, but not before teaching his son the secrets of form and line. Baudelaire made his name as a poet, but was also a gifted art critic who was always at home in the company of artists, making him a key figure in the history of French art. His mother married again, to an army officer, General Jacques Aupick, who opposed Baudelaire's literary ambitions and had the young Baudelaire sent abroad, though he returned on his own.

Baudelaire had decided early to be a poet, so as soon as he was 21 and came into his own inheritance he set up on his own in Paris. He was therefore present for the first kindling of excitement over absinthe among the bourgeoisie and artists. With his background, his wealth and sophisticated tastes, he was a crossover figure between the two. The young Baudelaire was a dandy, dressing all in black excepting an open-necked white shirt and an ox-blood cravat, spending half his inheritance in two years. Baudelaire had a black girlfriend, Jeanne Duval, the 'venus noire' of his poems, at a time when mixed-race relationships were considered an outrage, akin to bestiality. His work for her is some of the finest erotic verse in French, though their relationship was doomed to agonising scenes and suicide attempts.

They were both considerable drinkers; indeed, Baudelaire recommended in his poem 'Enivrez-vous [Get drunk]', 'Il faut être toujours ivre [It is necessary always to be drunk]', though he added 'on wine, on poetry, on virtue…not to be the martyred slaves of Time: get drunk endlessly!'

His distinctive and original art criticism was encouraged by the many artists he knew, including Delacroix and Courbet. In 1845 and

1846 he published reviews of the Salons of those years, consisting of lucid, original art theory. 'The heroism of modern life surrounds us and urges us on,' he wrote, presaging the work of the impressionists 30 years before the exhibition which gave them their name, 'He will be truly a painter, the painter who will know how to draw out of our daily life its epic aspect'.[16] The revolution of 1848 which overthrew the monarchy found Baudelaire armed on the barricades.

He worked as a critic and as a translator of the works of Edgar Allen Poe after his discovery of the works of the American in 1852 and his realisation that the gothic writer was a kindred spirit. However, Baudelaire suffered numerous disappointments in literature, and feared that his estranged family may have been right in dissuading him from this path. In 1857 his landmark collection of poems *Les Fleurs du Mal* was published, including erotic work and poems of lesbian sex and of repulsion and decay, showing how he found inspiration in the streets, the secret life of Paris, and in revolt and blasphemy. He wrote of it, 'In this dreadful book I have put all my heart, all my tenderness, all my religion (disguised), all my hatred'.[17]

One of the poems, 'Spleen' (LXXX) has the poet saying, 'I am like the king of a rainy country [Je suis comme le roi d'un pays pluvieux]'. No sex nor luxury can rouse this potentate from his lassitude; even baths of blood can't raise this bewildered cadaver, 'Where instead of blood flows the green waters of Lethe [Où coule au lieu de sang l'eau verte du Léthé]'. The green waters of forgetfulness, with their lethargy-inducing effect, could only be absinthe.[18]

Baudelaire was prosecuted, along with his publisher and printer, and fined for offences against public morals; six of the poems were banned. He was not feted as the great and innovative poet he believed himself to be: the consuming disappointment of his life. The failure of *Les Fleurs du Mal* was a bitter blow from which Baudelaire never recovered. By his thirties he was worn out by drink, drugs and syphilis. There is a reminiscence of his arriving with a struggle at the Café du Madrid on the Boulevard Montmartre and turning over a carafe of water on a table next to him, saying, 'the

sight of water is insufferable to me', then taking two or three absinthes
– one presumes without water.[19]

In his 1861 essay to artificial paradises he hymned opium, hashish,
brandy, wine and absinthe. Baudelaire's life became increasingly
desperate and sordid. When his money ran out, he went to Belgium
in 1864 in a hopeless effort to raise cash by lecturing. He drank
absinthe and took opium to dull the pain of his syphilis until finally
he fell down in the street outside the Saint-Loup church in Namur,
while out walking with the artist Félicien Rops. Rops, one of
Baudelaire's staunch supporters, had drawn the frontispiece for
Wreckage, a book printing the six poems from *Les Fleurs du Mal*
which had been censored in France. Baudelaire was brought back
in 1866 suffering from general paralysis – a frequent concomitant
of advanced syphilis. A year later, at the age of 46, he was buried
in Montparnasse cemetery with such friends as Manet, Verlaine
and Théodore de Banville in attendance.

Much of his work was unpublished or out of print at the time
of his death, but both his life and his work became the inspiration
for the next generation of French poets, such as Rimbaud and
Verlaine, and a generation of English decadents, including Ernest
Dowson, who were not born when *Fleurs du Mal* was published.
It was in painting, however, that the impact of his thought had
immediate effect.

Baudelaire, though 11 years older than Edouard Manet, had
become his good friend, and was the first to praise Manet's work
publicly. From 1858 they would dine together, and Baudelaire
accompanied the artist on sketching expeditions. It was in part in
an attempt to please Baudelaire that Manet painted his first major
work, *The Absinthe Drinker*, in 1859 in a ground-breaking style
which crossed from the classical to the art of realism.

Manet was from a well-to-do family, the son of a civil servant
who became a judge. His brothers were to become a civil servant
and a prison inspector, while Edouard was selected by his father to
be the lawyer of the family. After drawing lessons paid for by his
uncle, however, the 16-year-old told his father he would not be a

lawyer but a painter. His father compromised and sent him to naval college. His repeated failure to pass the college examinations led him at the age of 18 in 1850 to join the studio of Thomas Couture, who was given to painting subjects such as *The Romans of the Decadence,* which combined classical subject matter with titillating treatments of nudes to appeal to bourgeois taste. A career in art was not, in the middle of the nineteenth century, considered unsuited to a bourgeois existence: a classical artist could have his work hung at the Salon, enjoy commissions from rich patrons, and eventually be elected to the Institut de France.

Manet's desire to paint with greater realism meant he frequently clashed with his tutor, however. He wanted to draw from models posed naturally, and even fully clothed rather than conventionally nude. Manet railed, 'I don't know why I'm here. Everything we see around us is ridiculous. The light is false. The shadows are false. When I come to the studio, it seems to me that I'm entering a tomb.'[20] Manet tried to please, including taking a trip to Italy to copy the old masters, but if anything this increased his wish to find a style which he could reconcile with what he saw rather than what he was told to paint. Couture finally told Manet that if he had the pretension to be the leader of a new school in art, he had better do it elsewhere.

Manet did set up his own studio in the Rue Lavoisier, where he painted *Boy with Cherries.* When the model for this, Alexandre, hanged himself from a nail in the studio, Manet was deeply shocked and became obsessed with images of wretchedness. Baudelaire wrote a poem, 'La Corde', about the suicide, which he dedicated to Manet.

Manet moved studios to the Rue de Villiers, and at 27 painted his first radical masterpiece, *The Absinthe Drinker*, a portrait of a drunken rag-picker named Collardet whom Manet encountered near the Louvre, where he had been studying Velasquez. It is a stark painting with a limited palette of browns and blacks, painted directly from the model with a fierce immediacy. Collardet is not ashamed of his condition, he simply exists as a literal truth with no intervening moral gloss, he is not asking for pity, he has, indeed, a somewhat arrogant dignity with his tall hat and his blanket wrapped around him like a cloak. Indeed, Collardet was so unapologetic about his condition that once Manet had made his acquaintance the rag-picker took to calling round and making a nuisance of himself in the studio.

Under the influence of the classical masters and Couture's precise training, Manet had developed a modern style in which the technical simplicity he had studied in Velasquez and Hals mixed with Baudelaire's theories about the correspondence between nature and art. His understanding was deepened by the suicide of his boy model and his observation of the misery of life, which he saw on his sketching walks.

While the painting seems always to have been known as *The Absinthe Drinker*, the item which visually identifies it as unequivo-cally connected to the drink – the rather incongruous glass on the brick wall – was added later, between 1867 and 1872. Manet first painted the full-length figure, with the bottle at his feet. He later cut the picture down, removing the bottle and feet, and it was exhibited thus for a retrospective exhibition in 1867 at the Paris Universal Exposition, an exhibition which was put on at his own expense. He then added 16 inches of canvas, with the intention of making a three-quarter length portrait into a full-length image to form part of a series of full-length images of beggars. The glass of absinthe was now added, so that in 1872 the picture was as it is currently depicted, when it was sold to the art dealer Paul Durand-Ruel.[21]

If Manet hoped to win over Couture with his combination of the techniques of Velasquez with the themes of everyday life, he was disappointed. Couture was disgusted: 'An absinthe drinker! And they paint abominations like that! My poor friend, you are the absinthe drinker. It is you who have lost your moral sense,' he said, clearly indicating the link between absinthe, the new art and immorality.[22]

Encouraged by Baudelaire, Manet continued with confidence; the picture was the first he submitted to the Salon. It was refused because its subject matter was taken as vulgar, though, significantly, Delacroix voted for its admission. Baudelaire was with him when Manet discovered he had been rejected for the Salon, and the poet consoled his friend by saying that he must be himself.[23] As the Salon was the only public exhibition of any standing in France, a refusal could curse an artist's career, and the judges, almost all members of the Institute, could stifle any incipient artistic innovation under their expectations of conservatism. The rejection of *The Absinthe Drinker* was an important step in the downfall of the Salon as an arbiter of style, signifying the vast division between the Institute's preference and that of the most progressive artists. Protest over this and other refusals became so great that Emperor Napoleon III ordered a special exhibition of them, known as the Salon des Refusés, where many of those who later became known as impressionists were first seen by the public.

Manet, at 37, was the oldest of the group of new artists including Degas, Renoir, Monet and Pissarro, and was accepted as their leader. He and his followers met at the Café de Bade until 1866, when they moved to the Café Guerbois near the Place de Clichy, with a large front hall in white and gold and full of mirrors, leading on to a darker hall of billiard tables and card players, so the conversations of the artists were held against a background of the soft smacking of billiard balls.

Later they were driven out by the noise of a new generation of billiard players, and were to frequent the Nouvelle Athènes in the Place Pigalle. George Moore, who was to become a leading writer, but who studied painting in Paris, described the life of the cafés in tones of vivid excitement:

> I did not go to either Oxford or Cambridge but I went to the Nouvelle Athènes...Ah! the morning idlenesses and the long evenings when life was but a summer illusion, the grey moonlight on the Place [Pigalle] where we used to stand on the pavements, the shutters clanging up behind us, loath to separate, thinking of what we had left said, and how much better we might have enforced our arguments...With what strange, almost unnatural

clearness do I see and hear – see the white face of that café, the
white nose of the block of houses, stretching up to the Place,
between two streets, and I know what shops are there. I can hear
the glass door of the café grate on the sand as I open it. I can recall
the smell of every hour. In the morning that of the eggs frizzling
in butter, the pungent cigarette, coffee and bad cognac; at five
o'clock the fragrant odour of absinthe; and soon after the steam-
ing soup ascends from the kitchen; and as the evening advances,
the mingled smells of cigarettes, coffee and weak beer.

Moore describes how the door scrapes on the sand and Manet enters:

Although by birth and by art essentially Parisian, there was something in his appearance and manner of speaking that often
suggested an Englishman. Perhaps it was his dress – his clean-cut
clothes and figure … He sits next to Degas, that round-shouldered
man in a suit of pepper and salt. There is nothing very trenchantly
French about him either, except the large necktie; his eyes are
small and his words are sharp, ironical, cynical. These two men
are the leaders of the impressionist school.

Pissarro calls in, and Catulle Mendès after he has finished correcting
his proofs; meanwhile, Villier de l'Isle-Adam is chatting up 'that fair
girl with heavy eyelids, stupid and sensual'.[24]

Manet's pictures of women in bars illustrate the increased use
of cafés by women. It became possible for two respectable women
to sit and talk on a *terrasse* at the *heure verte*. It was daring for women
to take to this modish concoction in preference to the small, sweet
liqueurs which had previously been the lady's drink. Absinthe
drinking for women came to be seen as a sign of their emancipation,
akin to smoking cigarettes.[25]

The café remained, however, a place for women of uncertain
virtue, who frequented the places in the hope of finding a bourgeois
man to treat them. Manet's café scenes show women both serving
and drinking, demonstrating the increasing use by patrons of women
to attract business. A shocked English visitor described this as
one of the examples of 'immorality staring you in the face on the
Boulevards at night; you see it in the cafés; in the Brasseries, where

women are waiters instead of men'.[26] Even more direct means were used to pull in customers at a time of intense competition when new cafés were springing up all over the city. Henri Balesta in 1860 describes a situation in which a bar owner employs two or three women whom Balesta describes as the 'commercial travellers, agent provocateurs of absinthe'. Their mission, at three francs a day, was to frequent balls and public places, to find men and bring them back to their patron's bar, staying with them to keep them drinking.[27]

Félicien Rops, a Belgian who had settled in Paris around 1860, drew *La Buveuse d'Absinthe* (meaning specifically the female absinthe drinker) in 1865 at the age of around 32 and frequently afterwards drew the same subject over the next 30 years. The picture always shows a slender woman leaning against a pillar outside a dance-hall, her low neckline and fine dress showing she is part of the nightlife. Her insouciant attitude, accompanied by her staring eyes, slightly opened mouth and haggard expression suggest she is a prostitute. She became the archetype of the female absinthe drinker: hungry, vampish, wasted to the soul.

Joris-Karl Huysmans, writer of *A Rebours* (meaning 'against the grain'), often said to be the supreme expression of the decadent spirit, described Rops's absinthe drinker:

> M. Rops has created a type of woman that we will dream of, dream of again and be drawn back to, the type of absinthe drinker who, brutalised and hungry, grows ever more menacing and more voracious, with her face frozen and empty, villainous and hard, with her limpid eyes with a look as fixed and cruel as a lesbian's, with her mouth a little open, her nose regular and short... the girl bitten by the green poison leans her exhausted spine on a column of the bal Mabille and it seems that the image of Syphilitic Death is going to cut short the ravaged thread of her life.[28]

Huysmans is wrong: it was not the Bal Mabille aux Champs Elysées but the Bal Bullier, which was set up in the Avenue de L'Observatoire, half way between the Latin Quarter and Montparnasse in 1838 by François Bullier. In 1847 he moved his establishment to the other side of the avenue, where it opened with decor celebrating the 1001

Nights with Moorish decor, individually designed booths, private rooms and decorative fountains.

On exhibition of his absinthe drinker at the International Exhibition of Fine Art in his home town of Namur in Belgium, Rops felt himself 'spat upon':

> Namur was as one: the Société du Casino, the college of the mayor and his aldermen, the society of industry and commerce, the board of arbitration, the congregation of St Ives, the Sodality of St Peter in Chains, the Association for the Relief of China, the barons and retainers of high society were united to inflict a well deserved rebuke to an artist who 'far from consecrating his talent to the reproduction of gracious and elegant works, prostitutes his pencil complacently to the reproduction of scenes imprinted with a repellent realism'.

With unconcealed glee at this notoriety, Rops continues to tell his friend Jean d'Ardenne how his *La Buveuse d'Absinthe* blew the minds ('les têtes… s'epanouissaient') of his bourgeois countrymen.[29]

Still, his work had its appreciators. The mystical writer Joséphin Péladan wrote a poem in praise of Rops, one stanza of which reads:

> What lightening has flashed around your sleek little girls?
> What perverted debauchery, what devastating love
> Filled their melancholy with the glittering lights of absinthe!
> [Quels éclairs ont nimbé tes fillettes polies?
> Quel stupre assez pervers, quel amour dévasté
> Met des reflets d'absinthe en leurs mélancolies!][30]

Rops used different models for his *Buveuse d'Absinthe,* but it seems they had to live the part. He offered a newly drawn *Buveuse d'Absinthe* for exhibition in 1876, explaining to a friend: 'it's a girl called Marie Joliet who arrives every evening drunk at the Bal Bullier and who sees with eyes of electric death. I had her pose and I worked to take down just what I saw.'

The Goncourt brothers' novel *Manette Salomon* of 1867 has the eponymous protagonist, an artist's model, moving in with the artist Coriolis, where her avarice ruins his art and his life. The novel has a picture of those 'women without profession' who hang around towards dinner-time in the hope of meeting a man who does not wish to dine alone. Most often, around six, they fall back on pooling their resources so they are able to return to the café, drinking absinthes and anisettes.

The wretched nature of such an existence was described by a journalist, Maxime Rude, seeing a group of three women in a café staring longingly at his meal late at night. A man comes in and buys them an absinthe each then finishes his own drink and leaves. One of the miserable woman sighs, 'An absinthe, not even an onion soup! I really need an absinthe! I've had seven since last night and I haven't even had breakfast.'[31]

The acceptance by the Salon in 1880 of Marius Michel's sluttish female absinthe drinker, staring directly across her absinthe at the viewer with a cigarette in her hand, is an indication of how far official acceptance of such subjects had changed since Manet's *The Absinthe Drinker* was rejected 20 years previously. Emile Zola described it, 'A tart is sitting on a couch in a café and drinking steadily and miserably the morbid liqueur standing green and thick before her'.[32]

Poems addressed to female absinthe drinkers often drip with a contemptuous pity which disclose that the writer, a bohemian, is clearly of a superior class and able to stand in judgement on drinkers of the 'ghastly green liquid' even if, like Maurice Rollinat, who wrote 'Poor Woman Drinker', he was an absinthe drinker himself (though the son of a deputy to the Constituent Assembly). Part of it runs, 'When she had a feverish/ cough [presumably from consumption] oh, how she suffered/ She was always pregnant!/ She raged, "That tires me out!/ I am already in hell."/ Poor absinthe drinker!'[33]

Rollinat took his inspiration from Poe and, as Sherard said, he 'seemed to be modelling his life also on that of his unhappy master. It was drugs, absinthe: absinthe, drugs.'[34] It was part of bohemian life that artists would take for their muse girls like Rops's *buveuse d'absinthe*. Manet's friend the poet and inventor Charles Cros wrote a poem about the girls who hung around the bars: 'Young girl of the taverns,/ from what country have you come,/ that you show off your bosom/ for the eyes of the stupid public?...Young girl of the taverns,/ you prefer to the plough,/ to hear the sounds of the street,/ where we pour absinthe in torrents...'[35]

Cros, while by no means the finest poet of the period, wrote what is arguably the best absinthe poem ever written, 'Lendemain', 'The Morning After' (the poem appears in full in French on page 251):

With flowers and with women,
with absinthe and with fire,
we can divert ourselves a little,
acting our parts in the play.

Absinthe drunk on a winter evening,
lights up in green the smoky soul;
and the flowers on the darling one
exude perfume before the bright fire.

Then kisses lose their charms,
having lasted a few seasons,
reciprocal betrayal means
you leave one day without tears.

You burn letters and flowers
then the love-nest catches fire
and if the sad life is spared,
only absinthe and indigestion remain.

The portraits are eaten up in the flames,
the shrivelled fingers are trembling,
you die having slept too long
with the flowers, with the women.

Cros was the son of a doctor of law and philosophy who had lost his university post in 1849 because of his revolutionary views. He had three sons: Antoine, a doctor, Henri, a sculptor who exhibited with the impressionists, and Charles, a poet, inventor, musician and scholar, and eventually a 20-a-day absinthe drinker. He had been a child prodigy, teaching himself Hebrew and Sanskrit at the age of 11 and studied philology, then medicine, then astrology in Paris. He was a prolific inventor: the phonograph he developed in 1877, called a Paréophone, preceded that of Edison, by whom he was eclipsed as Cros lacked the funds to patent his device.

He invented an 'automatic telegraph', wrote on possible communication between planets, and discovered a method of synthesising rubies. Cros was a pioneer of colour photography, publishing on the theory as early as 1869 and going on in 1882 to make a colour print of Manet's painting *Jeanne*. A good friend of Manet, he attended Manet's mother's Thursday soirees in the Rue de Saint-Pétersbourg in the company also of Zola and Degas.[36]

Cros met other poets, including Verlaine, in the salon of Nina de Callias (née Villard), the daughter of a Lyon barrister. She had married a journalist, Hector de Callias, but the marriage was doomed by his greater affection for absinthe than for family life, and they separated. She consoled herself with talented young men, including Cros, who became her lover from 1868 until 1877.

Cros's poetry famously included symbolist monologues such as 'The Green Day', in which the green man goes through a day experiencing nothing but green, his drink inevitably being absinthe. One of his best known works, 'The Red Herring' ('Le Hareng Saur') is about a blank wall on which a ladder is rested in order to hammer a nail in and suspend a smoked herring. The last stanza remarks that he wrote it to put 'Serious, serious, serious people into a fury [Pour mettre en fureur les gens – graves, graves, graves]'.

Cros formed the Zutistes in 1883, devoted to 'incoherence and paradox', one of the organisations preceding the symbolists, which led the surrealists to regard him as an important predecessor. When he created the Zutistes, Cros left behind a poetic grouping who, not to be outdone, called themselves the Jemenfoutistes (the 'Idon'tgiveafuckists').[37]

Absinthe also figured largely in the lives of other artists of the time who, if poorly remembered today, made a real contribution to the carnival of art. Absinthe had been a fascinating and stylish drink, but what made it diabolical, the gateway both to artistic creativity and madness? One of the attractions for artists of depictions of absinthe drinkers was that it sent drinkers into a reverie, so what was generally depicted in, for example, the work of Jean-François Raffaëlli was a still life of decanter and glass with a static drinker looking into space. For all the controversy which was to develop over absinthe, all could agree that what was being experienced was a personal feeling rather than a communal one: no one ever proposed an absinthe sing-song.

3 Absinthe for the People

THE IMPORTANCE OF MANET'S *ABSINTHE DRINKER* in the history of painting understandably obscures its documentary relevance. The 1859 painting shows a model who is clearly neither an artist nor a representative of the military nor the bourgeoisie, but an impoverished alcoholic who has chosen absinthe as his drink of choice. The bitterness of the drink and the wretchedness of the rag-picker's life make an appropriate artistic metaphor which justify Manet's use of this subject and indicates a developing social truth: absinthe was becoming a drink of the poor.

As a drink of the boulevards, absinthe had been out of the financial range of the poor, but patrons of the little 'caboulots' or drinking shacks caught on to a new trend quickly and started to produce adulterated and highly alcoholic drinks which they called absinthe.

The British writer R.H. Sherard, who lived in Paris for long periods between 1883 and 1906, made a very clear distinction between the absinthe sold in the cafés and adulterated material sold cheaply to the poor: 'fourteen distinct poisons enter into the composition of good absinthe, such as is retailed at the best cafés', attests Sherard.

> Of what the stuff is made which is sold in the popular bars in
> Paris and the provinces at a penny ha'penny [Sherard translates

centimes for an English audience] the glass one shudders to think. I have heard that in the distilleries the workers take delight in throwing filth into the pots in which *la verte* is being manufactured, on the principle that nothing is too dirty for people with such a dirty habit as that of drinking absinthe…I have seen men, aye and women too, drink fifteen 'goes' of this mixture in the early morning on empty stomachs. 'Killing the worm' they call it, or 'strangling a parrot.'[1]

The hedonistic Second Empire (1852–70) had seen a *de facto* liberalisation of the licensing laws which led to a vast increase in the number of *débits de boissons* (drink sellers) – not only in bars and cafés, but also in places where drink was sold, including groceries and pastry shops. A lithograph of 1862 by Emile Benasset shows the poor gathered around the sort of fountain from which they would generally take drinking water, but in this case the fountain has a death's head and is disgorging absinthe.

The poor were much in evidence as the 1860s wore on, losing work in the wine and silk industries as a result of vine lice and a silkworm disease; in the cotton industry, as a result of the effects of the American Civil War; and suffering from the effects of a crisis in credit as confidence in the regime ebbed. All contributed to a general impoverishment of society.

Henry de Kock's popular novel of 1863 *Les Buveurs d'Absinthe* hardly mentioned the drink, but its appropriation for the title shows how absinthe had become a potent literary symbol. A Dr Legrain, describing the descent of absinthe from the boulevards to the shacks said, 'The most serious contamination phenomenon is that which led the worker on the path of the bourgeois'.[2]

The most degraded alcoholics were seeking out absinthe as they will always seek out the source of alcohol which combines potency with low price. In noting a connection between absinthe and degradation, Henri Balesta, the playwright and writer of short stories about Parisian life, published in 1860 the first literary description of 'absinthism' as a supposedly distinct condition in his book *Absinthe et Absintheurs*.

After describing the drink on the boulevards, Balesta directs his reader to search in the *caboulots* to find the absintheur, which means that the suggestion that absinthe was 'still a fairly exotic drink in France' in 1863 must be qualified.[3] In 1860 absinthe was 15 centimes a glass, when 3 francs a day was a good labourer's wage.[4] Balesta describes the absinthe drinker to be found in one of these wretched places:

> Gloomy, overcome, falling under his own weight, his complexion marbled by reddish marks, his eyes dim, his lips discoloured, his shoulders bowed by premature age, he stays there entire days in the same place, alone and a stranger to those who pass around him, drinking, drinking, emptying his glass only in order to fill it again.
>
> Don't believe that absinthomania is a special vice of the idle rich. The man of the people, the worker, is not spared the contagion. He also gives himself up, bound hand and foot, to the demon who calls for him. Yet how the vices of the poor bring disasters with them. The rich, the idle, the useless, strive to kill time, their most mortal enemy. If they kill themselves sometimes, what does it matter? They die alone, no one relies on them.
>
> But the poor man, he drags five or six lives with him: his invalid father and mother, who had looked after him while young so he would look after them while old, his wife and his children. He borrows against his week's wages to satisfy his vice and there are four, five, ten miserable creatures who go hungry...There is no pleasure for the father which does not cost a tear for the mother.[5]

One night the sodden worker comes back to his hovel, his children calling for bread, his wife reproaching him for his laziness. 'Fury takes him, a fury made the more terrible because he is wrong and he knows it: he raises his hand to the poor woman who has linked her misery to his, he hits her as the reward for ten years of devotion.' Soon the shabby apartment is denuded of what articles can be sold: pictures, the bed on which his children were born, his father's watch. The mother dies, exhausted by poverty and weakened by worry. The son becomes a vagrant, begging for his bread and the girl becomes a prostitute in the taverns. Balesta assures the reader that this is the cost of a glass of absinthe.[6]

Absinthe was specifically blamed for alcoholism in a previously temperate nation by, for example, the novelist Alphonse Daudet, no mean absinthe drinker himself, who said,

> This habit was acquired by our soldiers in Algeria and Tunisia during our wars there, and was by them brought back to France. Before those wars we were a very sober people. In the South especially, an intemperate man was altogether an exception. We used to boast that we were born drunk, that is to say intoxicated with the light and warmth of our sun, and so stood in no need of alcoholic stimulants. But all that, *hélas*, is changed now.[7]

According to Alexandre Dumas, the ravages of absinthe had not spared the army which had introduced the drink to France. He wrote, 'There is not a regimental surgeon who will not tell you that absinthe has killed more Frenchman in Africa than the flittá, the yataghan, and the guns of the Arabs put together'.[8]

Absinthe was believed to have particular qualities to undermine moral fibre, not apparently shared by other forms of alcohol. Taking his images from the contemporary horror of venereal disease, Balesta maintains that 'absinthomania' is essentially contagious, that 'it is by the man that the evil is transmitted to the female'.[9] Sherard also makes a point of remarking on the vile spectre of the *absintheuse*: 'The absinthe woman is that dreadful female who only emerges from her nameless lairs in times of popular disturbance, gaunt, haggard, a Fury of death and destruction'.[10]

In the progressive manner of such literature, Balesta's 1860 tract now goes further, to give an example of a child destroyed by absinthe: a cabinet-maker called Aubin has lost his wife to illness, leaving him with a ten-year-old child. Previously he had worked indefatigably, but now he spends his nights in a tavern with five or six idlers. Unwilling to leave the child behind, he takes her too, and she waits miserably in a corner during his revels. One night he has a 'diabolical idea': he offers the girl absinthe to give her 'strength and colour'. She thinks the taste revolting, and his friends find it amusing to repeat the gesture and offer her more. The absinthe does the trick: she loses her habitual torpor and becomes a bright, animated child.

The poor giving absinthe to children – generally to quieten young ones, rather than to liven them up – became a common theme. It was the subject of Jean-François Raffaëlli's picture *Au Café, l'absinthe pernod* of around 1885, in which a woman of the barrier region of outer Paris sits at a wooden table and leers as she doses a child in her arms while her husband slumps on the table, head in his hands and pipe in his mouth, looking on in an absinthe stupor.

In Balesta's story, Marie continues drinking a little absinthe with her father, and comes to enjoy it and ask for the drink, until one day she progresses to her own glass: 'true triumph for her father'. Soon she begins to develop terrible symptoms: 'anxiety, heaviness around the heart, insomnia, febrile movements, paralysis of the stomach'. Aubin calls in a doctor, who with a single examination divines the cause, saying, 'You have used up the strength of your daughter in over-excitement, in a month she will have finished her life and it is you who will have killed her'. The girl lives for three weeks more and Aubin hangs himself in their garret.[11]

This sort of improving story was familiar to Anglo-Saxon audiences from the temperance movement, a movement which found little favour in France, where viniculture and wine drinking was part of life. In France, anti-absinthism was to take the place of temperance, though the symptoms complained of were not peculiar to absinthe, but common to all alcohol.

Such considerations, of absinthe drinking having become an activity indulged by entire families, including children, preceded the vast increase in absinthe drinking which was to occur in the last three decades of the nineteenth century. Up until then among the poor, absinthe, or whatever adulterated versions of it were in currency, was the drink of a hard-drinking minority. The appearance of the tiny phylloxera insect on vines in 1863 was the first sign of a general disaster for French viniculture which was to become widespread after 1875. The plant-lice or vine-pest, somehow imported from America, damaged the vines and led to a serious shortage of grapes.

Absinthe had been made with alcohol extracted from wine. Thus, as a drink made with several processes after wine had already been produced, it was of necessity more expensive than wine. The wine blight obliged manufacturers to turn away from wine alcohol, to cheaper 'industrial' alcohol made from beets, molasses or grains. The result was an inexpensively produced absinthe which could be bought for 10 centimes less than a glass of wine but which was many times stronger – absinthe had an alcoholic content of 55–75 per cent alcohol by volume, as compared to 8 or 9 for table wine, though of course it should be borne in mind that absinthe would usually be diluted.[12]

The effect on absinthe drinking was immense: wine had been the drink of choice of the poor; now they could not afford wine, and absinthe became ubiquitous. Taxes were levied on the new distilled spirits in an attempt to protect the wine industry, but improvements in techniques for making *alcool d'industrie* improved, and absinthe therefore remained cheaper than wine. Moreover, a taste for absinthe was retained even after the first infestation was over, and the relative position of wine against absinthe was not improved by another attack of phylloxera in the 1880s.

As if a blight on wine were not enough of a curse for France, the Empire fell at the same time. Napoleon III's position had been confirmed by a plebiscite supporting him by seven million to one-and-a-half million on 8 May 1870, but two months later he allowed the Prussian chancellor, Bismarck, to goad him into an attack for which France was ill-prepared. Napoleon III was forced to abdicate in the face of military defeat.

Paris was besieged by the Prussians from September 1870. Food quickly ran out, and the cellars of the decamped bourgeoisie were raided, the alcohol needed more for calories than inebriation, but the result was that the days of the so-called commune resembled a long debauch of danger and drunkenness. In the seven months from October 1870 to May 1871 the consumption of alcohol was five times as much as it was in an ordinary year.[13]

The conservative National Assembly which came into power to conclude a peace with the invaders was deeply mistrusted by republican Paris. Resistance broke out in March 1871 in response to attempts to disarm the National Guard, largely composed of workers who had fought during the siege.

French regular forces moved in on the commune after 10 weeks and rounded up the communards, massacring thousands, most notably in Père Lachaise cemetery. Many of the artists of the period had taken part in the defence of Paris – Manet, Degas, Tissot, Cros and the sculptor Cuvelier were active; Verlaine was press officer for the commune and Courbet headed the Artists' Commission.

The beginnings of the Third Republic were a miserable affair, with shame for France's ignominious defeat mixed with maudlin regret for the sacrifices of the army. The incompetence of the army and the French leadership which had led the nation into conflict were forgotten in the lachrymose stupor. The defeat was taken absurdly personally: one French army officer refused to go to the theatre or any place of enjoyment as long as Alsace and Lorraine were still in German hands; Degas was once confronted by one of Whistler's unusual hats and remarked, 'Yes, it suits you very well, but that won't get us back Alsace and Lorraine'.[14]

It was in this atmosphere that Degas produced his undoubted masterpiece known as *L'Absinthe*. Degas, born into a banking family in 1834, abandoned study of the law to enroll at the Ecole des Beaux-Arts, where he was probably planning a career as a painter of heroic historic subjects, such as *Seramis Founding Babylon*, which he painted in 1861. In the later 1860s, however, probably influenced by Manet, he began to seek his inspiration in contemporary urban life, and started to paint scenes of race meetings and the ballet with the ease and naturalism which were to become his standard.

The tale told of the first meeting between Manet and Degas is that Manet saw his fellow artist in the Louvre copying a Velasquez directly onto the plate, with no intervening sketch, so confident was he of his skill. 'You've got guts, you'll be lucky if you carry it off,' Manet said and they began a friendship which was later to be punctuated by quarrels.[15] Manet loaned Degas Baudelaire's writing on art from his private library collection, finding the poet's work so profound that he wished his new friend to come under its influence.[16]

Degas's displaced figures, unorthodox cutting and perspective styles give the impression of scenes he has come upon and grabbed as a photographer might, giving his skilful craftsmanship a distinctive, modernistic edge. With the same concentrated detachment he was to depict ballet dancers, laundresses, racehorses and, most importantly in this context, the interior of cafés. He was always an observer, without pity or shame, as if depicting private moments of his figures gave him the private life he lacked. He depicted the world around him as if he were not a part of it, and indeed his private income and irascible nature did give him greater detachment than was enjoyed by his fellow artists.

He organised and took part in the first impressionist exhibition in 1874, and became impatient with fellow artists (including Manet) when the need for sales meant that they felt obliged so to compromise avant-garde principles as to exhibit with mainstream artists. Renoir, one of Degas's companions, said, 'All his friends had to leave him,' and described him as 'vitriolic, violent and uncompromising'.[17]

He was to become one of the central figures of impressionism, meeting with Manet and his acolytes in the Café Guerbois, where the smell of absinthe mingled with that of tobacco and they talked of technique and composition. Later they moved to the Nouvelle Athènes, which Degas used for the scene of what became known as *L'Absinthe*.

He made a series of studies in his notebook titled 'Hélène [*sic*] et Desboutin dans un café'.[18] The male model was Marcellin Desboutin, a painter and etcher who had studied under Couture (as did Manet). From 1854 he spent most of his time in Florence, entertaining friends and buying Italian art. He invested heavily in land and lost a fortune, returning to Paris around 1873 at the age of 50. He failed to find a publisher for his translation into French of Byron's *Don Juan* and a historical drama in verse which he had written for the stage failed to open because the Franco–Prussian War closed the theatre. He finally settled to the life of a professional artist and printmaker. He became friendly with Degas, Manet, Renoir and Zola, doing etchings of his artistic friends and exhibiting with them in 1876. He also met and drew Watts, Millais, Alma-Tadema and Leighton in London in 1873. Desboutin did not drink absinthe and took some exception to being castigated as an *absintheur*.

The woman is Ellen Andrée, an actress who frequently modelled for artists – two café scenes by Manet, for example, *Au Café* and *Chez le Père Latuille*, feature her. She occasionally had lunch with Degas, and the artist often went to the Théâtre des Variétés to see her. In the late 1880s she was a member of André Antoine's Théâtre-Libre company which helped to introduce Ibsen and Strindberg to French audiences. Notwithstanding this willingness to embrace naturalism, Andrée complained that Degas had 'massacred' her in *L'Absinthe*, and had wilfully placed the glass of absinthe before her and not Desboutin, an example of Degas's quirky sense of humour.[19]

Commentators have suggested Andrée is playing a street prostitute who has come in for a drink between one trick and the next, but this is a reading, and not indicated directly in the painting.[20] She does seem to have a relationship to the male figure – her left foot is touching his, and even though he has occupied so much of the table that she has to stand her water decanter on the next one, she does not move up to an empty place, as if she finds even the presence of this indifferent man better than no company at all.

Their isolation in the café is emphasised by the zig-zag images of empty tables, the exhausted decanter on an adjoining table, the reflection of their heads in the mirror behind, and their total lack of interest in each other, as if they are in different worlds. The gloom and loneliness of the scene was doubtless influenced by Degas's inner suffering as an artist after his realisation, during the winter of the siege of Paris at the age of 36, that his sight was failing. Degas was never again to be free from the fear of blindness. Added to his miseries were the death of his father in 1874, with his bank in financial chaos, and the bankruptcy of his brother Achille. Degas assumed the debts as a matter of family honour.

The choice of subject matter was probably intended to be a rejoinder to Manet, whose *Le Bon Bock* , a picture of his friend Belot enjoying a beer, had been the first picture of his to score an unqualified success at the Salon. Manet was on his way to realising his dream of being accepted by the establishment as a master, which is why he did not join with Degas, Monet, Renoir, Sisley, Pissarro and Morisot in the second impressionist exhibition, where *L'Absinthe* was shown.

The exhibition opened at Paul Durand-Ruel's gallery in Rue Le Peletier on 30 March 1876, an event which marked the polarisation of attitudes over impressionism which had begun at the first impressionist exhibition two years previously. The picture was shown under the title *Dans un Café* – that is, the drink was not the focus of attention. Eighteen years earlier Manet's *Absinthe Drinker* had been greeted with outrage for its subject matter and treatment. Degas's woman drinking absinthe, a model in similarly wretched circumstance treated in the impressionistic style, was now placed before the public.

The critical comment is interesting from the point of view of the history of art, but it is significant that, whether with faint praise – 'Monsieur Degas has found some interesting effects' – or condemnation – 'Try to talk reason with Monsieur Degas, tell him that in art there are certain qualities called drawing, colour, technique' – *Dans un Café* was not singled out, and the presence of the drink was not remarked upon.[21] In France absinthe had become part of the scene.

Reflecting on the changes in absinthe consumption at the end of the century, Doctor Eugène Ledoux of Besançon wrote 'in our fathers' time absinthe was an elegant drink: on the terraces and cafés only old warriors from Algeria and the idle bourgeoisie consumed this queer drink that smelled strongly of toothpaste. The bad example came from above: little by little absinthe was democratised.' Now, he worried, the scent of aniseed was everywhere.[22]

By 1876, the time of Degas's painting, all the elements of the absinthe story were in place: it was the hallucinogen for artists, the poison for the poor, and the sophisticated drink for the bourgeoisie. There was also the dreadful but unconfirmed fear that absinthe rendered its drinkers both bad and mad.

Medicine progressed uncertainly between one nation and another in its understanding of alcoholism. The study of alcoholism was more advanced on the continent of Europe than in Britain, where the zealots were in the ascendant after the teetotal takeover of the temperance movement in the 1840s, leaving it anything but temperate. The British temperance movement, founded to restrain and civilise alcohol use by limiting drinking and substituting weaker for stronger drinks, was quickly subsumed by extremists who demonised all alcohol and alcohol users. Their 'all or nothing' attitude towards alcohol did not encourage discussion or a spirit of enquiry into drinking.

A more thoughtful approach was adopted in other parts of Europe, where 'alcoholism' was adopted into medical parlance from 1852–53. It had been coined by the Swedish doctor Magnus Huss, who is said to have started his studies in the subject after a night of drinking as a student when he had the familiar experience of feeling so ill that he swore never to drink to excess again. Alcoholism for him was a form of poisoning, though until late in the nineteenth century he did not include wine and beer as a cause of alcoholism. The confusion surrounding drinking in general was manifest at the ceremony in France awarding Huss a special prize for his contribution to medical science, at which it was said from the platform, 'There may be a good many drunkards in France, but happily there are no alcoholics'.[23]

Balesta described a conversation with an unnamed doctor who informed him that

> there is almost no illness which the abuse of alcohol in general and of absinthe in particular is not able to bring about. Which one depends on the temperament and the predisposition of each individual. Apoplexy, paralysis, chronic illness of the stomach, intestines, liver, gout, dropsy, mental derangement, sterility, impotence, convulsions, epilepsy, depression, hallucinations and finally spontaneous combustion.[24]

Urged to proceed with the eye-popping last remark of this exposition, the doctor offered,

> examine the urine of your absinthe drinkers…the aqueous matter is disposed of by ordinary routes yet the alcoholic portion does not

undergo a complete decomposition and is absorbed throughout the body. Even the muscles are impregnated. Do you understand now that a body saturated with alcohol in the right condition bursts into flames at a given moment, and almost by itself?[25]

Spontaneous human combustion, or 'preternatural combustibility of the human body', was a well-described curio of medicine. Theodric and John Beck in their *Elements of Medical Jurisprudence* of 1842 cite a long list of cases, many taken from one Pierre-Aime Lair, who wrote an article titled 'On the combustion of the human body, produced by long and immoderate use of spirituous liquors'. The Becks, though not questioning the phenomenon, queried whether alcohol was the accelerant which produced human combustion, saying there is no proof of 'saturation of the organs', and that even if it were so it would not render a body combustible. An experimenter called Julia Fontenelle 'immersed pieces of meat for a long time, in alcohol, but on firing it their external surfaces alone was scorched'.[26] Others remarked that a person would die from alcohol poisoning long before imbibing enough alcohol to have even a slight effect on the body's flammability.

Human combustion found its way into world literature with Charles Dickens's *Bleak House* of 1852–53 and Emile Zola's 1893 novel *Doctor Pascal*, both involving characters with a high alcohol intake. There is a genuine correlation between high alcohol intake and bodies being consumed by fire, in that heavy drinkers are more careless around smoking materials and fire, and less likely to be in a fit state to respond promptly to accidents. Late-twentieth-century fire investigators have attributed apparent corporeal combustibility to a 'wick effect' of clothes slowly smouldering and burning body fat, frying away the body's moisture in advance of the heat source.[27] These bizarre phenomena were described by anti-absinthe and temperance propagandists as fitting within their exaggerated expectations of harm.

To witness the madness supposedly caused by absinthe, the anonymous doctor cited by Balesta advised him to 'go to Charenton', which is a large mental institution outside Paris.[28] This was a further development in the tale of the ravages of absinthe: that it not only stupefied with alcohol and hallucinogenic substances, destroyed the health of the individual and undermined the moral fabric of the family, but also sent a drinker mad. It is interesting that this voluble, anonymous doctor does not himself expound on the mental effects of absinthe, but refers the hearer to a specialist.

An American observer was able to report in 1878 that 'the immoderate use of absinthe is said to have caused much of the insanity that now peoples the asylums of Paris'.[29] Doctors in France were hampered in attempting to describe links between alcohol consumption and mental illness, because of the divisions caused by their different specialisations. Doctors in the urban and university hospitals were interested in organic disease; in alcoholics therefore they were concentrating on the different types of cirrhosis and tendon reflex, while the alienists (later to be termed psychiatrists) tended to work outside the towns with long-term psychiatric patients. They were thus using different terminology and looking at different manifestations of illness, so there was no natural unification of their findings.[30]

It is also significant, as Jean-Charles Sournia remarks in his study of alcoholism, that only one theory was entertained in relation to alcohol and mental illness: that alcohol led to mental disturbance. Other hypotheses, such as that alcohol might conceal mental disorders or that mental disease predisposed to alcoholism, were not considered.

Absinthe's position was complicated by the suspicion that it was a unique substance with a unique action, not simply a drink with a high alcohol content. Doctor Auguste Motet examined *absinthistes* at Bicêtre, a leading mental hospital, for a thesis published in 1859, *General considerations on alcoholism and specifically the toxic effects produced in man by the liqueur absinthe*. He considered delirium and epileptic attacks to be evidence of absinthism.

He cites the case of a 34-year-old stonemason who suddenly, and with no obvious reason, left his life of industry and took to drinking 10–12 glasses of absinthe a day, as well as eau-de-vie (alcohol distilled from fruit) and wine. He developed paranoid fears, believing the police were coming to arrest him and that the people looking after him were his enemies. When he went to hospital he assured the attendants repeatedly that he had not killed anyone. He was given the usual treatments for madness (hydrotherapy and rest) and was eventually released, cured.

This is actually a description of what seems to be a paranoid schizophrenic episode, complicated by alcohol. The sudden onset of these symptoms and the fact that they continued even after there was no alcohol (or when the amount in his system was diminishing) suggests this was neither alcoholism nor absinthism. However, the thesis's importance lies in the fact that Motet thought alcoholism and absinthism existed, that they were distinct, and that they were worthy of study.

The earliest report in a medical journal was published in 1864, and in it Louis Marcé defined the 'double action' of absinthe – that is, something in addition to the action of alcohol – in laboratory animals. The dogs and rabbits suffered convulsions, involuntary evacuations and other unpleasant symptoms.[31] As early as 1865 the *Dictionnaire de Médecine* defined absinthism as a 'variety of alcoholism, acute or chronic, caused by the abuse of absinthe and leading (more frequently than alcoholism) to mania and softening of the brain'.

Marcé's research assistant at the Hôpital Bicêtre in Paris was a student, Valentin Magnan, who was to make a considerable career out of his investigation of absinthe, both there and at St Anne's Asylum, also in Paris. Magnan's investigations with animals did not meet with universal approval. An English scientist writing in the *Lancet* in 1869 reported how 'the question whether absinthe exerts any special action other than that of alcohol in general, has been revived by some experiments by MM Magnan and Bouchereau in France'. The experiments placed animals such as guinea pigs in glass jars, some with a saucer full of essence of wormwood, others with one of alcohol. The animals which inhaled wormwood vapours experienced excitement: 'epileptiform convulsions'; the ones which experienced only alcohol became lively then drunk.

'Upon these facts,' the superior Anglo-Saxon wrote,

> it is sought to establish the conclusion that the effects of excessive
> absinthe drinking are seriously different from those of ordinary
> alcoholic intemperance. It is not the first time that we have had
> to notice discussions on this subject, and to comment upon the
> inadequacy of the evidence produced in order to prove that
> absinthism, as met with in the Parisian world, is something
> different in its nature from chronic alcoholism. We have never
> denied the possibility of an ultimate discovery of such differences;
> but we do maintain that as yet no symptoms of absinthism have
> been described which are not to be met with in many of the
> victims of simple alcoholic excess.

He remarked that the sleeplessness, tremor, hallucinations, paralysis, and even epileptiform convulsions, are all well-known symptoms frequently met with in the alcohol drinkers of England. The fact that concentrated fumes of wormwood were peculiarly toxic is evidence of little, as wormwood is present in small proportions in absinthe – no absinthe drinker drinks, or inhales, concentrated wormwood.[32]

Magnan did not take the rebuke, and in 1872 was still reported to be doing nothing more experimentally than distilling essences of absinthe and injecting them into dogs to produce fits.[33] Magnan in the early 1870s attempted to see the fits of acute alcoholism as almost invariably connected to absinthe (to be fair to him, they may often have been, in his practice) though the fact that they sometimes were not caused him problems: 'The fit, then is ... due to a distinct cause, which from the antecedent history is usually absinthe, more rarely bitters, vermouth, or vin blanc, the adulterated white wine which is sold retail in Paris by most of the wine merchants'.[34]

Magnan's answer was to look more closely at the precise action of absinthe and suggest a mechanism for the delirium of absinthe, as distinct from the *delirium tremens* ('trembling', as he describes it) which is common to all alcoholism.

> Absinthe acts in the same way as belladonna, henbane, datura, and
> haschisch (*cannabis Indica*) and does not require, like alcohol, to
> prepare its way, for, as is shown by physiological experiment,

it can rapidly give rise to hallucinations and delirium before the alcohol contained in the liqueur of absinthe has had time to produce trembling in man.[35]

Magnan was concerned to establish a specific absinthe effect, unknown to other forms of alcohol, as the notion of absinthism continued to be contested. A leading academic pharmacist, B. Dupuy, published a detailed monograph in 1875 titled *Absinthe: Its Properties and its Dangers,* which dealt in detail with all known facts about absinthe, and summarised, 'It is not possible to attribute to absinthe essence exclusively the principal morbid effects that are observed in those who partake freely of that drink namely epilepsy and epileptiform attacks. We repeat that alcohol plays the greatest role in their production.'[36]

Magnan and others worked within a framework of prevailing notions that beer and wine were harmless and even beneficial, while spirits such as eau-de-vie or cognac could cause alcoholism and drive a drinker mad. The contested belief was that excessive absinthe drinking was the quickest route to madness – it remained to be demonstrated, and was regarded with some humour by drinkers whose empirical experience showed that 'madness in a bottle' was an excessively simplistic way to describe the supposed dangers of absinthe. It became popular to order absinthe under the nickname 'un train direct' or 'une correspondance', from the phrase 'train direct à Charenton' or 'correspondance à Charenton': a fast route to the madhouse.

The peculiar qualities of absinthe were widely discussed. A French aphorism noted that absinthe gave genius to those who were not blessed with that quality, and took it way from those who were. The humorous magazine *Pêle-Mêle* depicted a bedraggled but cheerful artist saying that he didn't have a sou after the seventh absinthe, but his genius came only after the eighth. It was a joke endlessly repeated; the humorous magazine *La Vie Pour Rire* had a variation: the poet who sits at a café table complaining that it is astonishing – he has drunk four absinthes and has still not written a quatrain for his sonnet, as if this is the fault of the drink.[37]

Balesta has a defender of absinthe speaking of 'a journalist who was obliged by his job to have inspiration at a fixed hour and the only way in which he could never fail to tap his natural spring, as rich as that of Voltaire, was to search for inspiration in a glass of absinthe'. Even Balesta accepts the inspirational powers of absinthe:

> Putting the best face on it, for one, two, five, ten years all will go well and he will have a hundred times, a thousand times the inspiration that he would have had without your absinthe, I grant you. But at the end he would have a hundred times, a thousand times less than if he had never sought inspiration in absinthe, even to the point where inspiration never comes.[38]

What was absinthe doing to them? As early as 1839 some physicians were ascribing a narcotic property to wormwood by virtue of its action in occasioning headache and producing disorders of the nervous system.[39] An American pharmacologist in 1868 tried to define the feeling of taking absinthe:

> you seem to lose your feet, and you mount a boundless realm without horizon. You probably imagine that you are going in the direction of the infinite, whereas you are simply drifting into the incoherent. Absinthe affects the brain unlike any other stimulant; it produces neither the heavy drunkenness of beer, the furious inebriation of brandy, nor the exhilarant intoxication of wine. It is an ignoble poison, destroying life not until it has more or less brutalised its votaries, and made drivelling idiots of them.[40]

Less biased observers claimed that absinthe evoked euphoria without drunkenness, new views, different experiences and unique feelings. In 1859 Jules de Goncourt treated his mistress with absinthe as if with a magic potion and watched the result with clinical interest, the sinister alchemist above the sleeping form, performing an experiment with life. He writes, 'My mistress was lying there beside me, dead drunk with absinthe. I had made her drunk and she was sleeping.' She talked in a somnambulistic stupor:

> little by little, word by word, and recollection by recollection, as if with the eyes of memory, she looked back into her youth, seeing things and faces emerge, under her fixed gaze, from the darkness

in which the past lay sleeping, 'Oh yes he loved me alright!...Yes, they used to say that his mother had a look...He had fair hair... But it wouldn't work...We'd be rich now, wouldn't we...If only my father hadn't done that...But what's done is done...I don't like to say so...' There was something terrifying about bending over that body, in which everything seemed to be extinct and only an animal life lingered on, and hearing the past come back like a ghost returning to a deserted house.[41]

Later pharmacological analysis showed it was the wormwood in absinthe which provided not only its bitter taste but the chemical thujone which was responsible for its unique characteristic: the psychological effects which made it beloved of artists and others seeking new sensations.

Scientific attempts were made in the twentieth century to establish precisely what the effect of thujone was. Researchers in Puerto Rico and Idaho in 1975 published work based on their observation that there are striking similarities between the psychological actions of absinthe and experiences reported by users of marijuana. Researchers compared the properties of thujone and tetrahydracannabinol, the active principles of absinthe and cannabis respectively, and found they have a similar molecular geometry. The paper proposed that both absinthe and cannabis exert their psychological effects by interacting with a common receptor in the central nervous system.[42] Scientific commentators endorsed the approach, one remarking, 'The similarities in molecular structure, described effects, social denouncement, and other related factors between absinthe and cannabis raise many interesting questions which indicate the need for a comparative study of the two'.[43] Absinthe was said to act as an aphrodisiac, which would concur with the suggestion that its effect is caused by an action on the same receptors as cannabis, which heightens sexual (and other) sensations.

Later researchers have questioned this link, however, reporting on experiments to show that thujone did show some affinity for 'cannabinoid receptors' in the brain but did not activate these receptors at 'physiologically relevant' concentrations.[44] For most of the twentieth century there was insufficient interest in wormwood (or thujone) to subject it to modern analytical techniques. A modern pharmacologist analysing published research wrote in 1990, 'The literature on the pharmacology of thujone is, to put it bluntly, second rate, and conclusions as to its effects have been extrapolated far beyond the experimental base'.[45] This is particularly true of the literature from the nineteenth century, when poor experimental techniques were frequently subject to justifiable criticism from the experimenters' peers.

Personal observation tells, however, that absinthe has what pharmacologists call a dose response. That is, the more that is taken, the greater the effect. This is by no means the case with every substance; some have an optimum effective level, after which there is no further effect and some, like cannabis, produce a reverse tolerance, so that a frequent user needs less than someone who has never taken the drug before. Many remarked on the stages of absinthe drinking, including Oscar Wilde, who said, 'The first stage is like ordinary drinking, the second when you begin to see monstrous and cruel things, but if you can persevere you will enter in upon the third stage where you see things that you want to see, wonderful and curious things'.[46] Wilde also remarked on the oddness of the absinthe experience in trying to explain its effects to Ada Leverson, 'Take a top hat. You think you see it as it really is. But if you had never heard of one before and suddenly saw it alone, you'd be frightened or laugh. That is the effect absinthe has, and that is why it drives men mad.'[47]

Absinthe undoubtedly had a psychoactive effect, though this was but one ingredient in the absinthe legend. There was clearly more to the wormwood liqueur than a mildly hallucinogenic green liquid.

4 Poets Breaking the Rules

THE POOR, THE BOURGEOISIE AND THE BOHEMIANS all drank absinthe in their own circles by the 1870s, but they adopted different approaches to the drink, so that the use of absinthe by different groups came to reflect the social status of the drinker.

The democratisation of absinthe caused a problem for the bourgeoisie: they did not wish to abandon the pleasures of the drink, but decorum dictated that they could not be associated with the activities of the lower class. Distinctions had to be made to preserve the refinements of affluence, or the wealthy might appear to be no better than the rest, and that would not do.

The rich would therefore drink higher-quality or 'healthier' absinthe made from wine alcohol rather than 'industrial' alcohol, which made their absinthe satisfyingly expensive, but their sense of propriety called out for other means of determining class. Adherence to *l'heure verte* was one restriction: the bourgeoisie could drink absinthe only as an aperitif, so unlike impoverished absinthe drinkers, who would take it at any time, they had it before dinner – risking social condemnation from the waiter and other dinners if they ordered it after dinner, or ordered more than one or two. This led to the absinthe stroll, where the middle classes would engage in what was effectively an absinthe pub-crawl, with a glass or two taken in one café, then a move on to another for more. It was this constant movement and the changing faces at the tables on the *terrasses* of the boulevards which made *l'heure verte* so magical and such a spectacle. *L'heure verte* was not a scene of people sitting having an aperitif, it was a moving pageant of middle-class life.

R.H. Sherard noted of the absinthe drinker ashamed of his habit, 'He takes his first drink at one café, his second somewhere else and his tenth or twelfth at some tenth or twelfth other café. I know a very distinguished musician who used to start off at the Café Napolitain and finish up at the Gare du Nord…'[1]

The other way to differentiate between the classes was by the addition of absinthe paraphernalia. The extent to which a differential could be made in the cost of the drink was limited, but this was not true of the impedimenta used to drink it, which could be delicately crafted and decorated with expensive materials. All that was required to drink absinthe was a bottle of it, some water and perhaps some sugar to sweeten to taste. Sugar was used to render the drink palatable to most people, though it will not dissolve in alcohol at the concentrations that are common in absinthe, so a drinker could pour water in to lower the alcohol content and then add sugar.

A more elaborate method of doing this, which did not lower the alcohol content so much, was to pour water through a spoon on which a cube of sugar rested. Absinthe spoons had existed for the discerning drinker as early as the 1840s, but their extensive development coincided with the increase in absinthe use by the poor in the last three decades of the nineteenth century, the rich effortlessly asserting their superiority with a display of costly objects. The absinthe ritual was essentially a decorative act: the elaborate vessel to drip absinthe and the spoon with its intricate patterns accompanied the bourgeois increase in acquisition and a passion for the fussy over-decoration of everyday objects. Absinthe impedimenta was not (like the heroin addict's spoon and syringe) integral to the activity. It was a method of demonstrating social superiority, the costly nature of the equipment matching the finesse of the drinker.

Spoons were made in silver, silver plate and copper, zinc and nickel alloys, which were silver in colour and called white metal, and in pewter, nickel and aluminium. Absinthe spoons were increasingly delicate, elaborate and inventive. Many were produced in the shape of the Eiffel Tower after 1889 to commemorate its opening.[2] In place of a jug, cafés began to offer 'absinthe fountains': water dispensers with tiny taps to drip water on the sugar.

Marcel Pagnol described in *Le Temps de Secrets* observing the absinthe ritual for the first time in a bourgeois family where the father of a playmate has declared his wish for 'green-eyed absinthe':

> In a profound silence a sort of ceremony started. He placed before him the glass which was large and strong, after having checked that it was clean. He next took the bottle, uncorked it, scented it and poured an amber-like liquid glinting greenly in a dose which he appeared to view with suspicion because, after examination and reflection, he added several drops.
>
> He then took from the tray a sort of little silver shovel, narrow and long, and decorated with a fretwork of holes in an arabesque design. He placed this item like a bridge on the edges of the glass, and loaded on it two pieces of sugar. Then he turned towards his wife, already holding by the handle a 'gargoulette', an earthenware jug in the form of a cock, and he said, 'To you, my dear'.
>
> One hand on her hip, at the end of her graciously curved arm, she raised the pitcher high then, with infallible aim, allowed a tiny stream of fresh water to fall from the beak of the jug on the morsel of sugar which began slowly to disintegrate ... in the liquid whose level slowly rose I saw forming a sort of milky fog in turning fringes which swirled together while a refreshing odour of aniseed deliciously assailed my nostrils. Two times the master of ceremonies interrupted by raising a hand the falling liquid, which he had judged without doubt too harsh or too abundant. After having examined the draught with an anxious air, then reassured, he gave with a single look the signal to resume the operation.
>
> Suddenly he stopped, and with an imperious gesture he halted the stream of water, as if a single drop more would have instantly despoiled the sacred drink.[3]

As this was clearly a man of higher education and refinement, Marcel deduced that the drink could not be the same as the Pernod widely drunk by farm workers in his part of the world, which he knew reduced men to stammering insanity; it must be something different, 'without doubt a poet's beverage'.

Pagnol's amused scorn is for the pretentiousness of this bourgeois affecting of an artistic temperament. As the lower classes aped the upper-middle class with cheaper imitations of their objects, the bourgeoisie looked to the excitement and freedom of the emotional jungle of bohemia, to a world which shimmered with beauty and glistened with danger. The bohemian legend was celebrated in tales of the lives of those such as Verlaine, Rimbaud, Gauguin and van Gogh who dared to leap out of bourgeois life and face the world with no shield but their talent.

While the bourgeoisie wanted the frisson of danger and a taste of the licence which the bohemian life supposedly offered, the bohemians felt the need further to distance themselves from their middle-class roots. As the bourgeoisie separated themselves with the impedimenta of absinthe and a carefully ordered life, bohemians such as Verlaine and Rimbaud defined themselves by uncontrolled drinking and deliberate disorder: 'dérèglement', a rejection of the nice rules of society. If it was necessary for the bourgeoisie to differentiate themselves from the poor, it was imperative for the bohemians to distance themselves from the bourgeoisie. The way they used absinthe was a defining activity in this distancing, and Verlaine was the cynosure.

Paul Verlaine was born in 1844, the only child of a moderately well-off army officer. The future poet was spoiled as a child by his mother, who had suffered three miscarriages previous to his birth, and he developed a precocious talent, writing his first published poems when he was a teenager. He developed his cynicism and love of the obscene at puberty, which was accompanied by his already ugly features becoming more pronounced. He was using the services of prostitutes before the age of 20.

He became a clerk in an insurance company, then went into the service of local government in Paris, at the same time frequenting literary cafés, where he met poets of what came to be called the Parnassian group. The artistic objective of the Parnassians was initially similar to that which motivated the early impressionists: to represent the spirit of a scientific age in reaction against romanticism. The first series of *La Parnasse contemporain*, to which Baudelaire contributed shortly before his death and Verlaine contributed eight pieces, was issued through 1866. Through his association with the Parnassians, Verlaine met such contemporaries as Mallarmé, Catulle Mendès, Villiers de l'Isle-Adam and Anatole France.

Verlaine's friend Edmond Lepelletier remembers waiting for Verlaine at the door of his office at 5pm and going to the Café d'Orient, a vast establishment with billiard tables on the Rue de Clichy, where they would have heated discussions on literature, art and politics. Even at a young age, Lepelletier thought it worth remarking on the avidity with which Verlaine would drink his absinthe and replenish the glass. Another friend remembered that every time Verlaine visited a particular bookshop he would stop at a nearby bar, sometimes taking more than one absinthe, which made it difficult to drag him away.[4] Less than a model town-hall employee, he would leave his hat in the office to imply that he was still in the building but skip out at midday to the Café du Gaz to meet his poetical friends, who were already publishing his work in literary reviews.[5]

Two shocks rocked the life of the young Verlaine: the death of his father when Verlaine was 21, and that of his beloved cousin Elisa two years later. He now established a pattern of drinking heavily, for days and nights at a stretch, in times of emotional stress. 'I fell back on absinthe, absinthe in the evening and at night,' he wrote.[6] His biographer Joanna Richardson worked out from an extant tavern bill that over a two-and-a-half-day period he drank a hundred glasses of spirits, but it is important in terms of the context of the claims made about Verlaine's absinthe addiction that this, the only quantified evidence of Verlaine's drinking, was specifically noted as gin (called 'gnief' in patois).[7]

Over the same period his first book of poems was published, *Poèmes saturniens* (*Saturnine Poems* or *Poems Under Saturn*), its publication funded by the doomed Elisa. His drinking now transformed the likeable, fun-loving boy into a demon, a downfall for which Verlaine specifically blamed absinthe.

> Absinthe! How horrible it is to think of those days, and of more recent days which are still too near for my dignity and health...A single draught of the vile sorceress (what fool exalted it into a fairy or green Muse?): one draught was still amusing, but then my drinking was followed by more dramatic consequences.
>
> I spent hour after hour in that house of ill fame...I used to go there with friends, among them the dearly lamented Charles Cros, to be swallowed up in the taverns of the night where absinthe flowed like Styx and Cocytus...this horrible drink: this drink, this abuse itself, the source of folly and crime, of idiocy and shame, which governments should tax heavily if they do not suppress it altogether: absinthe![8]

He believed that a stable relationship would save him from the debauchery into which he was sinking, the *breuvages exécrés* ('execrable beverages') of his verse. At the age of 25, in 1869 Verlaine fell in love with Mathilde Maute, a pretty, musical 16-year-old who was introduced to him by her brother, the musician Charles de Sivry. Lepelletier said that he was so taken with Mathilde after first meeting her that when he went to the café afterwards and ordered an absinthe he forgot to drink it. Love indeed.

Verlaine described the scene: 'I sat at table with the illustrated papers which were and still are my favourite reading, and to the great astonishment of the good Sivry, who was unused to such a spectacle, I drank no absinthe. Absinthe, like "virtue abandoned", was to take severe revenge.'[9]

His good behaviour did not last: over one week in July 1869 he twice returned to the family home drunk and threatened to kill his mother and himself. In a destructive rage he opened the cupboard where his mother kept the foetuses from the three miscarriages she had before his birth and smashed the jars which contained them. He spent the next few days suffocating his shame in the bars and brothels of Arras.

His mother continued to adore Verlaine and to forgive him, while he always made promises and always relapsed. He proposed to Mathilde, and for a while, with a supreme effort of will, stayed off the absinthe, stayed away from brothels and wrote verse, much of it to Mathilde. He even became more punctual at work. Despite the initial opposition of her father, they married in 1870, and Verlaine's good behaviour made his previous outbursts seem like youthful indiscretions to be put behind him now he had assumed the responsibilities of manhood.

Mathilde quickly became pregnant, which the child in Verlaine found difficult to cope with: she was both changing and introducing another person into their relationship. He recommenced drinking and again became violent. The deterioration in his character was not improved by the turbulent political situation; in the excitement of the 1870–71 war and revolt Verlaine joined the National Guard in defence of Paris, then served as press officer to the commune.

Verlaine's connection with the revolutionaries lost him his town-hall job, and the young couple had to move in with Mathilde's parents. It was there in 1871 that Verlaine welcomed Arthur Rimbaud. If Mathilde was the angel who might have saved the poet, Rimbaud was the demon to take him to hell.

Rimbaud was 16 when he arrived in Paris to see Verlaine. He had a similar background to Verlaine: he was the offspring of an army officer who left home when Rimbaud was six, so he was largely brought up by his mother, who was described as being incapable of giving affection, an austere and humourless authoritarian. She would supervise her sons so closely as to wait for them at the school gate so they would not learn bad behaviour from other boys. Arthur later described his 'repugnance' for his mother in verse, and his relief when he gained brief freedom from her in 'la fraîcheur des latrines' ('the freshness of toilets').[10]

He showed precocious talent, being a brilliant pupil and a published poet in his teens. Shortly after his fifteenth birthday, however, he began to revolt, stopped washing and changing his clothes, stopped going to school and started frequenting cafés, where he would smoke and drink, and, more importantly considering his later notoriety, was increasingly given to obscenity and blasphemy. His chief poetic influence was Baudelaire, particularly his dreams, visions and advocacy of substances to unlock the soul. Rimbaud took the message further, however, maintaining that to become the absolute poet he must experience all love and madness and suffering in a life which was beyond rules. As Henry Miller, a later admirer, said, 'Baudelaire merely laid his heart bare; Rimbaud plucks his out and devours it slowly'.[11]

Rimbaud ran away from home repeatedly, often without money, begging food on the way, once falling in with some soldiers who got him drunk and raped him or (in some interpretations) had sex with him with his consent. It may be that his neglect of personal hygiene started after this event, and therefore related to his sense of defilement.

Rimbaud sent some of his poems to Verlaine, who responded with a train ticket to Paris. Rimbaud at 17 met all the well-known poets of the day, and they set up a fund to defray his living expenses in Paris, to which Verlaine, Charles Cros and Banville donated, among others. Rimbaud briefly lodged with Cros, but his bad behaviour made the teenager unwelcome. Everyone except Verlaine was soon to turn against Rimbaud for his vile personality, for he was an arrogant and insolent character filled with his own self-importance. In a literary circle in which others were reading their works, he punctuated their verses with 'Shit'; and he early showed his tendency to violence when he used Verlaine's sword-stick to scratch the photographer Etienne Carjat.

The person who most took against Rimbaud, and with good reason, was Mathilde, though only later discovering the youth's power over her husband. Her original distaste was for his indecent behaviour and because he deliberately broke some things of which she was fond. Rimbaud left their rooms, but Verlaine continued to see him, while lying about this to Mathilde. Violence in the home increased, and continued both before and after the birth of their son. Verlaine's drunken violence was usually followed by tearful contrition and another offence. Mathilde wrote that from October 1871 to January 1872 her life had been threatened every day.[12]

Mathilde consulted Antoine Cros, the physician brother of Charles and Henri Cros, about Verlaine's behaviour, and he explained that both Verlaine and Rimbaud were unbalanced by their abuse of absinthe.[13] Mathilde's fears for her husband were well founded. Verlaine left the family home and became Rimbaud's lover, probably first in the attic he rented for Rimbaud in the Rue Campagne-Premiere, the so-called *nuits d'Hercules*.

Like many who are exclusively close, they developed a private argot which emphasised their togetherness and excluded others. Absinthe in this was 'absomphe' and L'Académie on Rue Saint-Jacques, the café they most used, was 'L'Académie d'absomphe'. De Musset and Murger had previously frequented L'Académie, so the bohemian tradition was maintained, despite the contempt of the waiters for Rimbaud and Verlaine's behaviour.

Another café they frequented was the Rat Mort, a lesbian haunt at night, which after 1868 became popular with writers during the day. It was opposite the Nouvelle Athènes, where Manet and Degas would be meeting. One time in the Rat Mort (really called the Café Pigalle), where Verlaine and Rimbaud were sitting with Charles Cros, Rimbaud said he would show them an experiment and asked them to stretch their hands out. When they did, Rimbaud pulled an open clasp knife from his pocket and stabbed Verlaine's wrists deeply. Cros withdrew his hands so he was not hurt, and Verlaine went off with Rimbaud, who later that night stabbed him twice in the thigh for his devotion. This was one evening when Verlaine went home to his wife, and Mathilde dressed his wounds.

Such passionate affairs as that between Verlaine and Rimbaud were not limited to a homosexual sub-culture, and absinthe was frequently cited as a factor in relationships where there was violence. The novelist Alphonse Daudet in 1880 had no qualms at telling Zola and Edmond de Goncourt about his affair with a woman who used the sobriquet Chien Vert ('Green Dog'), Marie Rieu, whom he had 'inherited' from the photographer and caricaturist Félix Nadar. 'A mad affair', Goncourt writes,

> drenched in absinthe and given a dramatic touch every now and then by a few knife-thrusts, the marks of which he showed us on one of his hands. He gave us a humorous account of his wretched life with that woman, whom he lacked the courage to leave and to whom he remained attached to some extent by the pity he felt for her vanished beauty and the front-tooth she had broken on a stick of barley-sugar.

Eventually Daudet wanted to get married, and had to break with Marie, but was afraid of the scene she would make when he told her. So he took her deep into the woods and told her the bad news, at which she 'rolled at his feet in the mud and snow, bellowing like a young heifer crying, "I shan't be nasty to you any more..."'[14] Daudet was to novelise the impossible affair in *Sapho*, published in 1884, in which a young artist comes to Paris from Provence and forms a liaison with the model Sapho of the title.

The somewhat bizarre behaviour of such individuals as Baudelaire had come to be endemic among the bohemians, but Baudelaire had always maintained bourgeois friends. Verlaine and Rimbaud took their behaviour to further extremes to alienate former friends and supporters. Verlaine and Rimbaud became exemplars of what to expect from heavy absinthe use, but much of their behaviour was hardly hallucinogenic, it was merely adolescent, such as when they were involved in such juvenile misdemeanours as being arrested at a station café for drinking too much and disturbing the other passengers.

They made their lives a deliberate challenge to the bourgeoisie, spurning all the things their middle-class French backgrounds held dear: home, family, industry, sexual restraint, heterosexual romance, class difference and cleanliness.

Central to this was alcohol. The drinking became public evidence of Verlaine's uncontrollable poetic soul, too great for the mundane things of this world, to be expressed not in everyday terms but the heightened reality of drunkenness. It is easy to scoff at this pretension, but it is clearly the case that some of the best verse Verlaine wrote, *Romances sans paroles* (*Songs Without Words*) were written in this chaotic period of his life with Rimbaud, and his time of married harmony produced no notable work.

Rimbaud was explicit about the relationship between drinking and his higher purpose as a poet. He wrote in a prose poem called 'Morning of Drunkenness' in *Illuminations*:

> Petite veille d'ivresse, sainte!…Nous t'affirmons, méthode!… Nous avons foi au poison. Nous savons donner notre vie toute entière tous les jours. Voici les temps des Assassins.
>
> [Little drunken vigil holy!…We pronounce you method!…We have faith in the poison. We know how to give our entire life every day. Now is the time of the Assassins.]

Rimbaud's poem 'Comedy of Thirst' celebrates absinthe as part of a wild, heroic drunkenness: 'Vois le Bitter sauvage/ Rouler du haut des monts!/ Gagnon, pèlerins sages,/ L'absinthe aux verts pilier [See the wild Bitter/ rolling from the top of the mountains!/ Wise pilgrims let us reach/ The Absinthe with its green pillars]'.

Some of Rimbaud's work owed much to alcohol in general, such as 'Le Bateau Ivre' ('The Drunken Boat') written before he even knew Verlaine. However, some are clearly works of synaesthesia which show a merging of colour, sound and meaning attributable not to alcohol alone but perhaps to absinthe. His sonnet 'Voyelles', for example, giving the value of colours to vowels, takes poetry to meanings impossible without a true leap of the imagination: 'A, noir corset velu des mouches éclatantes…I, pourpres, sang crache, rire des lèvres belles [A, black velvet corset of clattering flies…I, purples, spat blood, laughter of beautiful lips]'. He remarked, 'I flattered myself on devising a poetic language accessible one day or another to all the senses.'[15]

Rimbaud had many admirers among those who did not have to suffer his bad behaviour. In the twentieth century, Henry Miller said, 'one might say that contemporary French poetry owes everything to Rimbaud.'[16] This is a hard claim to justify, but Rimbaud certainly stands as godfather to the singer-songwriters of the twentieth century in the heavily metaphorical, self-flagellatory tradition of Leonard Cohen and Patti Smith.

Verlaine and Rimbaud's habits became woven into the cultural life of France. As the jolly song goes, 'Ils buvaient de l'absinthe comme on boirait de l'eau/ L'un s'appelait Verlaine, l'autre c'était Rimbaud/ Pour faire des poèmes, on ne boire pas de l'eau [They drank absinthe like you drink water/ one called Verlaine the other called Rimbaud/ for you don't drink water to write poetry]'.[17]

The couple left Paris in 1872 and began travelling in France and Belgium. Mathilde applied for and was granted a legal separation from her husband, citing difficulties because Verlaine had 'altered his behaviour, associating with bad companions and giving way to drink and to absinthe,' abuses which have 'thrown him into a state of over-excitation resembling delirium tremens'. The document remarked on 'the most monstrous immorality' of his relationship with Rimbaud, noted that 'Verlaine gave way to absinthe drinking and was associated with Rimbaud who already had the greatest influence over him'. It charged that Verlaine spent too much time at the café, 'often passing whole days there and a part of the night, drinking alcoholic liquors and absinthe principally'.[18] In being effectively cited as a co-respondent in a divorce case, absinthe was clearly fully recognised as a dangerous substance, distinct from alcohol in general, which was also mentioned.

Verlaine and Rimbaud passed autumn and winter 1872 in London, living in a house in Camden, where Verlaine was to learn the drinking habits of the English. Ordering an absinthe in one establishment, he was astonished to be told, 'we don't serve spirits'.[19]

Rimbaud's sadism and the mere passage of time – he was growing up and his life was to develop very differently from Verlaine's – drove the lovers apart. Verlaine left London for Brussels and attempted reconciliation with his wife, threatening suicide if she did not come to him. She did not, and he summoned Rimbaud, who came but refused Verlaine's pleas for reconciliation. Wild with the anguish of rejected love, Verlaine had obtained a revolver, with which he shot Rimbaud twice, wounding him in the wrist, in

Brussels on 10 July 1873. When Verlaine pursued Rimbaud, holding the revolver in his pocket, seemingly about to kill him, the young poet found the forces of the hated bourgeoisie had their uses after all, and called the police to arrest his friend.

Verlaine was charged with attempted murder. Rimbaud did not want to pursue the charge, but the courts have their own logic, and when the report of the medical examination of Verlaine was produced, it showed what they took to be evidence of sodomy – a relaxed anal sphincter. Verlaine was sentenced to the maximum penalty: two years' hard labour and a fine of 200 francs. He served 18 months and rediscovered Catholic faith in prison, the poetic result of this contrition *Sagesse* (*Wisdom*) published in 1881.

On release, he considered joining a Trappist retreat but was, as ever, torn between the spiritual and the carnal, and instead in 1875 hurried to Stuttgart to see Rimbaud, who was working there as a teacher, having spent some time at his family home in Ardennes, where he wrote his masterpiece *Une Saison en enfer* (*A Season in Hell*). He rejected Verlaine violently, leaving him beaten and unconscious, and they never met again. Rimbaud took to wandering as an itinerant labourer, then took up as an explorer and trader in Africa, dying from cancer in 1891.

Verlaine crossed over to England, where he led a blameless life working as a teacher of French and drawing at Stickney and Boston in Lincolnshire, then in Bournemouth. He returned to France to teach there, and made an attempt at farming with Lucien Létinois, a favourite pupil who reminded him of Rimbaud. Lucien died in 1883, the first of a series of new blows for the now mature poet. Verlaine's mother died in 1886 and all attempts at reconciliation with Mathilde failed. She divorced him, and remarried when the law permitted her to do so.

His precarious respectability collapsed progressively under the weight of these woes, and Verlaine retreated into drunkenness and debauchery. Fortunately for him, the period of decline coincided with his fame as a poet, so young literary types sought him out and bought him drinks. A witness to this, Edgar Saltus, wrote that

Verlaine was 'paying with enigmatic songs the food which young poets provided, distilling a mysterious music from the absinthe offered by them'.[20]

Verlaine returned to literary Paris, becoming the threadbare king of the Latin Quarter, which was again becoming a preferred haunt of poets, painters, musicians, comedians, lawyers and students. The Hydropathes ('Water-haters') club was one literary venture which flourished here with its journal, the *Hydropathe*, founded in 1879. Other groups were set up, often with mutually opposing views: the Fumistes, the Zutistes, the Hirsuites. This last was the most prestigious, having as members Verlaine and Charles Cros, meeting at the Café de L'Avenir (later the Café du Soleil) in Saint-Michel from 1883.

The most important establishment of the 1880s, however, was Rudolphe Salis's Chat Noir, set up in an old post office at Boulevard de Rochechouart in 1881, with a journal of the same name created the following year. Salis was a former painter with a love of paradox and show. He had his waiters dressed in the livery of the Académie française and was personally on hand to insult his patrons as they arrived. The Chat Noir's sign was a black cat with tail erect, symbolising Art, holding a terrified goose, the Bourgeoisie, under its paw. Its motto read, 'Passant, sois moderne' (roughly, 'Passerby, be modern'). It was advertised explicitly as an absinthe establishment, 'If you would drink an incomparable absinthe, come to drink at the Chat Noir'.

The large former post-office room was divided by a curtain, with the front half used by casual customers, the back called the Institut, used by regulars – artists, illustrators, poets, playwrights, musicians, journalists and various types of performers. The walls were decorated with the paintings of artists who were patrons. In a business plan of bracing audacity, Salis had the writers and performers gathered there put on their own works. Effectively, he had the audience entertain themselves at no cost to himself as the patron who would introduce the performers before they took the stage.

Salis had the poet Emile Goudeau relocate the Hydropathes, of which group he was convenor, from the Left Bank to the Chat Noir.

Goudeau organised literary soirees on Friday and Saturday evenings and 'absinthes littéraires' ('literary absinthe nights') on Wednesdays. As cabaret manager, Goudeau also organised a programme of readings, singing, recitals, plays and shadow-puppet performances. One of the pianists at the Chat Noir was Charles de Sivry, Mathilde Verlaine's elder brother, another was the composer Erik Satie, another Claude Debussy.

The Chat Noir reunited the disparate literary groups, and included the work of Verlaine, Villiers de l'Isle-Adam, Stéphane Mallarmé, Théodore de Banville and Cros, though the last of these, the great polymath of his age, was not to see the decade out. After his stormy relationship with Nina de Callias broke up, he married, in 1878, and had two sons, but his health was feeling the effects of the absinthe. The death of Nina in 1884 and the illness of his wife hit him hard, and his alcoholism worsened, as did his financial situation. At one point his library was sold at public auction to pay his debts. He died one night in 1888 while finishing a poem, 'surrounded by the very saddest circumstances of poverty and neglect' at the age of 46.[21]

Maurice Rollinat, hailed as a second Baudelaire, was of course nothing of the sort, but a histrionic imitator of Baudelaire and Poe. Despite being thin he had a harsh voice which he used to recite verses from his collections, with titles such as *Les Névroses* and *L'Abîme* (*The Neurotics* and *The Abyss*), full of opium and absinthe-filled images of the occult and the supernatural. His grimacing performances, his voice mewing and strident by turns, would be accompanied by the piano. He cultivated a fearsome appearance as a mad poet, and was determinedly perverse; he trained his dog to behave badly by rewarding anti-social behaviour and admonishing it for behaving well.

In the same vein, the poet Jean Lorrain, son of a ship owner, wrote of ancient and mediaeval legends and of homosexual love and the absinthe drinkers of the bars. His taste was for something stronger, however, attested by his 1890 volume *Stories of an Ether Drinker*.

Another of the writers in his element at the Chat Noir was Aphonse Allais, born to two pharmacists in Honfleur in 1854. He started training as a pharmacist in Paris but became seduced by the Montmartre cabaret. At '*l'heure verte*', Allais would sit before his absinthe and recount humorous stories to his friends. When he was happy that he had honed his story to perfection, he would go to the back of the café alone and write it out for one of the many journals for which he wrote. As well as the journals associated with the Hydropathes and the Chat Noir, he contributed to all the major humorous journals of the period. It amused Allais to sign some of his articles by the name of Francisque Sarcey, a strait-laced drama critic whose work was much in vogue and was certainly not comic, and who thus had the novel experience of reading for the first time the funny things he had supposedly written.

Allais was given to impersonating Sarcey, and once did so on first meeting a young admirer of Sarcey, inviting him to dinner the next day, but giving the address of the real Sarcey. Allais warned the young man that he had a brother who was under the delusion that he was Francisque Sarcey and that he might well answer the door, particularly as he was kept at home by the family because of his tendency to molest children. If the young guest should meet this imposter, he should deal firmly with him, and explain that he had come for dinner and knew all about his paedophilia.[22]

Allais also wrote poems and theatrical pieces. One of his pieces was perhaps the first use of 'stream of consciousness'. Called *L'Absinthe*, it is the thought processes of a struggling writer sitting on a *terrasse* talking about his rejections: 'very good, your article... subject interesting... well written but... not in our style'. He watches the sugar from his absinthe melt, then, after the first hour, and the first absinthe, he notes that the boulevards are coming alive and the women are so much prettier than they were an hour before. He sees the street sellers, has another absinthe, yearns for the women, ponders the people around him, and considers there is a book to be written there, 'unique, unforgettable... a book that everyone would have to buy... everyone!' Inspired by the thought, he calls for another absinthe, this time a large one without water. The piece ends there, with the reader knowing that of course this dreamer is never going to write a great novel or embrace the girl of his deepest desires. As Allais said, 'life is not funny'.[23]

If his literary style could be surreal, one of Allais's elaborate jests was a precursor of Dadaism. As it was constantly claimed that modern artists could not paint, Allais got together a school of artists who certainly could not paint, writers who were assembled under the title of the Salon des Incoherents. Allais's contributions included the black canvas, *Negroes Fighting in a Cave at Night*, a completely white canvas, *Anaemic Young Girls Going to their First Communion in a Blizzard*, and his masterpiece of 1884, *Some Pimps Lying in the Grass Drinking Absinthe*, which was, of course, completely green.[24]

A character in one of his stories, known only as 'the poor bastard', takes his last coins to a boulevard bar 'which served the best glass of absinthe for miles around. A place where, for four sous, you could get "a bit of Paradise in your belly".' The poor bastard meets a good fairy in the bar, who gives him one wish, at which he asks for 20 francs a day for life. She grants this happily, but goes on to give him the total all at once: 30 francs.[25] Dying as he had lived, Allais passed away in a booth in the Criterion Café at the age of 51.

The creation, demise and re-creation of sometimes tiny literary groups led to a significant movement: the symbolists, with the decadents as either another, related movement, 'the cradle of symbolism', or as the activist wing of symbolism, depending on one's point of view. Both were influenced by absinthe and con- tributed to the mystique of absinthe by their use of it and their representation of it in their work.

Symbolism, the most important movement in French poetry since the 1850s, offered a liberation from form: everything must be fluid, the function of poetry was to evoke, not to describe; its matter was impressions, intuitions, sensations. The poet's images should be symbols of the state of his soul, poetry aspiring to the condition of music, an emotional understanding being conveyed without the intervention of precise definitions. That is the theme of a poem could be 'orchestrated and expanded by the choice of words having colour, harmony and evocative power of their own'.[26] The synaesthetic approach was evoked and stimulated by absinthe. The drink both contributed to the sensations which gave rise to the verse and to the literary ambiance which sustained it.[27]

The *Décadent* was a literary magazine published between 1886 and 1889, founded by Anatole Baju and owing much to Verlaine. When contributions were lacking, the editors filled the pages with strident literary manifestos, abusive criticism and verse supposedly written by the legendary Rimbaud (by this time of course long since lost to literature).

The inspiration to use the term 'decadent' may have come from Verlaine's poem 'Je suis l'Empire à la fin de la décadence [I am the Empire at the end of decadence]'. The spirit of decadence was that of a civilisation having reached its apogee, enjoying the luxury produced by earlier endeavour, of languor, futility, disdain for moral restraint, a horror of banality and a seeking after novelty. Verlaine described decadence as 'thoughts refined to an extreme of civilisation, a high literary culture, a soul capable of intense volup-tuousness … a mixture of the carnal spirit and the sad flesh and all the violent splendours of the end of empire'.[28]

By the 1880s Verlaine was a literary monument to be pointed out to tourists, and for journalists to seek out for a quick quote on symbolism. As Paul Claudel described him, 'La vieux Socrate chauve/ Grommelle dans sa barbe emmêlée;/ Car une absinthe coûte cinquante centimes/ Et il en faut au moins quatre [The old bald Socrates/ Grumbling into his grizzled beard;/ Because an absinthe costs 15 centimes/ And he is at least four short]'.[29]

'We were all worshippers of Verlaine,' wrote an American, Vance Thompson, 'We had read *Sagesse*. We had lent the poet five franc pieces, had bought him absinthe, had helped him up the hospital steps when his diseases were too many for him.'[30]

The poet and dandy F.-A. Cazals was one of Verlaine's closest friends, though he was no match for the old incorrigible. His zeal to protect his friend, it was recounted, sometimes went to self-destructive lengths, as once when Verlaine was seemingly insensibly drunk and Cazals drank the old poet's absinthe to spare his friend's liver. Each time he did so, Verlaine, who was slyly observing the scene, ordered another glass. Eventually Cazals had to be taken home, dead drunk, to the great amusement of Verlaine.[31]

One of those who took the opportunity of seeing Verlaine in this period was the Anglo-Irish writer George Moore, who wrote,

> Verlaine is of all men of genius I have ever met the least fitted to defend himself in the battle of life. He is able for nothing except the occasional writing of beautiful verses...standing today on the last verge of life he sees glory rising out of the chasm beneath him...in the meantime, he lives in poverty, if not in absolute hunger.

Moore had gone to a vile slum in the company of a literary editor to whom Verlaine had promised work, to visit the decrepit literary monument:

> we saw the terrible forehead, bald and prominent, under a filthy nightcap; a nightshirt full of the grease of the bed covered his shoulders; a stained and discoloured pair of trousers were hitched up somewhere about his waist.
>
> The disorder of his private life has reckoned heavily against Verlaine. For many years hardly any newspaper dared to print his name...He has lived the prey of strange passions that have ruined and dishonoured him...I shall not forget the glare of the bald forehead, the cavernous eyes, the macabre expression of burnt-out lust smouldering upon his face.[32]

There is no doubt that Verlaine played up to his image. He was expected to be the drunken poet sitting before an absinthe, it was, so to speak, his job to behave thus, if he had not sung an 'absinthe-tinted song', as the title of one biography had it, he would have had no income.[33] As he put it himself in an ambiguous remark on celebrity, 'Me, my fame is nothing but a humble, ephemeral absinthe'.[34] He even adopted a name for this persona: Pauvre Lélian, an anagram of his name.

He was sometimes funded to travel, and took tours in England, Holland and Belgium. Maurice Maeterlinck gave an impression of his arrival in Ghent station to a welcoming committee of poets,

The Brussels train came to a halt in the almost deserted station. A
window in a third-class carriage opened with a great clatter and
framed the faun-like face of the old poet. 'I take sugar with it!' he
cried. This was apparently his usual greeting when he was on his
travels: a sort of war-cry or password, which meant that he took
sugar with his absinthe.[35]

The last years of Verlaine's life were spent in bars and hospitals and
with prostitutes. Between 1886 and 1894 he was in hospital 19 times.[36]
He was suffering from cirrhosis of the liver as well as gonorrhoea,
syphilis and diabetes, and a painful infection of the leg left him
frequently lame. In hospital he was allowed a lamp after lights-out
to write, and was given unlimited visiting rights by the authorities,
so he could entertain the writers, critics and portraitists who came
to see him. Society women and impoverished artists came to sit by
his bed, and the doctors and nurses overlooked the small bottles of
absinthe secreted under the pillow for him.

He was cared for by ageing prostitutes, Philomène and Eugénie,
the last lovers who received verses from him. He died at his
lodgings on the Rue Descartes in 1896 at the age of a little over 50.

In the context of this study, the question is how much of
Verlaine's life was dominated by absinthe? He certainly claimed
it was – he wrote in *Confessions of a Poet* of his problems being
caused when 'my bestial self turned towards the green and terrible
drink'.[37]

Lepelletier, the friend who knew Verlaine the longest and wrote
a long memoir of him, absolves absinthe from exceptional culpability when he remarks, '[Verlaine] always had a weakness for
drink, but during his travels, after his separation from his wife, he
developed an almost chronic drunkenness,' also stating that it was
in England that Verlaine developed the habit of steady drinking,
one hurried glass after another. This is almost certainly wrong
(Verlaine had been involved in bouts of continuous drinking at
least as early as 1867) but it is revealing that Lepelletier thinks
drinking took hold in a land where gin and whisky flowed freely
and absinthe was not easily obtained.[38]

Others, however, cited absinthe as a specific curse, as one commentator on the cafés of Paris wrote:

> There were many who had to suffer for their weakness for the 'green fairy': Villiers de l'Isle-Adam, Charles Cros, Glatigny, the artist André Gill, and the Communard Vermersch, whom it led to a padded cell. There were the musicians Chabrier, Cabaner and Charles de Sivry, and finally there was Verlaine, who abused it to the end of his days.[39]

Journalists were eager to give the public a peek into the world of thrilling artistic self-destruction. The American magazine *Bookman* produced in 1899 a five-page appraisal of Verlaine titled 'The Poet of Absinthe', which quoted approvingly from an English critic to demonstrate that absinthe had brought Verlaine down:

> The eyes were sodden, the body scarred with bad scars; drink, hunger, misery had ruined the frame, the clothes were ragged and foul; the hands, lean and filthy, shook with absinthe ague, but the mind triumphed, and even in his lowest degradation – degradation too awful to be set down – the absinthe voice formulated the speech of supreme genius.[40]

The connection of these common symptoms of excessive drinking with absinthe, and the explicit connection between genius and absinthe, serves to stoke a myth while supplying it with no evidence. Significantly, not a single line of Verlaine's verse is quoted in this account; it is the life which is celebrated by the journalist, not the work.

Verlaine was complicit in the creation of the Verlaine myth of the absinthe-sodden genius. Absinthe was not his only drink – he started on beer, though he also drank rum and water; absinthe was a source of cheap alcohol for a man who was usually poor. All those who were close to him, such as his wife, complained of his drinking generally, he was a violent alcoholic and would have been so with or without absinthe. Blaming the green fairy in his memoirs, however, gave him an 'absinthe defence': it wasn't his vicious character which made him reprehensible, but the green drink. Rimbaud sneeringly refused to excuse his bad behaviour, and did not blame absinthe for what he did – it was what he was. Verlaine, in contrast, was given to histrionic displays of contrition and was only too keen to blame some external factor for the suffering for which he would otherwise be entirely responsible. He wrote his memoirs in 1895, at a time when absinthe was subject to extreme criticism and an attack on it would fit in with prevailing attitudes that absinthe nurtured genius but made men mad.

Many others also blamed absinthe: 'Who can tell what damage was done by absinthe to this rash, unstable generation?' proclaimed Guy Michaud in *The Poetic Message of Symbolism* in 1947.[41]

The English poet Algernon Swinburne, whose work Verlaine very much admired (and who himself had been influenced by Baudelaire) behaved rather as the French poet did. Swinburne, from a comfortable family, would outrage the bourgeoisie with his drunken behaviour, but was also writing feverishly brilliant verse whose erotic content divided the literary world. Swinburne was drinking the spirits easily available in England. Would his poetry or his behaviour have been any better or worse had he been drinking absinthe instead of brandy as his principal stimulant?

Dylan Thomas's work is full of colour and of disparate images pulled together, of impressions rather than literal descriptions in the manner of the symbolists, yet though alcohol played a strong part in his life (and death) absinthe did not. No amount of such negative examples can prove the point, but it is obvious that alcohol of any type is certainly not sufficient for poetry, and images of surreal potency can be created without the aid of absinthe. While always associated with absinthe, the drink was not a necessary or essential part of Verlaine's creative life – and probably not an essential part of his destruction either.

Absinthe drinkers, a curious form of continental life, in the London magazine *The Graphic* in 1872.

'There's nothing like an absinthe to set you up', by Honoré Daumier. Bibliothèque nationale, Paris.

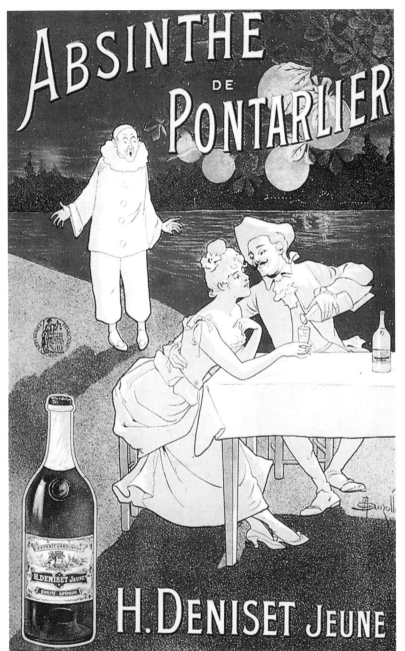

A courting couple get in the mood with an outdoor absinthe. Musée de Pontarlier.

A good-time girl explains that absinthe is one of her minor sins. Musée de Pontarlier.

La Buveuse d'Absinthe, by Félicien Rops – a vamp hanging around the dance-halls.
Collection Marie-Claude Delahaye.

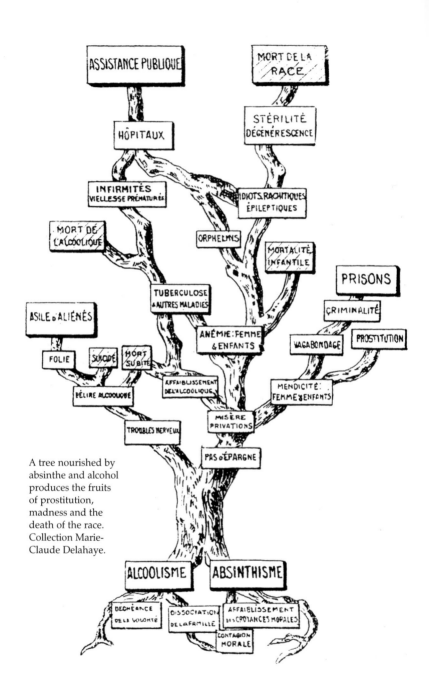

A tree nourished by absinthe and alcohol produces the fruits of prostitution, madness and the death of the race. Collection Marie-Claude Delahaye.

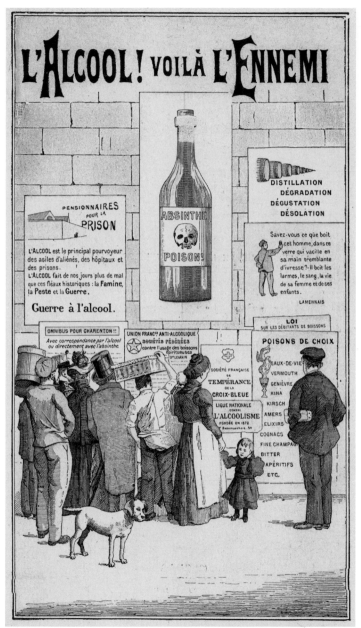

'Alcohol is the enemy' – but the enmity omits such 'patriotic' alcoholic drinks as wine, beer and cider ('fine champagne' is a brandy made from champagne). Collection Marie-Claude Delahaye.

Above
The Old Absinthe House in
New Orleans – keeping the
name of absinthe alive in
the US.

HOW TO PREPARE LA FEE ABSINTHE THE FRENCH WAY

1) *Pour one shot of La Fée into a glass*

2) *Place a slotted La Fée Absinthe spoon on the glass. Place one sugar lump on the spoon*

3) *Drip six to eight parts iced water through the sugar and into the absinthe*

4) *Stir mixture, which will turn cloudy, and drink*

Left
How to make an absinthe –
the old techniques have to be
relearned in a turn-of-the-
(twentieth) century card for
customers. Green Bohemia
Limited.

5 Madmen of Art

POPULAR HISTORIES, WEBSITES AND ADVERTISING for absinthe in the twenty-first century all list the same artists as absinthe drinkers, as if the drink and artistic genius were inseparable. Absinthe certainly formed part of the world in which the post-impressionists worked from the 1880s, but did absinthe really make a definitive contribution to the art of the late nineteenth century?

Van Gogh's Habits

The absence of any mention of addiction or abuse of wormwood throughout the long period of its use from classical times is intriguing. Rare and infrequent references are made in herbal manuals to damage caused by over-use. In his 1708 *On Poisons*, Johan Lindestolophe remarks that continued use of *Artemisia absinthium* will lead to 'great injury of the nervous system'.[1] Reports of damage and addiction emerged, and became common only when the drink was produced in large quantities and was made available cheaply.

A distinction has to be made between damage and addiction – many substances can cause damage by poisoning the body, but there is no addictive element. Some substances, such as heroin, are highly addictive but do no appreciable damage in a pure form (impurities will injure a user). Substances which are a real threat to well-being are those which are both addictive and damaging. Alcohol is both, though only damaging when taken in quantity. The question is whether absinthe is addictive (or whether some constituent part of it is) regardless of the quantity of alcohol which makes up most of its bulk.

The *Oxford English Dictionary* gives definitions of addiction going back to the sixteenth century, the early ones referring to 'addiction' to a party, person or principle. Other uses are abstract, 'addicted unto evil', 'addicted to a melancholy', 'addicted to virginitie'. Eighteenth-century uses of 'addictedness to drinking' and 'addiction to tobacco' move towards a present-day usage, but the emphasis is on the individual and personal proclivities, not the 'habit-forming' substance.

The late nineteenth century, the time of scares over absinthe use, was a period when the concept of addiction was taking hold, when the quality of wickedness was being transferred from the person to the substance; the explanation of excessive alcohol or other drug use had been that of gluttony, a personal sin. An improved understanding of chemistry and pharmacology led to the deduction that the substance itself might be 'wrong', in that it had a quality to stimulate excessive use.

Such observers as Sherard had no doubt that absinthe was addictive. He wrote, 'It is moreover an insidious drink, the habit of consuming it grows upon its victim, who sooner or later has to abdi- cate all will power in the control of his passion'.[2]

Absinthe certainly had a characteristic of addictive substances – that most people had no interest in it and used it never or rarely, while for others it was the subject of obsession, as if no other drink could satisfy them. Was it a drink of choice or a drink of necessity?

The best-documented examples of heavy absinthe users are artists who came into their own as absinthe drinkers in the last quarter of the nineteenth century. Such artists as Manet and Degas either did not drink absinthe or did so insignificantly: they painted people who did. It was the period of neo-impressionism and such artists as Paul Gauguin and Vincent van Gogh in which the artists themselves, rather than their subjects, drank absinthe.

Notwithstanding his personal fastidiousness, Degas liked these grubby bohemians, and despite the wanderings of Gauguin and van Gogh, they were part of a community of artists still very much at war with the art establishment in the 1880s. Van Gogh's close bond with his supportive brother Theo, an art dealer and proponent of the impressionists, gave him access to the vanguard of modern art.

Vincent van Gogh is sometimes called the greatest Dutch painter since Rembrandt, and certainly is the most popular and accessible of the impressionists. His reputation is based almost entirely on the last three years of his life, between 1887 and 1890, and it was at this time that he was drinking absinthe heavily.

Van Gogh was born in 1853, the eldest son of a Dutch pastor. He worked from the age of 16 at the Hague branch of the art dealers Goupil and Co., then worked for them in London and in Paris until 1876. An unrequited passion for an English girl when he was in London set the pattern for the loneliness and longing of his emotional life.

In England he became a language teacher and a lay preacher, then decided to become a minister. He studied theology, but broke this off in 1878 because he did not see the relevance of academic theology to the needs of the poor, and took short-term training as an evangelist. When he disputed doctrinal orthodoxy, he came into conflict with authority and left to do missionary work in the coal-mining region of the Borinage in Belgium. He was dismissed for being an inadequate preacher and for applying too literal an interpretation of Christianity, demonstrated by such actions as giving away all his possessions to the poor and living in extreme poverty and dirt.

Van Gogh was deeply moved by his experience of poverty, and yearned to make a spiritual contribution in the world, but his inability to relate to people at the banal level of human intercourse meant all his efforts were doomed. He was unsociable and lonely, but unable to understand other people sufficiently to be able to make an effort to render himself more acceptable to others. He was either in an exalted state of excitement or depressive and irritable. A century later he would have been diagnosed as suffering from bipolar affective disorder or manic depression.

It was only in 1880 that, desperately poor and isolated, van Gogh began to draw seriously, and decided that it would be through art that he would express his sense of spiritual mission. By teaching himself to draw and paint, with occasional lessons, he became an artist over the next six years while he lived in Belgium and Holland.

For a time he lived with a prostitute called Sien, who gave him gonorrhoea and spent the money Theo forwarded to him on drink, though there is no record of van Gogh drinking to excess during this period. Indeed, it seems to have been a time of quiet industry on gloomy pictures. His life had been disturbed and bizarre, but there was no scent of absinthe or alcoholism in it.

In the first years of professional painting he was confined almost entirely to drawings and watercolours, but increasingly began to paint in oils. In 1884 and 1885 he painted still lifes, landscapes and figures, all from the lives of the peasants of Nuenen in brown, ochre and black.

In 1886 he joined Theo in Paris, and under his care van Gogh began to reverse the effects of years of physical neglect. He came into contact with the work of the impressionists that his brother was valiantly attempting to sell, which hung in Theo's apartment and in the art shop of the former communard Tanguy, where painters would often meet.

Paris was the most exciting city in the world, for an artist a carnival of ideas and sensations: of Japanese art, the techniques of the pointillists, the ideas of the symbolists and the slow increase in influence of impressionism. Van Gogh met some of the most important impressionists, including Toulouse-Lautrec, Pissarro, Renoir, Raffaëlli, Seurat, Gauguin, Bernard and Degas. Cezanne's comment at their only meeting, 'Sir, you paint like a madman,' was grimly appropriate.[3]

Artistically he now lightened his palette and turned towards the flowers, landscapes, portraits and self-portraits for which he is best known, pictures bursting with vivid life. One important influence was the work of Marseilles painter Adolphe Monticelli, who had begun to specialise in still lifes of flowers painted with brilliant intensity, heavy with almost sculpted strokes of paint. It was fortuitous that van Gogh was impressed by this work, as Theo's apartment was too small to permit anything but still lifes; van Gogh painted over 30 canvases of flowers in his first year in Paris.

As he was not able to afford his own studio, van Gogh enrolled at a communal studio run by Cormon, a classical painter. Here van Gogh was to meet the young artistic radical Emile Bernard, and Toulouse-Lautrec, and to make applied experiments in vivid colour. Cormon had the greatest difficulty in maintaining discipline among his charges, to ensure that they would keep to classically posed models and the restrained colours he favoured.

Asserting himself in mid-1886, van Gogh prevailed on Theo to move so that he would have space to paint, and he also began to drink (or to make drink a part of his life). He had always used available drugs: he had relied on the appetite-suppressant properties of tobacco to help him through times when he did not have the money for both paint and food, and he had chosen to buy paint; for some of his flower pictures he would drink innumerable cups of strong, black coffee to over-stimulate himself in the hope that he could 'reach that high note of yellow'.[4] Van Gogh saw drugs in relationship to his work; therefore their recreational function (if such a driven man had what would generally be defined as recreation) was secondary.

Van Gogh's alcohol consumption was unremarkable until he moved to Paris, but now not only alcohol but absinthe was unmistakeably present. He painted a still life of a glass of absinthe and a pitcher of water in 1887, as one biographer put it, 'the painter's tribute to a new companion which was to be of increasing help to him'.[5]

In the same year, Toulouse-Lautrec, who is by many accounts responsible for introducing him to absinthe, painted van Gogh sitting with a glass of it before him at Le Tambourin on the Boulevard de Clichy. The café was run by Agostina Segatori, who was van Gogh's lover for a time and may have given him another venereal infection. In neither absinthe picture is there an absinthe spoon or other impedimenta – van Gogh seemed to take his absinthe straight.

As his use of absinthe coincided with van Gogh's development of colour in his work, it is reasonable to question whether the altered perceptions caused by absinthe had a direct effect on his art or, as Wilfred Niels Arnold puts it, 'the novel experiences of relative sizes, shapes and colours perceived under the influence of absinthe could have been recalled later and incorporated into a new font, palette or composition'.[6]

Overwhelmingly throughout the development of the impressionist movement the story is one of colour: the discovery of colour after staid classical representations, the need for brighter colours, the representation of colour. It is tempting to think of this as the result of absinthe-induced hallucinogenic experiences, and indeed the desire for brighter colours to represent what the painters saw in their mind's eye may have been influenced by absinthe.

There are other interpretations, however. Van Gogh and other impressionists were interested in advances in the understanding of perception, such as the effect of the complementarity of colours on the eye of the observer creating darker or lighter effects, from the application of knowledge of the spectrum.

The period also saw advances in chemistry which permitted not only the mass production of a wider range of oil-based pigments, but the manufacture of tube paints which could be carried about and resealed, thus vastly simplifying the process of outdoor painting and allowing artists to paint colours illuminated by the brightest light there was: the sun.

Van Gogh would be outside all the time, painting a canvas so large that when he was carrying it people would think it was a signboard. He would be sitting slashing away at his canvas with energetic brush strokes, shouting and gesticulating in his excitement, to the amused interest of passers-by, though van Gogh had long since learned not to care what others thought of him. Even other artists, he considered, 'disgust me as men'.[7]

Theo suffered agonies from van Gogh's disordered life. His brother was argumentative and appallingly untidy in his habits; he said Vincent seemed to be 'two persons; one, marvellously gifted, delightful, gentle, the other egoistical and hard-hearted'.[8] Van Gogh had a supreme sense of artistic mission coupled with a painful emotional sensitivity; he was never going to find living in the real world easy. To steel him for its rigours he drank more and more heavily. As he said, 'if the storm within gets too loud, I take a glass too much to stun myself'.[9] He was suffering the upset stomach characteristic of the absinthe drinker, though in van Gogh's case his poor eating habits and nervous irritation contributed to the gastric ulcer from which he suffered.

Van Gogh departed on February 1888 for Arles in Southern France on the advice of Toulouse-Lautrec, who had spent time in the Midi as a child and spoke of its light and wide open spaces. Coincidentally, Arles had the highest absinthe consumption of any region in France: four times the national average.[10] His departure from Paris was the beginning of van Gogh's most creative, and most disturbed, period. Paris had promised the security of a brotherhood of like-minded artists, but in fact had offered a parade of egoists and largely empty theorists. Away from the petty artistic politics and the theorising of Paris, van Gogh could concentrate on artistic technique.

Van Gogh wrote of Arles, 'In all honesty I have to add that the Zouaves [soldiers], the brothels, the adorable little Arles girls on their way to their first communion, the priest in his surplice who looks like a dangerous rhinoceros, the absinthe drinkers, all seem to me creatures from another world'.[11]

He wrote to his sister of the colours he was using: 'Now the palette is distinctly colourful, sky-blue, orange, pink, vermilion, a very bright yellow, bright green, wine-red, violet'.[12] Most of van Gogh's most successful paintings were created here, of boats at Arles, the bridge at Arles, a starry night on the Rhône, a café at night. Van

Gogh often worked from morning till night, with tremendous speed under the burning sun.

At night he would go to a café and drink and smoke with desperate determination. He depicted one of these low dives in *The All-night Café*, which depicts the Café de la Gare, where he slept when he first arrived at Arles because, though he had rented a house, he could not afford a bed. These all-night cafés were places where night prowlers could take refuge and sleep slumped over a table if they could not afford to pay for a night in a doss house, or were too drunk to be taken in. Van Gogh remarked that he 'tried to express the idea that the café is a place where one can ruin one-self, go mad or commit a crime'.[13] The artist stayed up for three nights, painting in the café and sleeping during the day, telling the landlord he would paint 'the whole of his rotten joint'.

The glare of the lights and the brilliance of the colours show something of van Gogh's vision:

> the room is blood red and dark yellow, with a green billiard table in the middle; there are four citron-yellow lamps with a glow of orange and green. Everywhere there is a clash and contrast of the most disparate reds and greens in the figures of little sleeping hooligans, in the empty, dreary room, in violet and blue.

He described to Emile Bernard how he saw colour:

> I was in a brothel here last Sunday – not counting other days – a large room, the walls covered with blued whitewash – like a village school. Fifty or more military men in red and civilians in black, their faces a magnificent yellow or organe (what hues there are in the faces here), the women in sky blue, in vermillion, as unqualified and garish as possible. The whole in a yellow light.[14]

He later advises Bernard, 'Painting and fucking a lot are not com-patible; it weakens the brain'.[15]

The artist Paul Signac visited van Gogh in March 1889 and later described the way he had lived, 'returning home after having passed all day in the sun, in torrid heat, and having no real house in that town, he took a place on the terrasse of the café. Then the eaus-de-vie and absinthe succeeded each other at a steady pace.'[16]

Van Gogh compared his drinking habits to those of the Marseilles impressionist Adolphe Monticelli, who had inspired him with his flower paintings. Monticelli lived in Paris from 1863, where he received a commission from Napoleon III for the Palace of the Tuilleries. The Franco–Prussian War in 1870 put paid to his career as a court painter, and he returned to Marseilles, living in increasing poverty and disorder, which worsened when he suffered a stroke and was paralysed in 1883. He was said to have had furtive drinking habits, as if he were ashamed of himself. One of his biographers described how he would tiptoe furtively onto the street, and suddenly duck into a café, where he would sit on a bench in a dark corner with an absinthe and 'head back, eyes ecstatic, sip in little mouthfuls of his Ambrosia'.[17] A fellow artist, Jules Monge, painted him in 1884, two years before his death, in the process of mixing his absinthe.

When he heard of Monticelli's death, supposedly from 'absinthe consumption' (though he was not in good health and was 62), van Gogh wrote that he 'doubted more and more the truth of the legend that Monticelli took enormous quantities of absinthe. Considering his work, it doesn't seem possible to me that a man weakened by drink can do such things.'[18]

Van Gogh's only good friend in Arles was Joseph Roulin, the Arles postal agent (whom van Gogh called the postman), also a man given to many absinthes. Van Gogh was obviously brooding on Monticelli for he wrote,

> I so often think of Monticelli, and when my mind dwells on the stories going around about his death, it seems to me that not only must you exclude the idea of his dying a drunkard in the sense of being besotted by drink, but you must realise that here as a matter of course one spends one's life in the open air and in cafés far more than in the North. My friend the postman, for instance, lives a great deal in cafés, and is certainly more or less of a drinker, and has been so all his life. But he is so much the reverse of a sot, his exaltation is so natural, so intelligent, and he argues with such sweep, in the style of Garibaldi, that I gladly reduce the legend of Monticelli the drunkard on absinthe to exactly the same proportions as my postman's.[19]

In this van Gogh plays the familiar alcoholic's mental trick of comparing himself (or Monticelli in his stead) not to sober people or to occasional drinkers but to other alcoholics.

He referred somewhat defensively to Monticelli when he wrote,

> You can be fairly sure that the Marseilles artist who committed suicide did not in any way do it as the result of absinthe, for the simple reason that no one would have offered it to him and he couldn't have had anything to buy it with. Besides, he would drink it not solely for pleasure, but because, being ill already, he needed it to keep himself going.[20]

The use of the term 'suicide' is a grim portent in terms of van Gogh's life. It is quite inappropriate in reference to Monticelli, unless there is some figurative meaning that Monticelli's drinking contributed to the cerebro-vascular attacks which left him paralysed. In fact he died in the early morning of 29 June 1886 at the home of his cousins, who were looking after him. Drinking may well have contributed, but this was the death of a man who had already suffered two strokes.[21]

Van Gogh painted a still life with onions showing a bottle of absinthe, a pitcher of water, his pipe and tobacco, a candle, a letter from his brother and a copy of *Health Annual*, whose advice about camphor in the pillow he used to treat his insomnia . Marie-Claude Delahaye and Benoît Noël suggest that the bottle of absinthe and the water, at opposite sides of the table, symbolise choices in life between good and bad for van Gogh to make.[22]

Van Gogh always hankered after inclusion, for a community which would contain and support him. He hoped to form a working community of 'Impressionists of the South' based at his house in Arles, but only Gauguin was willing to join him, more for personal reasons of poverty than because he shared van Gogh's vision of community; Gauguin was far from being a team player. Van Gogh was, moreover, completely lacking in the leadership qualities which would make the dream of a 'brotherhood of artists' possible. Van Gogh, in his usual, wheedling way, persuaded his brother to pay Gauguin's debts to free him to come to Arles, so poor Theo now had two unstable artists to support.

Gauguin thus went to Arles in October 1888. He was another egoist full of his own vision of himself and of art, but a man with striking differences from van Gogh, though like his friend Gauguin came to painting late. He was born in 1848, so was five years older than van Gogh and was a flamboyant, commanding figure, though small of stature. He was born in Paris, but his mother was Spanish-Peruvian and he spent some of his boyhood in Lima, so he was used to travel from an early age. He was sailing the world in the merchant navy from 1865 to 1871, and was on a fighting ship during the Franco–Prussian war. At the age of 23 he turned to a business career, taking a job with the stockbroking firm of Bertin on the Paris Bourse, where for more than a decade he made a generous income. He was an ideal bourgeois of the *belle époque*, making big money fast on speculative business ventures and establishing a home with his young wife, Mette Sophie Gad, from a comfortable Danish family.

Very much in the mould of the Second Empire bourgeois, Gauguin liked to dabble in art. The art which this bourgeois collected, however, was impressionist – the work of Cezanne, Manet, Renoir, Monet and Pissarro. He became a Sunday painter who developed such skill that his work, with Pissarro's sponsorship, was exhibited in the fourth show organised by the impressionists in 1879.

When the Paris stock exchange crashed in 1883, Gauguin decided not to look for another bourgeois job but to devote his life to art, a decision which his wife considered a monumental betrayal, for she had married a wealthy, middle-class man and had four children with him in good faith (with another on the way) and now found herself wedded to an impoverished artist. Soon the family moved to Copenhagen to stay with Mette's parents, and in 1885 Gauguin went alone to Paris to follow his chosen path.

By the time he met van Gogh, his savings long gone, Gauguin was virtually starving. He wanted to go back to the tropics, where he could engage with brilliant colour and with a notion he had of the elemental roots of art, which could be divined in 'primitive' societies. He travelled to Taboga and Martinique, dogged by poverty, disease and harried by the police. After four months he returned to Paris in poor physical shape but with several canvases.

He stayed with Emile Schuffenecker, another stockbroker-turned-artist, though one account says he had to leave Paris in a hurry when his benefactor started to suspect Gauguin was having an affair with his wife. In early 1888 he travelled to the Brittany port of Pont-Aven, which the colours of the picturesque landscape made a haunt of artists.

Here he found company with Emile Bernard, a teenaged artist from Lille who had been thrown out of Cormon's studio in Paris. He then experimented with pointillism under the influence of Paul Signac, but the two quarrelled and Bernard destroyed his pointillist works. Before he arrived at Pont-Aven, Bernard had been making drawings with the simplicity of stained glass or wood cuts, with flat colours and bold lines. A critic had named such work 'cloisonnisme', after the enamel work whose bold colours were separated by metal cloisons. Bernard's work, with its strong forms and excessively simplified drawing, was to influence Gauguin; the younger artist had made the conceptual leap in looking at stained glass and folk art that reality was being created in non-imitative forms. Gauguin and he therefore moved away from trying to re-create an actual scene with paint, and instead explored the capacity of pictures to induce the feeling inspired by the scene. Gauguin received the credit for this development, though Bernard was further advanced on the path when they met in Pont-Aven.

The movement thus created formed part of synthetism, an artistic expression of the literary movement symbolism (though confusingly Gauguin is sometimes referred to as a symbolist painter). The origin of the movement can be dated to 1886, with the inspiration of Rimbaud's *Illuminations*, published that year in the symbolist review *La Vogue*. The artistic objective (similar to the transcendent ambitions of Rimbaud's verse) was the expression of ideas, mood and emotion through paint and the rejection of naturalistic representation. As with symbolism in literature, synthetism was moving a section of creative life in a direction in which it was already proceeding, and it would be vain to quantify the contribution made by absinthe. However, the realistic edge given to thoughts, dreams and hallucinations by the green fairy also made its contribution to an art of ideas. In 1889 Gauguin and other artists from Pont-Aven were to exhibit their works as synthetist painters.

Van Gogh urged both Gauguin and Bernard to join his community in Arles, but Bernard was unavailable, as he had been called up for military service. Gauguin was destitute and not in good humour, as he had been unable to seduce Bernard's sister Madeleine, so was only too ready for Theo's offer to help send him to Arles.

The brief time van Gogh and Gauguin spent together (it was two months) is one of the most discussed in art history. It is worth dwelling on because it is a tale of madness, and if madness is the consequence of drinking absinthe, this is one of the prime and most frequently cited examples.

Gauguin's domineering, arrogant personality acted as a stabilising force on van Gogh, who was almost pathetically pleased to have a fellow artist to work with. Gauguin organised such essentials as van Gogh's chaotic working space, where tubes of paint were left without their caps on to be trodden underfoot, and van Gogh would spend money he could not afford on buying paint he already had but could not find in the mess. Gauguin also imposed some kind of discipline on their spending, with a shared petty-cash box and a list of necessary expenses, headed by such essentials as visits to the brothel and tobacco. Gauguin painted one of their haunts, *Café de nuit à Arles*, in which the manager sits at a table with her glass of absinthe, water and sugar cubes before her. Nearby three prostitutes sit with Roulin, and a man is slumped over another table with his head in his hands.

However much order was being injected into his life, Gauguin's presence also put van Gogh under intense pressure, because he so believed in the notion of a community of artists to make him feel less alone. It was his responsibility to please Gauguin in every way and keep him in Arles. This was a vain hope, for Gauguin was not an individual with a need for a fixed home; while he was with van Gogh he longed to be back in the tropics.

This fear of Gauguin's departure, coupled with differences in artistic approach, exacerbated van Gogh's drinking. Overall, Gauguin's influence was to increase van Gogh's intake of absinthe and his visits to local brothels. Both men drank, but Gauguin tended to binges, van Gogh drank solidly. He wrote to a friend describing van Gogh as 'an excellent fellow who is sick, who suffers, and who asked for me. Remember the life of Edgar Allen Poe who became an alcoholic as a result of grief and a nervous condition.'[23] One evening, after Gauguin had completed a portrait of his companion which Van Gogh lamented was 'I gone mad', they went to the café, where van Gogh (according to Gauguin's account with no provocation) threw his glass of absinthe at him. Gauguin frogmarched him back to the house, where van Gogh fell asleep, the next day having no good recollection of the event.

Both the sudden onset of this violence and van Gogh's quiescence and hazy memory afterwards suggest a psychotic episode. Whatever the cause, Gauguin had had enough, and wrote to Theo that he wanted to leave. He vacillated following van Gogh's exhortations, but both knew the end had come.

The crisis came soon after, on the evening of 23 December 1888. Gauguin's account is that he went for a walk in a nearby public garden after dinner and van Gogh came rushing up behind him with an open razor. He says he frightened van Gogh off and went to sleep in a hotel, returning to the yellow house the next morning to find a crowd and a policeman, who asked, 'What have you done to your comrade?' They followed a trail of blood upstairs to van Gogh's room, where he lay apparently dead under bloodied sheets. To general relief, he was alive.

It later became clear how the attention of the police had been attracted to the event: late on the night of 23 December, van Gogh, bloody and distracted, had gone to a brothel he frequented and asked for a prostitute called Rachel. On her appearance he gave her a part of his ear, saying she should 'guard this object carefully'. His friend Roulin was at the brothel, and dragged him home.

Gauguin left forthwith, a departure which has led to speculation that the notoriously hot-blooded Gauguin attacked van Gogh with one of the fencing foils he had brought with him after an absinthe-fuelled argument about his wish to leave.[24] It is significant in this interpretation that Gauguin did not tell the police van Gogh had approached him with an open razor; this element of the story appears only in Gauguin's memoir *Avant et Après*.

A benign explanation of this violent domestic dispute is that van Gogh began to flash the razor around the house, threatening to do himself damage if Gauguin left, and Gauguin went away in order that he was not responsible for the consequences. He had often awoken to find van Gogh in the room staring at him while he slept, so he had reason to fear attack, even though he was by far the stronger man.

The conventional view, and the most likely one, is that after Gauguin's departure from the scene van Gogh had mutilated himself by slicing off almost his entire left ear with a razor, causing a prodigious loss of blood. Theo arrived soon after Gauguin left Arles, and van Gogh was committed to hospital to the care of a Dr Rey. Roulin visited and wrote to Theo, 'I think he is lost. Not only is his mind affected, but he is very weak and downhearted.'

Dr Rey, not a specialist in mental illness, and struggling with the limited conceptual framework of contemporary medicine, diagnosed that his patient was suffering from a form of epilepsy (then considered a mental illness) provoked by a combination of bad diet and absinthe and aggravated by overwork and excessive amounts of coffee.[25]

He was allowed to leave the hospital after two weeks, and resumed painting but his behaviour was again bizarre, showing signs of paranoia such as refusing to eat because he believed his food was poisoned. The townspeople of Arles were also alarmed at his conduct: they accused him of drinking too much and of being a threat. Women were said to be frightened because he 'indulges in touching them and also makes obscene remarks in their presence'.[26]

He had some understanding of his state, saying 'I am unable to look after myself and control myself, I feel quite different from what I used to be'.[27] He agreed to be admitted as a voluntary patient to St Paul-de-Mausole Asylum for the Alienated where he was diagnosed as 'suffering from acute mania with hallucinations of sight and hearing'.[28]

A diagnosis of insanity gave van Gogh the freedom to cease his internal struggle to keep up appearances, and he became prey to intermittent bouts of psychosis: he went into Dr Rey's bathroom once when the physician was shaving with an open razor and offered to do it for him; after a walk with an attendant who accompanied him while he painted, van Gogh kicked the man in the stomach, saying he was compelled to do it because the Arles police were after him. All this adds to the picture given by Gauguin and the Arles townspeople of an unstable and potentially dangerous individual.

Far more alarming, and perhaps more revealing than these general paranoid experiences, were the episodes which were peculiar to van Gogh as an artist. In March 1889 Paul Signac took his friend out of the hospital and to his old house to look at his pictures. He had to rush van Gogh back to hospital because he was trying to drink turpentine. On two other occasions van Gogh had an attack in which he started eating the paint from his tubes. His carers interpreted this as a suicide attempt. More creatively, one could see it as a psychotic delusion – perhaps a notion that he would become a greater painter by internalising the paint.

Van Gogh has been variously diagnosed, retrospectively, as having a psychosis, cerebral tumour, syphilis, magnesium deficiency, manic depression, temporal lobe epilepsy, toxic psychosis, acute intermittent porphyria, chronic sunstroke, poison by digitalis (which could have provoked the yellow vision) and glaucoma (some self-portraits show a dilated right pupil, and he depicted coloured halos around lights).[29] Even if some of these diagnoses are accurate (and there is general agreement on psychosis), they are hardly adequate to explain van Gogh's style, though they may have had some influence, as may the altered perceptions caused by absinthe.

In depictions of madness it is important too to allow the patient his voice. Van Gogh's view was that his insanity was caused by his desperate devotion to his work, to push himself further into the unknown in creativity. As he said in one of the last things he wrote, 'Well, my own work, I am risking my life for it and my reason has half foundered because of it'.[30]

The biochemist Wilfred Niels Arnold has made a study of van Gogh at this period, and he considers that family members and others have acknowledged the contribution of van Gogh's drinking habits to his failing health, 'but they have confused the literature by missing or underestimating his proclivity for absinthe (and its damaging components in addition to alcohol)'.[31]

Arnold points to the substance known as thujone for absinthe's addictive and psychodynamic properties. Chemists have defined the constituents of many essential oils, including the terpenes, a family of chemicals which are found in the basic constituents of absinthe: pinocamphone found in hyssop; fenchone from fennel and, most importantly, thujone from wormwood. Thujone is the major constituent of wormwood oil, making up 90 per cent of the oil's weight.

Arnold describes the action of thujone: 'the compound causes marked excitement of the autonomic nervous system, followed by unconsciousness and convulsions'.[32] Certainly wormwood, or the thujone in it, was the key ingredient of absinthe. However, Arnold elegantly fits other aspects of van Gogh's illness into a framework of the artist's physical dependence on terpenes.

While recovering in the Arles hospital from the damage he had done to his ear he was suffering from insomnia, but was fighting it himself 'with a very, very strong dose of camphor in my pillow and mattress'.[33] Camphor oil is a terpene with a similar structure to thujone, and indeed the margin between convulsant and fatal doses is narrower for camphor than for thujone.

The craving for terpenes also explains van Gogh's attempting to drink turpentine (containing pinene) and the bizarre episodes where he ate his paints (whose solvent was turpentine). Van Gogh's need for thujone, then, developed into a generalised craving for terpenes when the most easily accessible form – absinthe – was not available because of hospital restrictions.

Van Gogh therefore was demonstrating a pica, a craving for unnatural foods, which was associated with his heavy use of absinthe. This throws no light on van Gogh as an artist, but a great deal on the debate surrounding the addictiveness of absinthe. Were others similarly addicted not only to alcohol, but to the terpene oil in absinthe as well?

Arnold considers van Gogh's 'madness' was caused by porphyria, a metabolic condition characterised by a marked increase in the formation and excretion of porphyrins. His proposal has received experimental support from a team at the University of Massachusetts Medical Centre who tested camphor, pinene and thujone for their ability to produce porphyria in those with a liver condition which predisposed them to it.[34]

The rest of van Gogh's story is sadly familiar: he was deemed cured in 1890 after a year in the asylum and sent, in apparently good health, to the picturesque village of Auvers-sur-Oise, just north of Paris. There he was under the care of Dr Gachet, a specialist in mental illness and a friend to many artists. The daughter of the house where van Gogh lodged above a café later reported in a memoir of him that he did not drink while he was with them, and as he ate meals in the café where she helped out, she would have known. One of the village youths, however, said he was drinking with them, and grew talkative when he did so.

He painted around the town and in wheat fields in the surrounding countryside. His mental state began to decline, and he obtained a revolver, perhaps stolen from the hunting bag of the youths he met, perhaps loaned to him in order to scare off the crows which troubled him while he was painting. He went out into the fields on 27 July 1890 and shot himself in the chest. He did not die, but returned to the café where he lodged and made his way upstairs, to the alarm of the proprietor. The bullet had missed vital organs, but infection set in and van Gogh died after two days.

He was buried in the graveyard at Auvers-sur-Oise. Theo outlived him by only six months, dying of a kidney infection complicated by a weak heart. He was buried at Utrecht, but was later exhumed and reinterred beside his brother. The village is now home to a museum commemorating van Gogh's time there and a Museum of Absinthe.

Emile Bernard organised an exhibition of van Gogh's work, though he was expanding his creative horizons and began to study mysticism and philosophy. He left for Constantinople in 1893, then settled in Egypt for 10 years. He returned in 1904 to found and edit an arts review, *La Rénovation Esthétique*. He died in Paris at the age of 73 in 1941.

Theo's widow Johanna worked tirelessly to establish van Gogh's posthumous reputation. It is the stuff of art legend that the man who sold only one painting in his lifetime had produced work which, a hundred years later, sold for staggering sums: a self portrait sold for $65 million at Christie's New York in 1998.

Gauguin's Travels

After van Gogh's death, Gauguin struggled to return to the south seas, at one time hoping Theo would fund the trip. His life is often interpreted as that of a stockbroker who threw it all up to be an artist and to travel. In fact, Gauguin had been travelling all his life; it was settling down to be a stockbroker for 12 years which was the aberration, not his wanderings, which began in 1851 when he was four years old and on his way to Lima. Nor did he truly give up the bourgeois role of buying and selling for his bread: Gauguin was convinced that the time was right in modern art for him to be able to make a killing on the art market, a prediction which was nearly correct.

In recognition of their contribution to contemporary culture, and of their poverty, the Théâtre d'Art gave two benefit performances on 20 and 21 May 1891 in aid of Verlaine and Gauguin. They were a sell-out, though after expenses the returns were disappointing and Gauguin was not, as he had hoped, able to fund his trip to Tahiti with the money raised. He was already on his way by the time of the benefit, and what money was raised went to the visibly needy Verlaine.

Gauguin hadn't forgotten how to work the system to ensure favourable treatment – he obtained a letter of 'official mission' from the French government to give him a reduction in his fare and respectful treatment by colonial officials. However, when he arrived in the south seas, far from feting him as a great artist come to immortalise them, the French authorities regarded Gauguin with disdain.

He had made his voyage because he believed the primordial secrets of artistic truth were to be found in primitive cultures, and was looking for noble savages. He actually found drunkenness and syphilis. Moreover, there was no easy life in this supposed tropical paradise. The islanders grew their own food and a Chinese merchant sold such imported delicacies as canned food. Gauguin could have hunted, but the noble savage, he found, would spend his entire time in hunting, leaving nothing for painting.

Far from leaving the petty demands of money behind him, Gauguin was increasingly fixated on the monthly arrival of the mail boat with its promise of letters and money from France. He married a native girl of 13 in a local ceremony, and Teha'amana moved into his bamboo hut to cater for his needs, though she would still meet native lovers when she went out into the bush to gather fruit.

Gauguin produced 60 paintings, though was unable to keep himself by the sale of his art, and money left for him in France was embezzled. After two-and-a-half years he was granted free repatriation to France, leaving another young wife weeping for him.

Another symbolist exhibition was greeted with mirth by the critics, but at least Gauguin gained some financial security from the will of an uncle. He set up a salon, where Degas, Mallarmé and others gathered to hear his travellers' tales, and he was comforted by his new girlfriend, a 13-year-old Indian-Malay girl called Annah.

On a trip to Brittany, he responded to racist insults aimed at Annah and was brutally beaten by Breton sailors, receiving a severe injury to his ankle which was never to heal properly. Back in Paris after two months' convalescence in Pont-Aven, he found his apartment had been ransacked for any valuables by Annah, who had subsequently departed. He set up an auction of his work (Annah hadn't considered that valuable) and returned to Tahiti in 1895.

The syphilis from which he was probably already suffering when he first went to the island had worsened, his leg injury caused him suffering, and Teha'amana had since remarried. She returned to Gauguin briefly, but soon went back, appalled to find that her foreign husband was now covered with running sores.[35]

He was still able to tempt girls with alcohol and small gifts, however; he wrote 'every night skittish young girls invade my bed – three of them yesterday to keep me busy.'[36] He soon found another 13-year-old, Pau'ura a Tai, to live with him. In 1897 he wrote about the joys of south-sea life,

> just to sit here at the open door, smoking a cigarette and drinking a glass of absinthe, is an unmixed pleasure which I have every day. And then I have a fifteen-year-old wife who cooks my simple everyday fare and goes down on her back for me whenever I want, all for the modest reward of a frock, worth ten francs a month.[37]

Poverty again overcame him, and his difficulties were exacerbated by the death of his teenage daughter Aline from pneumonia. She was the only one of his family who kept faith with him, who had told him 'I shall be your wife'. In response to her death he produced one of his largest and finest paintings: *Where do we come from? What are we? Where are we going?* Shortly after completing it he walked into the hills behind his hut and swallowed the arsenic powder he had been prescribed for his syphilis sores. It was too great a dose and he regurgitated it, 'condemned,' as he put it, 'to live'.[38]

He took a job in the Tahitian public-works department as a clerk and did some work of satirical journalism. His poverty was alleviated in 1900 at the age of 51 when the Parisian art dealer Ambroise Vollard offered to buy all his future paintings and to give him an advance.

Sick and in pain, despised by the natives and Europeans alike, he left for Hiva Oa in the Marquesas, where he said he hoped to find 'unspoiled' native life. He may, however, have felt obliged to leave, as one of his acquaintances said, because no woman in Tahiti would have sex with him any more, so disgusting were his syphilis sores and 'the women of the Marquesas were poorer and more savage, and he would have better opportunities there'. Another friend was recorded as saying Gauguin one day returned triumphant from a trip to Papeete (the capital). 'He had heard that in the Marquesas you could still buy a girl model for a handful of sweets! He ordered a sackful.'[39]

He acquired a new girlfriend, Vaeoho, aged 14, and continued painting. He would sometimes have friends round, including a former infantry sergeant and a native carpenter, for dinner and an evening of absinthe. He had a bitter dispute with the local Catholic priest, who tried to stop native girls from going to his hut, which he had called Maison du Jouir, 'House of Pleasure'. The artist responded by trying to get the natives to stop sending their children to school.

The idyllic life included prodigious amounts of absinthe, and it was his favourite drink, but how important was it? Rum was 2.50 francs a litre, while absinthe was 7 francs a bottle. It is reasonable to assume that when money was tight, Gauguin drank rum. In one four-month period, according to the records of a Hiva Oa merchant, Gauguin bought '25 litres of absinthe *and assorted spirits*' (my emphasis). He also bought 202 litres of red wine and 80 bottles of beer.[40] If absinthe is claimed to have made a contribution to his artistic vision, why not beer or wine?

There was diminishing fun, and increasing quarrels with the local authorities, the church and the police. Finally Gauguin died alone in his hut at the age of 53 in 1903. At the auction after his death, one canvas sold for 7 francs; some canvases, deemed indecent, were burned.

Gauguin was always sufficiently a bourgeois to have an eye on the market which he declared was there for exotic pictures from the south seas. He was correct: after his death, his wife and children were able to live in increasing comfort because of the rising value of his paintings, which fed a market eager for a different kind of exoticism after enjoying itself to the full on the oriental. Whatever his failings as a husband and father while alive, Gauguin made up for it after death.

His contribution to the development of art was his move away from the conception of a picture as an image of an actual scene and therefore away from impressionism. He had continually nagged van Gogh to get away from representation in art and paint from his imagination. Gauguin was interested in the capacity of pictures not to re-create a scene but to invoke a feeling. He was more interested in a conceptual method of representation, and in this prefigured the development of art in the twentieth century.

As with Verlaine, it is questionable how much of Gauguin's behaviour had anything to do with absinthe, or even to do with drinking. Artists developed an admirable distancing to preserve the quality of their art from the contamination of bourgeois values. This quickly turned into an artistic moral exceptionism in which drinking to excess and sex without regard to the human consequences were acceptable, and even became a necessary part of the artistic pose. At least in Gauguin's case the art was valid; plenty who flocked to Paris claimed the supposed moral exceptionism of artists and produced nothing of value.

Gauguin was taken with the conviction that he was a genius and as such he was outside the rules which governed ordinary mortals, but his 'bad behaviour' consisted primarily of abandoning his family and, while infected with venereal disease, of taking up with a succession of teenagers; alcohol was not a major issue. For Verlaine and Rimbaud, the 'little drunken vigil holy' was a vital part of their lives and of Rimbaud's artistic endeavour. Gauguin drank a good deal but never wrote or spoke as if absinthe were overwhelmingly important to him; it is not a factor in his paintings. It is more realistic to examine what he said about the south seas and about art, and what he did both in his travels and his paintings, and devise a Gauguin world-view from that.

The most that can be said about Gauguin and absinthe is that his approach to colour, to seeing colours as representative of moods rather than direct representations of a scene, is an approach to artistic conceptualising for which the synaesthetic effects of absinthe had prepared the artistic community.

Strindberg's Inferno

Gauguin's brother-in-law Fritz Thaulow is credited with introducing impressionism to Norway; and Gauguin's relationship to Copenhagen (his wife Mette's home city) was another route to the Scandinavian avant garde. Gauguin's artistic influence was particularly strong on two of the most brilliant of the Scandinavians, Edvard Munch and August Strindberg.

Munch was born in Löten, Norway in 1863 into a family which was politically and culturally prominent, but its many tragedies were to form the backdrop to his emotionally blistering work. His mother died of tuberculosis when he was five, and before his twenty-sixth birthday his sister, father and brother also died; later another sister became mentally ill. Some of his strongest work was concerned with death-beds, sickness and corpses. His first major painting, *The Sick Child*, created after he first visited Paris in 1885, is a radical break from his previous realistic works. He was now using techniques of expressing emotion direct from the canvas without an attempt at realism, the birth of what came to be called expressionism.

On this and subsequent visits to Paris he was first inspired by the work of Pissarro and Monet; later he was to come more strongly under the influence of Gauguin and the concepts of synthetism which Gauguin and Bernard had developed with artistic colleagues at Pont-Aven. Gauguin was the artistic link between the work of the impressionists, still featuring what was *seen* by the artists, and the harsher vision of the Scandinavians, Germans and Austrians of what was *felt*.

Munch was at the forefront of anti-naturalist thinking in art, which was also a reaction against the replicas of life, which photography could provide. 'The camera cannot compete with a brush and canvas,' he wrote, 'as long as it cannot be used in heaven and hell'. Munch's best-known work, *The Scream,* demonstrates his depiction of hell in the form of a single, anguished individual.

He was one of a circle of bohemians gathered around the anarchist thinker Hans Jaeger, who wrote of this Scandinavian cenacle in a book *From Christiania's Bohemia,* for which he was prosecuted and imprisoned for 60 days for 'immorality'. Munch depicted Jaeger and another friend, Jappe Nilssen, in 1890 in a café drinking absinthe; it was called by the artist *The Absinthe Drinkers,* though in common with other pictures with this title it had a troubled history. It was due to be exhibited along with nine other works in the Oslo Autumn Salon but before the exhibition it was sold to an American millionaire, Mac Curdy, who insisted that this picture (now his picture) was not exhibited under a name which drew attention to absinthe, so it became known as *The Confession.* It survived the subsequent fire at the exhibition, which destroyed five of Munch's paintings.

In 1892 Munch was invited to exhibit in Berlin by the Artists' Association, but the exhibition was greeted with outrage, as conservative painters and the public interpreted Munch's work as an anarchistic provocation. Just over half the Artists' Association members (in a close vote) forced an early closure after a few days, in a gesture considered outrageous behaviour to an invited guest, leaving Munch at 29 such a star of the avant garde that he decided to remain in Berlin. He joined the bohemian circle comprising sculptors, painters and writers who gathered at the tiny, dark Black

Piglet Café (Zum schwarzen Ferkel) on the corner of the Unter den Linden and Potsdammerstrasse.

Here Munch first met, and painted, Strindberg, who was a kindred spirit in being suspicious of impressionism, wanting to see modern movements take art further into an exploration of the artist's soul. Together they would discuss Nietzsche, the occult, psychology and sex. Strindberg was a fascinated observer of the impressionists; Gauguin describes him sitting in a corner of the artist's studio playing the guitar and singing; 'your blue Nordic eye studied attentively the pictures on the walls'. Gauguin asked Strindberg to write a foreword to the catalogue for an auction of his Tahiti paintings in 1895 when he was selling up for his final return to the south seas. Strindberg refused in a long, considered letter, saying, 'I cannot understand your art and I cannot like it ... But I know that this avowal will not surprise or hurt you, for you seem to me to be strengthened by other men's scorn.' Gauguin sent his effusive thanks, printed the letter in its entirety and sent it to the press.[41]

In March 1893 Munch introduced to the Black Piglet circle an old friend from Christiania (later to become Oslo), 25-year-old musician Dagny Juel. He had known Dagny there, where he had painted her and her sister as *Two Music-Making Sisters*. Dagny, who was to be the tragic muse of the Black Piglet bohemians, was born in 1867 in Kongsvinger in the south of Norway, where her father was a doctor and the town mayor. The family was musical, and in the mid-1880s Dagny and her sister went to Christiania to study music.

She went to Berlin to continue her studies in 1892 and met up with Munch. Finnish writer Adolf Paul described his first sight of her:

> One day she stepped into the Black Piglet at Munch's side – blonde, slender, elegant and dressed with a sense of refinement that understood how to hint at the body's sensuous movement but simultaneously avoid revealing too definite contours ... A classic, pure profile, her face overshadowed by a profusion of curls! ... A laugh that inspired a longing for kisses, simultaneously revealing two rows of pearl-like white teeth awaiting the opportunity to attach themselves! And in addition, a primeval, affected

sleepiness in her movements, never excluding the possibility of a lightning attack.[42]

An advocate of free love and female equality, Dagny was soon to be the lover of several of the Black Piglet circle. An anonymous writer described her attraction:

> She was by no means beautiful, yet few women were more seductive...A much too large mouth with narrow lips, which gleamed so redly over her pointed weasel teeth that those who did not know her swore they were artificially coloured...spirit shone in her smile, in every movement of her supple limbs, that were wrapped in a loose hanging gown. She needed only to look at a man, and put her hand on his arm, and he at once found himself able to express something he had long carried within him without previously having been able to give it form. She was the intellectual mid-wife for these poets born in pain.[43]

Art historian Julius Meier-Graefe described her as being 'very slender with the figure of a fourteenth century Madonna and a smile that drove men mad...she drank absinthe by the litre without ever getting drunk'.[44] She was given various nicknames including Aspasia, after Pericles's lover, and Ducha, meaning 'soul'. Munch painted her several times, most exceptionally in five versions of the *Madonna*, which, according to some critics, show Dagny 'naked and at the point of orgasm'. Certainly Munch believed that sexual ecstasy was the moment 'when life and death join hands'.[45]

She was said to have had affairs with Munch, Strindberg, the Swedish writer Bengt Lidforss, the German doctor Carl Schleich who pioneered local anaesthesia, and finally with the Polish writer Stanislaw Przybyszewski.[46] 'She rested in men's arms as lightly as a veil, a flock of clouds,' a woman friend said.[47]

When Strindberg arrived at the Black Piglet in 1892, a short time before Dagny, he was 43 and had already written his revolutionary plays *The Father* and *Miss Julie*. They had both been played in Berlin, where the former was shut down by the censorship office, the second mainly by outraged women in the audience. When he met Dagny he had just proposed to a young Austrian journalist, Frida

Uhl, and was writing to her every day. He was, however, unable to resist Dagny's charms.

Strindberg's biographer Michael Meyer admits the story of their first night is on the authority of two dubious witnesses (one of them Strindberg himself), but justifiably feels it is too good a tale to omit. Strindberg and Dagny spoke for hours, fuelled by beer, wine, toddy, Swedish punch and absinthe. Dagny had a good head for drink, and Strindberg boasted he never got drunk, but there was clearly some effect. They went to her hotel room, where they had sex and fell asleep. Waking up, Strindberg found himself, as he often did in an unfamiliar hotel room. He noticed the hairpins on the carpet and the face powder on the sofa and his familiar disgust for everything that was woman rose in him. Then he noticed the woman in bed beside him and was unable to control himself. He dragged Dagny out of bed and pushed her out of the door and bolted it, then went back to sleep. It had not occurred to him that it might be her hotel room he was in. Quite what Dagny did is not recorded, except that they met again the next night, and their relationship was thought to have gone on for several weeks, so she was not discouraged by this early evidence of the playwright's attitude to women.[48] 'I fucked her so had no revenge to seek,' he explained in a letter to a friend, who presumably was expected to understand Strindberg's bizarre logic of the sex war.[49]

Dagny was soon, however, enmeshed with Stanislaw Przybyszewski, a Polish medical student, writer and newspaper editor a year younger than herself. He was steeped in mysticism, satanism and sex, had published essays on Nietzsche and Chopin in 1892, and the following year brought out his first novel, *The Mass of the Dead*.

Przybyszewski left his common-law wife and the mother of his two children for Dagny. When his former lover knew he was gone for good (after he had returned for a time and given her another child), she killed herself. The writer was thought by the police to be implicated in her death and Strindberg wrote manically, underlined in red ink, 'Przybyszewski has been arrested for the murder of his wife. Soot in my absinthe.'[50] But no charges were laid, and he was released.

Dagny and Przybyszewski married in summer 1893 and had some happy, if impoverished, years as the king and queen of bohemia in their one-roomed apartment on the Louisenstrasse, where the artistic review *Pan* was conceived, Berlin's equivalent of the Parisian *Revue Blanche*. In this room, with its battered furniture they would entertain their friends, with Dagny playing Grieg and Przybyszewski playing Chopin on their rented piano, which had been baffled to reduce the complaints of the neighbours. Meier-Graefe described one of these evenings:

> One of us would dance with Ducha while the other two looked on from the table: one spectator was Munch, the other was generally Strindberg. The four men in the room were all in love with Ducha, each in his own way, but they never showed it. Most subdued of all was Munch. He called Ducha 'The Lady', talked dryly to her and was always very polite and discreet even when drunk.[51]

Munch painted a sequence of *Jealousy* pictures, with a woman tempting a man in the background and another figure, unmistakeably that of Przybyszewski, staring out gloomily. These paintings were considered to be an allusion to Munch's relationship with Dagny; Przybyszewski's novel *Overboard* is felt to be a reply, in its story of how a jealous painter commits suicide after his beloved is seduced by a writer.

Dagny began to write short plays, stories and prose poems. As the rejected lover Lidforss put it to Strindberg, 'Juel has now chosen her occupation, and seized the pen instead of the prick'.[52] The Przybyszewskis had two children, born in 1895 and 1897, and lived in desperate poverty, largely on the gifts of their family and friends, with Dagny pawning summer clothes in winter and vice versa. Neither practised sexual fidelity, though Przybyszewski was more flagrant about it and resented Dagny's sexual freedom. He was obsessed with the occult, sex and drinking, and though descriptions of their married life have tended to concentrate on his to the exclusion of her behaviour, she also needed alcohol and lovers to maintain her emotional equilibrium.

They moved to Krakow in the autumn of 1898, where Przybyszewski was the centre of the Polish bohemians, though Dagny did not enjoy her former celebrity, partly because she was isolated by not knowing Polish. Their drinking and promiscuity put an unbearable strain on the relationship, and they frequently parted but remained in contact. Finally, at the age of 33 Dagny set off to travel with a new young admirer, Wladyslaw Emeryk, a rich, idealistic but unstable Russian Pole. On 5 June 1901 in Tiblisi he shot her in the back of the head, then shot himself, leaving a letter to her husband that he was 'killing her for her own sake'.[53]

Przybyszewski never recovered from the shock of her death, and left Krakow to live an obscure life as a railway or postal clerk in the Prussian zone of Poland.[54]

Munch wrote kindly in an obituary notice about Dagny, stressing her own creativity and the encouragement she gave to other artists. He had a major exhibition in 1895 on the themes of love, jealousy and anxiety which had inspired him during his time with the bohemians, which he developed as *The Frieze of Life* during the 1890s. He continued exhibiting his work across Europe and America, making his living mainly from the entrance fees. Munch put on 106 exhibitions between 1892 and 1909 in a painful and unsettled period of his life in which he was drinking excessively, though absinthe is not mentioned by biographers as a drug of choice.

The crisis of what he called 'the battle called love between a man and a woman' came over a tragic love affair with the beautiful aristocrat Tulla Larsen between 1899 and 1902. She wanted to marry him, though he had reservations, writing,

> you must understand – that I am in a unique position here on earth – the position imposed by a life filled with illness – unhappy relationships – and my position as an artist – a life in which there is no room for anything resembling happiness and which does not even desire happiness.[55]

This ill-starred relationship came to a dramatic end after an argument with Tulla, when Munch fired a revolver in his cottage in Åsgårdstrand, taking the top of his finger off. He was bitterly disappointed when Tulla did not visit him in hospital, and was overwhelmed with jealousy when he discovered she had gone off to Paris with a rival painter, whom she subsequently married.

Munch painted Tulla in pictures such as *Hatred* and *The Murderess* as he became increasingly obsessed and disturbed. His pathological jealousy and bitterness against her, combined with his paranoid feelings of being persecuted in Norway because of his art, led to a breakdown in 1908. He feared he was going to be interned in an asylum, and suspected everyone of spying on him and intending to deliver him to the police. He left Germany for Denmark, and dosed his paranoid anxiety with alcohol:

> I drink one whisky and soda after another. The alcohol warms me up and, especially in the evening, excites me. I feel it eating its way inward, inward to the delicate nerves. Need tobacco too. Cigars, lots of strong ones ... Whisky and soda, whisky and soda. Burn up the pain.[56]

This is a good description of how the mentally ill can use the anaesthetic qualities of alcohol. Munch was eventually admitted to a clinic, where he underwent treatment for eight months, after which he gave up alcohol for the rest of his life.

His friend Strindberg was an even heavier drinker and an even more disturbed individual, but one for whom absinthe rather than whisky was often the drink of choice. Strindberg had been born in Stockholm in 1849, the son of an aristocrat and a former servant. His childhood was marked by misery: his father went bankrupt when he was a small child; when he was 13 his mother died and his father quickly remarried. He described the poverty, insecurity and religious fanaticism of his life in a bitter autobiography, *Son of a Servant*.

The first 12 years of his adult life were to see study for the ministry and in medicine, then failure as a teacher, and as an actor and as a journalist, until a period of comparative calm when he became a librarian and married Siri von Essen, a Finnish actress, in 1877. After a number of unsuccessful plays, he now wrote an auto-biographical novel, *The Red Room*. This satirical account of fraud and abuse in Swedish society established him as both a great talent and as an enemy of the establishment, a critical opinion confirmed with his volumes of stories, which led to fierce attacks on him and an unsuccessful prosecution for blasphemy. Partly because of the attacks, in 1883 he left Sweden and for six years travelled restlessly around the continent.

The family lived in Grez near Nemours in 1885, where his daughter remarks that in 1885 he began to drink absinthe after a long period of complete temperance. It is typical of Strindberg's extreme personality that he went from not drinking at all to drinking the most highly alcoholic drink available.[57] A Norwegian writer, Johanas Lie, said Strindberg was already addicted to absinthe when they met in Paris in 1884; certainly he was an alco-holic after his return to Sweden in 1889.

Strindberg had problems in his family life, which he blamed on a Danish friend of his wife Siri, Marie David, who encouraged Siri to stand up to her husband, and became for him the embodiment of everything he hated about feminism: 'these damned modern women who for a time made my marriage unendurable'.

Consequently, Strindberg attempted to smear David to the church committee which was deliberating on his divorce from Siri, writing that she was a lesbian and that she drank heavily, 'cognac with her breakfast coffee, absinthe before lunch and cognac again throughout the day'. On the basis of such testimony, the committee declared that in the interests of the children David should cease all contact with the family.[58]

Strindberg and Siri were divorced in 1891, whereupon this un-happiness, coupled with the lack of artistic recognition in Sweden, led Strindberg to Berlin. While nominally a socialist, he had become undemocratic and anti-feminist, a state of mind in which he found Germany congenial. 'France is absinthe and self-abuse,' he remarked, 'Switzerland matriarchal sentimentality' but Germany was 'patriarchal and male-dominated; army recruits six feet tall with fat cheeks'.[59]

It was in this mood that he participated in the Black Piglet cenacle and briefly became Dagny Juel's lover while still keeping up a relationship with the journalist Frida Uhl, whom he married in 1893. That relationship soon failed, and they parted within a year, with Strindberg entering his 'inferno' period, the years between 1894 and 1897 of his teetering on the brink of insanity.

Strindberg was impoverished, and engaged in months of heavy absinthe drinking during his disappointment at the failure of *The Father* to bring him any real money. Each time it was performed in a new country gave him renewed hope, which was always dashed. The outcry from the press and public in Sweden was so vehement that it came off after nine performances, though it was not without its supporters. The French doctor and poet Marcel Réja, who saw a lot of Strindberg in 1897–98, said alcohol 'probably played a not unimportant role in the inferno crisis'.[60] One of Strindberg's letters describes 'I drank one whole day from morning till late at night. With L – one evening and half the night. To be sure this is swinishness. But when I am alone in a great city, the tavern alone saves me from suicide.'[61]

Drinking without eating properly left him emaciated through poor nutrition and even more open to mental disturbance, in which there was to some degree a physical cause. His illness tended to follow a pattern of an initial period of restlessness and disquiet, a feeling of illness, persecutory and suicidal ideas, followed by sudden flight from the scene where the symptoms subside.[62] He suffered auditory hallucinations of such things as three pianos playing in neighbouring rooms; he believed his neighbours were persecuting him with 'electric currents'; and he made wild accusations of his wife's infidelity and his friends' treachery. He believed friends such as Munch and Przybyszewski were trying to kill him with domestic gas.

Part of his madness was Strindberg's conviction that he was a great scientist, or alchemist, for Strindberg made no distinction between the two. Frederick Delius said,

I believed implicitly in his scientific discoveries then. He had such a convincing way of explaining them and certainly was very ambitious to be an inventor. For instance, Röntgen rays [X-rays] had just been discovered, and he confided to me one afternoon over an absinthe at the Café Closerie des Lilas that he himself had discovered them ten years ago.[63]

Strindberg's biographer Michael Meyer tells how the women who owned the restaurant across the road from Strindberg's lodgings went downstairs one morning to find him in the middle of the room, having moved all the chairs against the walls and arranged the pots and pans in a circle.

Wearing only underpants and a shirt, he was performing a dance of exorcism around them. He explained he was doing this to chase away the evil spirits which might poison the food. During hot weather, he would usually climb in through the window, since evil spirits stood watching in the doorway; and one day everything in the kitchen exploded just before lunch was to be served. This was a consequence of Strindberg trying to make gold in a saucepan.[64]

He made occasional references to absinthe as one of a number of drinks he was taking, only once ascribing to it special effects: 'several times this month I have drunk absinthe with Sjöstedt, but always with unpleasant results'; the café 'became filthy with horrid types,' people 'covered with filth as though they had come out of the sewers' appeared on the streets and stared at him.[65]

Rather as with van Gogh, there is no shortage of theories as to what caused Strindberg's strange behaviour. Diagnoses for Strindberg's 'hallucinatory delusional psychosis' include schizophrenia, manic depression, paranoia, alcoholism and, invariably, given the medical preoccupations of the time, 'absinthism'.

E.W. Anderson, who has studied Strindberg's case, remarks that there is no question as to the schizophrenic character of the playwright's crises, 'but this is not the same as a diagnosis of schizophrenia'. He feels the sense deceptions, elementary hallucinations, mortal panic, heart tension, and the fact that the symptoms occurred most intensely at night 'are strongly suggestive of a toxic delirium'.

He maintains that with 'the definitive history of alcoholism, especially absinthe, the diagnosis of an alcoholic delirium or more probably one of those more commonly seen mixed forms, intermediate between a delirium tremens and an alcoholic hallucinosis, seems compelling'. He notes the probably impure forms of absinthe Strindberg would have been drinking, 'well known for its highly toxic effects'. In support of this, Réja made a diagnosis of 'alcoholic delirium', but it appears did not specifically implicate absinthe.[66]

When Strindberg recognised the damaging qualities of alcohol, he foreswore the spirits he had been used to drinking, notably putting absinthe far down the list: 'Today I promise myself never again to touch schnapps, cognac or whisky! My God help me to keep this vow! Including rum, arrack, absinthe.'[67]

By 1896 Strindberg emerged from mental crisis with a renewed vigour for creativity, and in the 11 years from 1898 wrote 35 plays and founded his own theatre in Stockholm, as well as writing *Inferno*, his own account of his descent into madness. In his later years he was to enjoy the acclaim of the public in Sweden, though never of the Swedish establishment. Strindberg married a Norwegian actress almost 30 years his junior, though they were parted within a year, and he was to propose to a 19-year-old painter before he eventually died from stomach cancer in Stockholm at the age of 63.

Despite his stormy emotional life, Munch was a survivor, and lived on to the age of 80 in deliberate self-isolation in Norway. Norway's National Women's Museum has now been established in Dagny Juel's childhood home in Kongsvinger.

Van Gogh, Munch and Strindberg were all manically devoted to their art, all heavy drinkers, and all suffered periods of mental illness, but absinthe was not a prime mover in any particular case. Strindberg drank what was available and attached no particular importance to absinthe.

If a case can be made for absinthe's involvement in the post-impressionist use of colour, as in van Gogh's work, or to some extent in the creation of synthetism, as in Gauguin and Bernard's experiments, its influence can equally be said to be absent from

Munch's expressionism. Moreover, though he drank it, absinthe mattered little to Gauguin and not at all to Bernard. The case for absinthe's involvement in the artistic process dwindles away into a mass of qualifications. It was a colourful contribution to a scene which would have existed and progressed along the same lines with or without the green fairy.

6 The Absinthe Binge

BY THE 1890S A PATTERN BECAME CLEAR in the use of absinthe by artists: some, such as Raffaëlli, delighted in it and used it as a major symbol. Others, notably Toulouse-Lautrec, may have used the drink to excess but paid scant attention to it artistically. In the better artists creative imagination supplied images of the time where their lesser contemporaries used absinthe as a handy image. This became apparent at a time of unprecedentedly high and rising absinthe use.

While there had always been heavy absinthe users, such as Verlaine and van Gogh, nothing short of an absinthe binge was underway in the 1890s. A relaxation of the French licensing laws relating to retail shops in 1880 led to an extra 10,000 shops selling alcohol being established in Paris. By 1909 there was a liquor outlet for every 30 adult males in France. Consumption of spirits was about one-and-a-quarter litres per person annually in 1854; by 1900 it was more than four-and-a-half.[1] That this was largely an increase in absinthe consumption is demonstrated by the fact that between 1885 and 1892 the consumption of all forms of alcohol increased in Paris by 5 per cent, but absinthe consumption increased by 125 per cent.[2]

Heavy drinking by an entire society is often considered to relate to the anxiety attendant on social dislocation and consequent personal uncertainty. In terms of the absinthe story, it was the relative cheapness of *alcool d'industrie* which meant much of this drinking was of distilled spirits, and absinthe was the most popular of the distilled spirit drinks. Taxes were raised to discourage drinking in the 1870s and 1880s, but as industrial processes improved and economies of scale continued, prices continued to fall. In 1873 a glass of absinthe was 15c, while a kilo of bread was 50c. In 1894 in the 'great cafés', the price was only 10c, while in 'working men's quarters' absinthe could be had for 3c.[3] Moreover, it was easier to obtain than bread; a starving character in Zola's *Le Ventre de Paris* (*The Belly of Paris*) comments that there is a far greater willingness of people to buy an acquaintance a drink than food.

Two artists were significant in chronicling this, Raffaëlli, who painted the poor in miserable and drab drinking establishments, and Toulouse-Lautrec, who depicted the gaiety of the *belle époque*. Jean-François Raffaëlli was born in 1850 to an Italian family in Paris. He kept himself going with jobs as a shop-boy, a bit-part actor and an itinerant singer as he trained to be an artist. It was only after the war of 1870–71 that he could give himself full-time to art. He painted for years in a flashy, academic manner, then switched to impressionist constructions under the influence of Degas. As one of Degas's 'gang' at the Café Guerbois and then the Nouvelle Athènes, he participated in the impressionist exhibitions of 1880 and 1881.

He took to painting the poor of Paris in an impressionist style, but with dulled-down tones which contributed towards making the scenes picturesque. Zola and the other naturalistic writers were impressed by Raffaëlli, but others sneered at his work as 'misérabilisme'. Renoir, working on his gloriously coloured scenes of hedonism, sniffed 'Everything is poor in his pictures, even the grass'.[4] Raffaëlli's most successful picture, *Les Déclassés* (*The Social Rejects*) of 1881, shows two melancholy men in late middle age, wearing smart but now battered clothes, obviously with no work or other reason to live except to sit in front of their glasses of absinthe. It was another of those pictures which were later renamed to highlight the absinthe featured in them, so it now goes under the title *Les Buveurs d'Absinthe*.

Poverty itself, with its many symbols of wear, want, misery and decrepitude, had been the defining characteristic of social rejection, now absinthe drinking so characterised the poor that many of Raffaëlli's pictures of the street-cleaners, the unemployed and other poor show them with the drink. Raffaëlli would hunt down subjects in the 'zone': inhabitants of the military barrier around Paris, comprising fortifications, toll-gates, close-packed dwellings and tiny cafés called 'estaminets'. He also frequented the industrial Asnière region for his picturesque characters.

Le Figaro published 10 of Raffaëlli's drawings of 'Parisian types' in 1889 with a description of different characters by such great naturalistic writers of the day as Zola, de Maupassant and Mirbeau. Joris-Karl Huysmans contributed 'patrons of the café', which included 'the old captain of the line whose flowing moustache is yellowed by the cigarette under his nostrils, who loves to splash his absinthe into muddiness by pouring drop by drop the iced water from a carafe'.[5]

Raffaëlli had made himself unpopular among the impressionists by stealing the show at the 1881 exhibition with an enormous submission of 34 paintings (he had shown 41 at the 1880 exhibition, but not made such a splash). His success with the public and the critics promoted strong suspicion that he was not an impressionist at all. One critic put it frankly, after praising the artist's skill: 'Why the hell did Raffaëlli join this enterprise?'[6] Gauguin and Pissarro campaigned to exclude him from the seventh, 1882, exhibition, Gauguin arguing that Raffaëlli's work had nothing to do with the concerns of impressionism from a technical point of view. Other artists also resented his success and despised his vanity and pushiness. The rejection of Raffaëlli led to his patron Degas also withdrawing his work, making the 1882 impressionist exhibition a very different affair from previous shows, and arguably more theoretically 'impressionist' than ever.

As he grew more successful and established, with his niche of melancholy rag-pickers and absinthe drinkers, Raffaëlli began to distance himself from the impressionists, and was considered excluded from the group by the time of the long-delayed eighth exhibition of 1886. His work indicates a change in circumstances with regard to absinthe; now a generation had grown up with heavy absinthe use. It was not so much the social scourge of earlier times as a defining part of the cultural scene: where there was wretchedness, there was absinthe.

For Toulouse-Lautrec, absinthe was an ever-present ingredient, in his pictures as much as his life. He was born into an aristocratic family at Albi in 1864 and was named Henri-Marie-Raymond de Toulouse-Lautrec-Monfa. As a child he was able to indulge his family's love of sport and art, but his happy childhood was cut short when first a trifling accident broke a thigh-bone, then another accident broke his other leg, disclosing an underlying disease, presumed now to be an adrenal dysfunction. His legs atrophied, but the enforced leisure of convalescence left Toulouse-Lautrec more than enough time to devote himself to art.

Added to this handicap, which meant he always walked with the aid of a stick, as he grew he showed other signs of abnormal physical development consistent with adrenal dysfunction. Sexual development speeded up, but the long bones stopped growing, so his trunk was out of proportion to his limbs, and his arms and legs were spindly, while he had an adult man's head, chest and hands.[7] Presumably as a result of the same disease process, he now developed large nostrils, a thickened tongue and tendency to lisp and drool, and a habitual sniffle.

By the age of 17 he had resolved to become an artist, and his family paid for private tutors. In the early 1880s he was enrolled in the studio of Fernand Cormon in the Rue Constance, where, as mentioned, he met van Gogh and Bernard. The reception given to a peculiar-looking aristocratic cripple in the greater world can be imagined, but Toulouse-Lautrec's boisterous personality, his evident courage and his dedication to his work made friends of his colleagues.

The newly created boulevards and parks for the bourgeoisie had pushed back the poor from the centre of Paris into outlying areas such as Montmartre. Artists had only in recent years been colonising Montmartre from their previous haunts of Montparnasse and the Latin Quarter. The bohemians were advancing in search of cheap rents to the steep packed-earth footpaths and narrow lanes with clusters of dance-halls and cafés and street prostitutes working in the shadow of the scaffolding used to build the Sacré-Coeur church, which was erected to the memory of the victims of the communards. Montmartre's former mayor, Georges Clemençeau, worked tirelessly for an amnesty for the communards who had survived the bourgeois reprisals (they were allowed to return from exile in 1880). Montmartre had always been known as a lawless region, and now it became the principal territory of the state of Bohemia. Though in his early years as a student Toulouse-Lautrec lived with his parents, his entertainments and increasingly his inspiration came from night-time jaunts in Montmartre with his friends from the studio.

Toulouse-Lautrec's enthusiasm for absinthe is first mentioned in the context of his relaxation with fellow artists after a day at the studio, when they would all go to an artists' bar 'étouffer un per-roquet', literally 'to choke a parrot', to drink an absinthe. In her biography of Toulouse-Lautrec, Julia Frey remarks that it is bizarre that the artist's childhood symbol of evil, which had haunted his sketchbooks, was a parrot. He also suffered an eerie obsession with green, saying once, 'Do you know what it is like to be haunted by colours? To me, in the colour green, there is something like the temptation of the devil.'[8] It was as if in the green liqueur known as a parrot Toulouse-Lautrec met the nemesis he had been waiting for all his life.

He was always described in terms of absinthe: a minor poet friend, Romain Coolus, described Toulouse-Lautrec as talking incessantly 'through his drooping moustache, damp with vermouth or absinthe', and the painter Gustav Moreau said, 'his paintings were almost entirely painted in absinthe'.[9] Toulouse-Lautrec walked with the aid of a hollowed-out walking stick with a reservoir of alcohol and a concealed glass, so that at the end of his life (when his drinking was being monitored by his family) he would never be without a drink. It is preserved in the Toulouse-Lautrec Museum in Albi.

His other lifelong preoccupation was sex, and particularly sex with prostitutes, uncomplicated by anything more than friendship. One of his student friends later boasted that he had been responsible for Toulouse-Lautrec's first sexual experience with a woman. Charles-Edward Lucas was sensitive to the handicapped teenager's predicament, and perceived that his bawdy talk belied sexual inexperience. He arranged for a 16-year-old model, Marie Charlet, to seduce Toulouse-Lautrec. She called him her 'darling coat-hanger' and talked widely of the nights they spent together.[10] Toulouse-Lautrec was soon to contract syphilis from a prostitute, it was said from one called Red Rosa – he always had a predilection for women with red hair. Prostitutes were said to have called him the Tripod because of his small legs and long penis.

Tired of the academic regimen of copying in Cormon's studios, Toulouse-Lautrec's attendance became more infrequent, and he rented his own studio in Montmartre and busied himself doing portraits of his friends and others he met in bars and cabarets. The 1880s were the heyday of Rudolphe Sallis's Chat Noir, and Toulouse-Lautrec and friends were usually to be found there, but when Sallis moved further up the Boulevard de Rochechouart to another location, he left behind the old post office, which was taken over as the Cabaret Mirliton by Aristide Bruant, who Toulouse-Lautrec immortalised in a poster with his black cloak and hat and red scarf.

For 15 years Toulouse-Lautrec was the chronicler of Montmartre life at the height of the *belle époque*, painting ecstatic dancers, debauched bourgeois gentlemen, blowsy women and prostitutes at rest. The very names of the performers he depicted gives an idea of the vitality and earthiness of Montmartre. They included La Goulue ('the greedy one'), Nini Patte en-l'Air ('Nini with legs in the air', a play on a slang term for sex), La Môme Cri-Cri ('the crying-out girl', who squealed when she did the splits), La Môme Fromage ('cheese girl'), Valentin le Désossé ('Valentin the boneless'), Grille d'Egout ('sewer grating', from her gapped-teeth), Chocolat (a black dancer) and Cha-U-Kao ('chahut-chaos', dance of confusion).

Entertainment was often explicitly sexual, with dances such as the can-can, effectively a fast moving peep-show, dancers doing the vertical splits and hopping on one leg to expose their vaginas (pantaloons came in the later, professional form of this dance). In the early days dancers were amateurs like Louise Weber, laundresses or from other working-class occupations, who went to dance-halls after their labours. Weber was known as La Goulue, because of her habit of finishing off any half-empty glasses on a nearby table. Her language was also coarse, but when dancing she became transformed into the spirit of gaiety and fluid movement, which made her image, as depicted by Toulouse-Lautrec, known throughout the Western world – if not always in the highest circles. The singer Yvette Guilbert described the look:

> blonde, with a fringe cut across in line with her eyebrows; her long hair in a coil on the back of her head, tightly twisted to stop it falling during the dances. The classic kiss-curls hung by her ears and from Paris to the New York Bowery by way of London and the dives of Whitechapel, every tart of the day had the same hair-style and wore the same coloured ribbon round her neck.[11]

Toulouse-Lautrec had found his spiritual home in the cabarets and dance-halls but though he was greeted warmly, a fellow student, François Gauzi, qualified his friend's social success, 'Lautrec is seen only as a midget – a miniscule being, a gnome, one of Ribera's dwarfs, a drunken, vice-ridden court-jester whose friends are pimps and girls from the brothels'.[12] Though his company was enjoyed, he was never far from the cruel jibe about his height or appearance.

Degas, one of the few contemporary artists Toulouse-Lautrec admired, had no time for Toulouse-Lautrec, despite the similarity of their subjects. Degas said to the model Suzanne Valedon, also Toulouse-Lautrec's lover, 'He wears my clothes, but cut down to his size'.[13] Valedon, also an artist, was probably the only woman with whom Toulouse-Lautrec had sex who was not a prostitute, and

Degas's objective in making a hurtful remark to her was clearly that it would get back to Toulouse-Lautrec.

Toulouse-Lautrec adored outrageous, attention-grabbing behaviour. Once, while staying in Arcachon, near his mother's home, he acquired a tame cormorant, which he promenaded along the bay. He would take the cormorant to the café with him and have the bird drink absinthe. 'It has developed a taste for the stuff,' he said, 'it takes after me'.[14] He enjoyed dressing up in exotic costumes and performing tableaux: pictures exist of him dressing up as a Japanese shogun, an Arab muezzin, a woman, and as principal figure in various photographic tricks, such as one in which he appears as both as artist and model.

Toulouse-Lautrec exhibited in the fifth annual Salon des Independents in the company of van Gogh, Seurat and Signac in 1889. He was already, at the age of 25, a well-known painter, though known as much for his appearance, his outrageous behaviour and his vulgar subject matter as for the quality of his work.

The windmills that had once worked to supply the village of Montmartre with flour were now bought up and converted into places of amusement, first the Moulin de la Galette then, in October 1889, the Moulin Rouge, destined to become the most famous nightclub in the world, and which Toulouse-Lautrec used as the setting for some 30 paintings.

Its director, Charles Zidler, had his establishment fabulously decorated with both gas and electric light, chandeliers, gilded bronze fittings and mirrors. The garden of the Moulin Rouge had an immense model elephant, in whose side the orchestra sat; tame monkeys played around the patrons. The corridors were set up like a fairground, with sideshows including belly-dancers, a shooting gallery and a fortune teller. Prostitutes freely plied their trade from tables around the ballroom, where they waited for clients.

In this main ballroom dancers provided a spectacle: Zidler had talent-spotted all the best dancers from the cabarets and put them under contract to him, so laundresses who had danced for entertainment and for drinks were now professional. Zidler's innovation was to turn a working-class entertainment into a show for all society. The Paris aristocracy, the bohemians, the bourgeoisie looking for salacious entertainment, women of the demi-monde, foreign tourists and the Paris working class on a night out all met at the Moulin Rouge. Zidler had succeeded in creating a form for all the fun-loving elements of French society.

H.P. Hugh, an Englishman, wrote in 1899,

> As the night closes in you watch with fascination the gradual streaks of light that crawl out, as avenue after avenue is lighted up, and the whole city is lined out in fire at your feet. The red sails of the Moulin Rouge swing round, the flash light from the Tour Eiffel touches the Sacré-Coeur and whitens the thousand-year-old church of Saint-Pierre. The other Montmartre awakens while the quiet inhabitants of the hill go to sleep.
>
> The sickly odour of absinthe lies heavily on the air. The 'absinthe hour' of the Boulevards begins vaguely at half-past-five and ends just as vaguely at half-past-seven; but on the hill it never ends. Not that it is the home of the drunkard in any way; but the deadly opium drink lasts longer than anything else, and it is the aim of Montmartre to stop as long as possible on the terrasse of a café and watch the world go by. To spend an hour in a really typical haunt of the Bohemians is a liberal education.[15]

Toulouse-Lautrec drew *L'Anglais au Moulin Rouge,* in which the awkward Englishman is almost a silhouette, observing from a distance the behaviour of the brightly dressed women.

Toulouse-Lautrec was not only there in person for the opening of the Moulin Rouge at the end of 1889, but at the entrance hung his huge circus painting, as if establishing it as his place. Zidler asked him to design a poster for the Moulin Rouge in 1891, which the 25-year-old artist did with a picture of La Goulue, bringing his work to a wider public as well as making a definitive contribution to the development of the poster. Artists had drawn posters previously, but regarded it as hack work; Toulouse-Lautrec treated his posters as works of art, transforming the medium.

A highly successful film of 2001, *Moulin Rouge,* gives a fanciful picture of life at the nightclub in terms of its storyline, but successfully conveys some of the exuberance of Toulouse-Lautrec's life: the camaraderie, the fondness for dressing up, for singing songs and mocking the bourgeoisie. The magical element of absinthe is provided by the green fairy, as represented by the singer Kylie Minogue, who pops out of an absinthe bottle in spangles and paints everything in luminous green.

One of Toulouse-Lautrec's contributions to *fin-de-siècle* life was the popularisation of cocktails, for he loved drinking mixtures which gave him, as he said, the sensation of 'a peacock's tail in the mouth'.[16] The French were not known for mixing their drinks to create new tastes, so the American cocktail craze had not caught on. Toulouse-Lautrec would create potent mixtures, delighting in the drunkenness of large groups of people. He once dressed as a bartender for a huge party, in a white jacket and stars-and-stripes waistcoat, and shaved his head to add authenticity, serving two thousand fearsomely strong cocktails.

One of his inventions was the Maiden Blush, a composition of absinthe, mandarin, bitters, red wine and champagne. Toulouse-Lautrec is credited with inventing a cocktail called 'tremblement de terre' ('the earthquake') for cabaret singer Yvette Guilbert. This was a remarkable absinthe, as it did not turn cloudy but stayed green. It was the action of freeing the oils from alcohol by adding water which made the liquid cloudy. When Lautrec added cognac the absinthe was diluted but the alcohol content remained high so the drink did not louche.

In fact this was not an original Toulouse-Lautrec idea; the notion of mixing brandy with absinthe predated him. Henri Balesta wrote in 1860 of the last stages of the chronic absintheur, 'He invents revolting refinements of drinking to save himself from having to think. Now it isn't mixed, tempered with water that he drinks that infernal absinthe, it is pure or reinforced with rum or cognac.'[17]

Toulouse-Lautrec began a close relationship with the experimental magazine *La Revue blanche* in 1893, thereby coming into contact with André Gide and with Léon Blum, who was its literary and dramatic critic and later prime minister. The music critic was Debussy, and Verlaine, Mallarmé and Proust were also contributors.

After another artist left their shared apartment to get married in 1894, Toulouse-Lautrec took to living in brothels where he would sketch scenes of women dressing or relaxing while waiting for clients, even in such poses as holding their dresses up to expose their vaginas in the regular medical examination. In such surroundings he had inspiration for his work and the comfort of such women as Big Mareille, who met his need for physical affection which need not involve sex.

With his love of spectacle, it was unsurprising that Toulouse-Lautrec should have contributed to the theatre, producing posters and programmes for such avant-garde venues as the Théâtre-Libre and the Théâtre de l'Oeuvre. The latter is best known for presenting *Ubu Roi* by the *enfant terrible* Alfred Jarry in 1896. The first word of this play was 'merde' ('shit') and it did not become more elevated thereafter. The play caused riots and was taken off after two nights. Toulouse-Lautrec immediately fell in with the scatological playwright, and helped paint the sets for his satire, which was originally written when he was 15; the grotesque Père Ubu was a caricature of a schoolmaster he hated.

Jarry, also a writer of symbolist verse, expressed a desire to empty the mind of intelligence so as to leave it open for hallucination, making him an important precursor of surrealism. The surrealist André Breton said Poe was surrealist in adventure, Baudelaire in morals, but 'Jarry est surrealist dans absinthe'.[18]

Jarry called absinthe 'holy water', 'essence of life' and 'sacred herb', and refused to dilute it with water, which he considered unclean. He once painted his hands and face green, and at another time dyed his hair green, supposedly in homage to absinthe. He carried revolvers, which he took a boyish delight in firing off at parties and in cafés. He developed a persona with rabelaisian distortions of words, a fixed face and a metallic, high-pitched voice in which he spoke incessantly – it was as if he had become his own character Père Ubu.

The novelist Rachilde, the founder with her husband Alfred Valette of *Mercure de France*, which took some of Jarry's writing, wrote that

> Jarry began the day by imbibing two litres of white wine, three absinthes spaced between ten and noon then, at lunch, he washed down his fish or steak with red or white wine, alternating with more absinthes. In the afternoon a few cups of coffee fortified with brandy or other spirits of which I forget the names; then, at dinner, after, of course, other aperitifs, he could still tolerate at least two bottles of any vintage, of good or bad quality.[19]

Clearly, despite his preoccupation with absinthe, he drank a good deal besides.

Jarry's primary objective was to go through the whole of life with a dislocation of the rational mind from the imagination. To this end he developed the 'science of imaginary solutions', which he called 'pataphysic'. This was partly reached by a conscious effort, a choice of the paradoxical and the surreal. With less effort, though more wear and tear, it was also achieved by always being drunk. As he became increasingly impoverished, having spent his inheritance and scorning to earn a living, the wine and steaks disappeared from Jarry's life. Visitors to his tiny hovel, where there was nothing but a pallet bed and a large plastercast of a penis, believed he lived entirely on fish, which he caught from the Seine, and on absinthe. When money for even this ran out, he used ether then methylated spirits to alter his consciousness to the desired state. Like a character he described in an unfinished fragment, drinking in the darkness, 'he often went without food, because one cannot have everything at once, and drinking on an empty stomach does more good'.[20]

Jarry died at the age of 33 in 1907, of tuberculosis exacerbated by malnutrition and alcoholism. If *Ubu Roi* symbolised the absurdity and greed of the bourgeois, Jarry's life could stand to represent the absurdity and waste of the bohemian at his most profligate. It is not merely that his life was shortened by personal abuse and neglect, but the means of his dissipation meant he achieved little: his primary contribution to artistic life was his own drunkenness, which impeded concentrated work.

This, then, was a standard by which Toulouse-Lautrec's life could be measured, for although he may have been a drinker, until his last two years he controlled his drinking to such an extent that he could always produce work of quality. By the late 1890s, however, Toulouse-Lautrec was showing signs of severe alcoholism, of delirium tremens and hallucinations. A shot once rang out, and friends rushed to find him sitting on his bed, in his hand the pistol he was using to shoot the spiders that he said were attacking him.

Thadée Natanson, one of the publishers of the *Revue blanche*, remarked, 'He loved to drink only too well ... at the crack of dawn to empty a glass of rot-gut rum, which he poured as if he were already leaning his elbow on the greasy zinc counter, into a thick-bottomed glass brought home from a neighbourhood bar'.[21]

Toulouse-Lautrec did not suffer the drawn and emaciated face supposedly characteristic of the absintheur, the melancholy expression, the ghastly pallor. He was a most boisterous drunk, given licence by his privileged position as an artist to behave outrageously. His drinking led him to such improprieties as openly propositioning a housemaid at a dinner table, and he would pick fights with strangers. His friends and relations, particularly his father, did not complain that he drank absinthe, but that he drank so much all the time. Count Alphonse was told his son had been seen drunk many times in Paris, and merely said, 'Why doesn't he go to England? They scarcely notice the drunks over there.'[22]

Like Manet, Toulouse-Lautrec maintained a bourgeois life separate from his existence as a bohemian. He would dine with his father most evenings in the 1880s. In the 1890s his mother lived as near as possible to Bohemia (it was unacceptable for her as a lady to live any closer than she did to Montmartre, maternal affection or no). She left in January 1899, unable to cope any more with her son's moods. This was the trigger for increasingly bizarre and paranoid behaviour in him. Finally he suffered a collapse in a brothel in the Rue des Moulins. This was probably primarily caused by tertiary syphilis. Unconscious, he was taken home and then committed to an asylum in Neuilly-sur-Seine. He stayed voluntarily after the initial period of commitment, but in the spring of 1900 he started drinking heavily again, and died the following year at the age of 33.

That Toulouse-Lautrec was fond of absinthe is beyond doubt; he lived and worked in an absinthe milieu, drank a great deal of it and painted a variety of pictures in which absinthe is present, including *Portrait de Vincent van Gogh* (1887), *Au Moulin Rouge* (1895), *A Grenelle: Buveuse d'Absinthe* (1886), *Monsieur Boileau au Café* (1893) and *La Buveuse d'Absinthe* (1888). Yet he did not adopt absinthe as an all-important image, as did Raffaëlli, Rops and other lesser talents.

The point is more clearly made in the absinthe work of a minor poet, such as Toulouse-Lautrec's friend Raoul Ponchon. Absinthe was everywhere in his work, as when he mocked the horror with which the absinthe drinker came to be seen: 'Moi, m'absintheur! Vierge sainte!/ N'en déplaise à mainte et maint/ Ce qu'ils croient être une absinthe/ N'est autre qu'un pippermint! [Me, to absinthe myself! Holy Virgin!/ With all respect to everyone/ That which they believe to be an absinthe/ Is nothing but a peppermint!]'

Like Gauguin and Verlaine, Ponchon stepped into Bohemia from the other side. A bank employee, he left his job on the death of his father in 1871 when Ponchon was 23 – now he had only himself to please. He set himself up in a garret with 'Painter and Lyrical Poet' chalked on the door. He would take his breakfast in the Café de Cluny, then return for the aperitif hour. The rest of the day he led a public life in different cafés, though he drank for only six days a week; he maintained the bourgeois Sunday by not drinking a drop that day. He was a most prolific poet, writing 150,000 verses, of which 7000 were about food and drink, some showing evidence of a pencil-sucking lack of inspiration, such as *L'Absinthe*, which begins 'Absinthe, je t'adore certes! [Absinthe, I indeed adore you!]' and continues in the same vein.

His poems were generally light and accessible, and their publication in such journals as the *Courrier Français*, to which he contributed for 21 years, made him the supreme 'poète-journaliste'.

An affectionate poem dedicated to Ponchon's nose by Georges de Lys described the evidence of many years of absinthe: 'Mon nez n'est pas couvert/ De la pourpre très sainte,/ Il est devenu vert/ A pomper de l'absinthe [My nose is not coloured/ With the holy purple/ It has grown green/ With boozing on absinthe]'.[23]

As a body of work by absinthe users built up through the nineteenth century, it becomes clear that it was the writers of light verse and comic versifiers who hymned absinthe, minor poets such as Ponchon, working hard on cultivating the bohemian ideal. Truly great poets such as Rimbaud and Verlaine wrote about absinthe only in passing, amid a range of other symbols of decadence. Baudelaire wrote of absinthe not at all, except obliquely. The suspicion must be strong that the connection between absinthe use and art was illusory, except with those such as Jarry, for whom the pose was the art, and who altered their lives with absinthe. But even Jarry could have lived the same life using other forms of alcohol or drugs such as ether to fragment his consciousness.

Similarly, it was Raffaëlli, always felt by his contemporaries to be a show-off and poseur, who made a point of painting pictures with absinthe as a definitive symbol. Degas, van Gogh and Toulouse-Lautrec, though they painted scenes in which absinthe played a part (and the latter two drank it to excess), did not single out the liqueur for special treatment. It had no supreme importance for them. Put it another way: remove the absinthe from the pictures or the titles of the pictures, and Toulouse-Lautrec's work is still supremely valid, Raffaëlli's loses much of its strength.

7 English Decadence and French Morals

IN FRANCE THE MILITARY TASTE FOR ABSINTHE had led it into the bourgeois camp and established it as a middle-class drink. An interest in the exotic introduced the rapidly expanding Paris art scene to absinthe. In England, however, no soldiers brought back a taste for absinthe from the outposts of empire and the middle class never took to absinthe as a group. It was the marginal bohemians who adopted absinthe, along with other equally suspect French habits.

France came to represent everything the British feared about changing society and the future of Empire. Respectable Britain had a low opinion of Paris, as described by Mary Corelli, favourite contemporary novelist of Queen Victoria and William Ewart Gladstone: 'Paris has long been playing a losing game. Her men are dissolute, her women shameless – her youth of both sexes depraved – her laws are corrupt – her arts decadent – her religion dead. What next can be expected of her?'[1]

William Somerset Maugham's book about art and moral responsibility *The Moon and Sixpence*, set in the 1880s and 1890s, uses absinthe as a symbol of the incomprehensible lure of French culture. It is indicative of the nature of the runaway stockbroker-turned-artist Charles Strickland's new-found freedom that almost the first words he uses to the narrator are 'Do you like absinthe?'

The narrator, English to the core, who has tracked the fugitive bourgeois, loosely based on Gauguin, to a shabby hotel in Paris, says (one assumes through clenched teeth), 'I can drink it'. Later he remarks how 'with due solemnity we dropped water over the melting sugar'; thus a man who took afternoon tea so seriously disdained the ritual of the foreigner.

'Englishmen dislike this poison, which they liken to paregoric', remarked Victor Plarr, but the serious Francophile had to learn to enjoy it.[2] For those who, like Philip Carey in Maugham's *Of Human Bondage*, yearned to blend in with the ambiance of Paris, coming to terms with absinthe was as much a part of becoming an artist as was finding a studio. Maugham has his would-be artist wondering what to do, to attain the character he desires until he seizes upon it: 'Absinthe! Of course it was indicated, and so sauntering toward the station, he seated himself outside a café and ordered it. He drank with nausea and satisfaction. He found the taste disgusting, but the moral effect magnificent; he felt every inch an art-student…' As his apprenticeship in bohemia continues, 'by virtuous perseverance he had learned to drink absinthe without distaste'.[3]

For the English decadent writers of the late 1880s and the 1890s, as the poet and critic Richard Le Gallienne wrote, absinthe was 'mysteriously sophisticated and even Satanic. To me it had the sound of hellebore or mandragora…in the 1890s it was spoken of with a self-conscious sense of one's being desperately wicked, suggesting diabolism and nameless iniquity.'[4] Le Gallienne's name had been Gallienne; he added the 'Le' for effect in 1887 when he left home at the age of 21, because to be French was suggestive of sophistication, artistic daring and sexual licence.

One of Le Gallienne's friends, Coulson Kernahan, described how they drank their first absinthe after walking along a street parallel with the Strand in London and seeing in the window of a restaurant a sign saying they sold absinthe. Le Gallienne confessed he had never drunk it.

I've only read of it in French novels or English short stories about Parisian or Bohemian life. Paul Verlaine is pictured always as sipping it – the source for his inspiration as a poet, I'm told. I believe the principal ingredient is some wicked but wonderful stuff called wormwood…It is said to be delicious to the taste, but deleterious, even deadly, to health and to the moral sense, if one forms the absinthe-habit. They say, however, that it has a marvellous, almost a magic, effect in producing a feeling of buoyant high spirits, and in lifting and dispelling any weight there happens to be on the mind.[5]

The story proceeds in a fanciful fashion with an improbable serving of absinthe by a French waiter who persuades them to have another, then another: 'Eet make you glad you are alive. Eet cheer you up.' By the 1930s, when this story was published as a tale of the folly of youth, the Frenchman in the role of diabolic tempter had become a figure of fun. At the time it was set, France had a sinister reputation in middle-England, and one which was more attractive to the adventurous.

Le Gallienne, the son of a Liverpool brewer, does not report anything of this version in his memoir, but says he was first invited to drink absinthe by the poet Lionel Johnson in his rooms. It is more likely that such a questing man, so keen on image, would have made the acquaintance of the quintessentially decadent drink before he had become sufficiently intimate with the rather reserved Johnson to go to his rooms. Moreover, Le Gallienne was alive and active when Kernahan published his piece, making a complete fabrication unlikely. Le Gallienne affected defiance by calling his slim volume *English Poems*, a self-conscious desire to rival French achievements.

Absinthe had to be sought out in most places, though it was available in the 1880s. The French apparently complained – and were mocked for complaining – about the 'inferior absinthe sold in the cafés in the locality of "Lee-ces-ter" Square'.[6] An American travel writer noted,

in large and closely packed towns and cities the consumption of absinthe is on the increase. In London it is decidedly on the increase. It is not possible to find a street in some parts of the metropolis in which the word 'absinthe' does not meet the eye in the windows of houses devoted to the sale of other intoxicating and lethal drinks.[7]

As late in the century as 1889 the *Times* was reporting in a short feature, as if no knowledge were expected of the reader, the most basic information about absinthe: the varieties of wormwood plants, where it grows and how it is made. It continued,

> Absinthe is a powerful but destructive nerve stimulant, which may be valuable in cases of exhaustion or extreme fatigue but, like chloral and opium, it is liable to abuses, which, in the aggregate, far outweigh all the benefits which are derived from its legitimate use. The effects of general and unrestrained absinthe drinking in France are coming to be recognised as forming the basis of one of the gravest dangers that now threaten the physical and moral welfare of the people.[8]

The examples, therefore, come from France, as if absinthe is rare in Britain, and the closest comparison is with opium, the major drug of addiction, after alcohol, in late-nineteenth-century Britain. Winter Blyth, public analyst and medical officer of health for Marylebone, found absinthe available for sale in a large number of places.[9] However, for the damage caused by absinthe, again the examples come from French rather than English cases. It has to be suspected that minor public health officials, aided by some elements of the press, were playing up an anticipated health hazard rather than warning of an existing one.

In his study of the English decadence, Matthew Sturgis has noted how the anxiety at the century's close was given a peculiarly French edge by the use of the term 'fin-de-siècle', where, 'for the insular English, France represented all that was naughty, dangerous and corrupt. It was the country of absinthe and the can-can, of Emile Zola and Paul Verlaine; it was the home to flaneurs, Bohemians and decadents.'[10]

'One had, in the late eighties and early nineties, to be preposterously French', remarked Plarr.[11] Yet for the progressive artist in

England, being Francophile was not enough, you had to reject your own backgound. George Moore, an Anglo-Irish writer who was educated in Birmingham, then became an art student in Paris, wrote of

> two dominant notes in my character – an original hatred of my native country and a brutal loathing of the religion I was brought up in. All the aspects of my native country are violently disagreeable to me and I cannot think of the place where I was born without a sensation akin to nausea … I am instinctively averse to my own countrymen; they are at once remote and repulsive; but with Frenchmen I am conscious of a sense of nearness; I am one with them in their ideas and aspirations, and when I am one with them, I am alive with a keen and penetrating sense of intimacy.[12]

The poet Ernest Dowson was splenetically Anglophobe. He complained that England was a country 'whose climate is unutterably horrible to me, whose cooking ruins my digestion and whose people, ideas, beliefs, prejudices etc are all either ridiculous, unintelligible or irritating to me'.[13] Across the Channel, however, on a crossing Dowson often made, was 'my fair France', where the food, art and manners were to his taste.[14]

Dowson was a central figure in the tragic story of the English decadents who emerged in imitation of the French, adopted French styles and lived in France whenever possible. Much of Dowson's verse was set in France and his home (or place of wandering, given his rootless nature) was often Paris or Brittany. Dowson assumed the mantle of Verlaine, the role of the accursed poet, the outcast obsessed by sanctity and by obscenity, whose poverty is a badge of the rejection of all except art. In the words of a character in one of Dowson's books, 'I may fail or I may succeed, as the world counts those things. It is all the same: I believe in myself.'[15]

Dowson was born in 1867 in Lee, Kent, the son of a dry-dock proprietor who so neglected his business that it was constantly in decline throughout Dowson's early life. Dowson's father suffered from tuberculosis, the only effective treatment for which was rest in a warm climate. Consequently Dowson's early years were spent travelling to salubrious climates in France and Italy with his parents.

Baudelaire, Verlaine and Swinburne were the principal literary influences on his verse, and the Latin poets Catullus and Propertius; English decadence always had a strongly classical tinge. Dowson had written exquisite verse from his teenage years, writing of love and death, particularly the death of children. His first published poem was composed when he was aged 17 or 18.

He had no regular schooling, but he studied for five terms at Oxford, where his acquaintance with Paris music-halls and the wider world in general made him the envy of other undergraduates. He was said to have already 'tasted' absinthe by the time he arrived at Oxford, but his usual drink was Chablis and soda. Latterly as a student, he tried dosing his depression with whisky, and also experimented with hashish.[16]

He declared he would live as an artist whatever the cost, and when he left Oxford without a degree in 1888 it was rumoured he had gone to Paris to take up a bohemian life. In fact he went to London to help his father run the ailing dock at Limehouse. His family lived in a series of rented rooms; the office above the dock where he often slept was the only fixed home Dowson ever knew.

In the evenings he was enjoying all the life London had to offer, going to music-halls and restaurants, having sex with prostitutes and going out with girls. He repeated the quip in a letter to a friend that 'absinthe makes the tart grow fonder'. As early as 1889 at the age of 21 he realised he was overdoing his consumption of absinthe. He wrote to a friend,

> On the whole it is a mistake to get binged on the verdant fluid. As a steady drink it is inferior to the homely scotch…awoke this morning with jingling nerves and a pestilential mouth… [absinthe is] extremely detrimental to the complexion. I believe that even in the full swing of the campaign of my last term [at Oxford] I never presented a more deboshed appearance than I do this morning.[17]

'We will absinthe,' he writes to a friend, 'be it never so deleterious. What is one more drink among so many?'[18] Dowson described one night on the town in 1894 with the actor Charles Goodhart and a drug-addict friend:

> we met at seven and consumed four absinthes apiece in the Cock till nine. We then went and ate some kidneys – after which two absinthes apiece at the Crown. After which one absinthe apiece at Goodie's club. Total seven absinthes apiece. These had seriously affected us – but made little impression on the opium eater. He took us back to the Temple [presumably where Goodhart lived] in a cab. This morning Goodhart and I were twitching visibly. I feel rather indisposed: and in fact we decided that our grief is now sufficiently drowned, and we must spend a few days on nothing stronger than lemonade and strychnine.[19]

Thus his nightlife was a cross between the refined French green hour, taking an absinthe or two in cafés along the boulevards, and the English pub-crawl.

Late in 1889, on one of his rambles round Soho, Dowson met the girl with whom he was to fall in love when he called in to a restaurant owned by a Polish couple and met their 11-year-old daughter Adelaide. Dowson had always been entranced by young girls in relationships which were not physical (and not remarked upon by his friends as being odd). It was, however, the contradiction between his love of the innocence of childhood and his need for an adult relationship which dealt him the crippling blow from which he was unable to recover. He continued to see Adelaide with her parents' approval for the next seven years, in varying degrees of hope that they might marry.

He dedicated his first book of poetry, *Verses*, to her, and his book of stories *Dilemmas*. He wrote stories about blighted love, the impossible union between teenagers and older men which are never consummated because, to pick one example, on the morning when the man comes to plight his troth, the girl first declares to him that she is to enter a convent and he is too pure of purpose to divert her from her spiritual mission.

Dowson's personal life veered between the spiritual (he converted to Roman Catholicism in 1891) and the dissolute. He was given to long nights of drinking, getting into brawls and having sex with prostitutes. One of his friends said that when Dowson could afford it he had a prostitute every night.[20] He would sit at a marble-topped table in the Cock tavern in Shaftesbury Avenue with a cigarette in his mouth and an absinthe before him, writing deathless verse, the very image of the bohemian poet, a legend which he to some degree created by living the life so completely.

Of the verse he wrote thus, the best known describes the contradiction between his perfect love and the life he leads, as the narrator has sex with a prostitute but thinks of his true love: 'thy breath was shed/ Upon my soul between the kisses and the wine;/ And I was desolate and sick of an old passion.'

He was welcomed to soirees of the Century Guild of Artists, which aimed to unify the arts and therefore was a location where writers would meet painters and architects. It was at a gathering at the Century Guild house at 20 Fitzroy Street, where several members lived, that Dowson was first to meet Oscar Wilde, fast becoming the defining figure of the decadence.

Dowson was also a member of the Rhymers' Club where, as Arthur Symons said, 'young poets, then very young, recited their verses to one another with a desperate and ineffectual attempt to get into tune with the Latin Quarter'.[21] The club was set up by W.B. Yeats among others, and met in the Cheshire Cheese off Fleet Street. Yeats had had his first book of verse published in 1889, and was with rather than of the decadents, but he has left a sympathetic memoir of them.

Yeats praised Dowson and his equally drunken Rhymer friend Lionel Johnson, who 'never made a poorer song/ that you might have a heavier purse, Nor gave loud service to a cause/ That you might have a troop of friends.'[22] Dowson and Johnson would sit up all night drinking and talking of religion and poetry. Johnson was homosexual by inclination, but led a celibate life.

Dowson's verse, often about lost love and death, first came to general public notice in the two books of collected poems produced by the Rhymers. While he led a lively nightlife, he was no more dissolute than the friends whose company he kept, and would often be in groups calmly and soberly discussing art. A friend did comment in a memoir about him, however, that 'in spite of the cheapness of the liquor...no one in the gathering – except, perhaps, poor Ernest Dowson – ever became drunk'.[23]

Dowson's love for Adelaide was no secret; he once took his mother to 'Poland', as he called the restaurant in Sherwood Street where Adelaide lived with her parents above the shop, and many times entertained literary friends there. As she grew into her teens Adelaide was described as being coquettish and cruel to him, failing to see in his sensitivity anything but a target for teasing.

The pathologically indecisive Dowson went to see Adelaide and her parents almost daily, and was always on the verge of coming to an understanding with her mother, who was the dominant figure in the household. He never did take the final step with Adelaide's mother and, as only he could, he chose the worst time possible to declare himself to Adelaide.

In April 1893, when she was just short of her fifteenth birthday, her father lay dying upstairs, and Dowson found himself alone with Adelaide. He had long connected the deep emotions of bereavement with those of love, and assumed others felt similarly. In the intense emotion of being alone with his love in a house of death, he asked her to marry him. He then realised the mistake, apologised profusely and told her to forget all about it. That was the nearest he came to marrying Adelaide. A curse concurrent with unrequited love also became apparent in 1893 when he was 26, and had the first haemorrhage from tuberculosis, from which his father and his mother now also suffered. He knew he was destined for an early grave.

Over 1893–94 Dowson was enjoying considerable literary success, with the publication of a novel, *A Comedy of Masks*, which went into two editions, the performance of his short play, *The Pierrot of the Minute,* a book of short stories, *Dilemmas: Stories and Studies in Sentiment,* in preparation, and the publication of his poems in various journals, with publishers requesting a book of verse from him. He had translated Zola's *La Terre* and was doing other translations which might give him a small income; the family dock was now unable to support them.

Dowson's aunt gave a view from the comfortable middle class on Dowson: 'Ernest was playing the fool, translating brilliantly and then taking awful drugs, absinthe and other things...he was a queer mixture, clever but [a] fearfully weak character and like a madman when he got drink or drugs.' Dowson's aunt Ethel shows the confusion in the English mind about quite what absinthe was: a drug or a drink?

She may well have been informed by Marie Corelli's novel *Wormwood,* which affirmed that the 'green-eyed fairy' was not merely a highly alcoholic drink with a hallucinatory effect, but a drug akin to opium, 'The action of absinthe can no more be opposed than the action of morphia. Once absorbed into the blood, a clamorous and constant irritation is kept up throughout the system, – an irritation which can only be assuaged and pacified by fresh draughts of the ambrosial poison.'[24]

In fact Dowson rarely took drugs other than alcohol, which he took to excess every night. In the early 1890s, absinthe was far from the only drink he indulged in, as his friend and fellow Rhymer Edgar Jepson wrote: 'As long as I could keep Dowson to wine or beer, he was sober enough. When his nervous irritation with life drove him to the poisonous juice of the potato, there was little to be done.'[25]

His parents were the English middle class in sad decline, fatally ill, burdened by debts, with the dock unprofitable and mortgaged. They lived in a series of rented rooms until Dowson's father died from an overdose of chloral hydrate in August 1894 and his mother, obsessed with the idea that the family's misfortunes were her fault, hanged herself six months later. Dowson, horribly bereaved, disappointed in love, fatally ill and impoverished, started on the downward cycle which, with increasing ferocity, was to carry off all the decadents from a world of absinthe and misery.

Though they were clearly identified by others, few people had adopted the term 'decadent' for themselves except in jest. Some were labelled with it as a term of abuse. Decadent was used of *fin-de-siècle* writers of whom a bourgeois speaker disapproved; no attempt was made by its critics to understand or define decadent art except in sneering terms. In newspapers it was often used with the accent, as 'décadence', to emphasise its French origins.

A working definition would be the art of the height of empire when the fruits of previous periods of stoicism are enjoyed. It was self-consciously exquisite, and gloried in the artificial and the exotic, particularly in religion. Many, such as Dowson, Lionel Johnson, John Gray and Aubrey Beardsley converted to Roman Catholicism, while Yeats and others such as Eric Stenbock went to more out-landish forms of ritual.

Arthur Symons, born in 1865 the son of a Wesleyan minister, became the chief celebrator of decadence. In writing of 'The Decadent Movement in Literature' in *Harper's New Monthly Magazine* in 1893, he defined it as almost entirely a French phenomenon, but Symons himself, Beardsley, Le Gallienne, Hubert Crackanthorpe, Dowson and Wilde were creating an English version which was in fierce combat with the bourgeois establishment. Arthur Symons invited Verlaine to lecture in London, and Dowson was one of those privileged to meet 'the master'.[26] Symons enjoyed a *succès de scandale* with his volume of poems *London Nights,* celebrating nightlife, music-halls and sex. Symons was not a poet of the first rank, and like many other such, he wrote a poem called 'The Absinthe Drinker', with such lines as 'The hours are all/ Linked in a dance of mere forgetfulness.'

The decadents did not take absinthe as a light aperitif, but indulged it as if they expected the drink itself to divulge the secret of the art of Baudelaire and Verlaine. Without doubt, there was a good deal of affectation in baiting the bourgeoisie by aping French manners and adopting eccentric costume; no one would defend

Wilde and Le Gallienne's velvet knee-breeches as a high point of artistic expression.

The decadents offered themselves up to ridicule; the most successful satire, *The Green Carnation*, which was published anonymously, sent up Oscar Wilde's aphorisms and his relationship with his acolyte Lord Alfred Douglas. The lure of absinthe is mocked when a society lady says to a friend, 'Come to my room, Emily, and we will drink some Bovril, and have a talk. I love drinking Bovril in secret. It seems like a vice...I feel so delightfully vicious when I drink it, so unconventional!'[27]

Wilde was the great poseur but, to the fury of his critics, was also a great writer. He was born in 1854 in Ireland, where his father was a prominent surgeon and his mother a nationalist poet. Making the transition from aesthete to decadent, he wrote one of the great decadent works, *The Picture of Dorian Gray*, in *Lippincott's Magazine* in 1890 (and expanded it as a book in 1891). The *Daily Chronicle* critic was not impressed: 'It is a tale spawned from the leprous literature of the French *Décadents* – a poisonous book, the atmosphere of which is heavy with the mephitic odours of moral and spiritual putrefaction'. 'Leprous', with its suggestion of contamination, was a common term of abuse used against literature coming from France. Another reviewer felt it would 'taint every young mind that comes into contact with it'.[28]

Significantly, neither *The Picture of Dorian Gray* nor Huysmans's *A Rebours*, 'the breviary of the decadence' as Symons called it, felt it necessary to dwell on absinthe. The implication of this is that if the real thing was presented: a concentrated decadent philosophy of life, then the symbols of it, such as absinthe, could be disregarded.

Wilde's attitude to absinthe varied. 'It has no message for me,' he told Bernard Berenson, but to Arthur Machen he said, 'I could never quite accustom myself to absinthe, but it suits my style so well'.[29] This was rather giving the game away; much of Wilde's life was a pose, and he had an Irish storyteller's manner of painting a fanciful picture with words in his everyday speech.

Wilde knew, as he promoted the pose of aesthete then of decadent, that the symbol was as important as the substance. Wilde used the symbol of the green carnation, an exotic improvement on nature which was used in the satire of that name, written by Robert Hichens in 1894. Wilde said green was 'always the sign of a subtle artistic temperament, and in nations is said to denote a laxity if not a decadence of morals,'[30] and he was given to saying such things as, 'Absinthe has a wonderful colour green. A glass of absinthe is as poetical as anything in the world. What difference is there between a glass of absinthe and a sunset?'[31]

Wilde said he could drink nothing but absinthe when Aubrey Beardsley was present:

> Absinthe is to all other drinks what Aubrey's drawings are to other pictures; it stands alone; it is like nothing else; it shimmers like southern twilight in opalescent colouring; it has about it the seduction of strange sins. It is stronger than any other spirit and brings out the subconscious self in man. It is just like your drawings, Aubrey; it gets on one's nerves and is cruel…When I have before me one of your drawings I want to drink absinthe, which changes colour like jade in sunlight and makes the senses thrall, and then I can live myself back in Imperial Rome, in the Rome of the later Caesars.[32]

Wilde was interested in the visions absinthe could produce. Various accounts of one have been recorded, for example,

> Three nights I sat up all night drinking absinthe, and thinking that I was singularly clearheaded and sane. The waiter came in and began watering the sawdust. The most wonderful flowers tulips, lilies and roses sprang up and made a garden of the café. 'Don't you see them,' I said to him, 'But Monsieur, there is nothing there'.[33]

In another version he said,

> One night I was left sitting, drinking alone, and very late in the Café Royal, and I had just got into this third stage [of drinking absinthe] when a waiter came in with a green apron and began to pile the chairs in the tables. 'Time to go, sir,' he called out to me. Then he brought a watering can and began to water the floor. 'Time's up, sir, I'm afraid you must go now, sir.'

'Waiter, are you watering the flowers?' I asked but he didn't answer. 'What are your favourite flowers, waiter?' I asked again.

'Now sir, I really must ask you to go now, time's up,' he said firmly. 'I'm sure that tulips are your favourite flowers,' I said, and as I got up and passed out into the street I felt-the-heavy-tulip-heads-brushing against my shins.[34]

As with most of Wilde's stories, this was refined and improved with telling, but a constant here is that even this mild hallucination happened after very heavy absinthe use: three nights of sitting up drinking in one version – though that has rather a fairy-tale ring to it.

Like all the decadents, he was close to France. Even his scandalous first play, *Salome*, which could not be performed in Britain, was written in French and later translated into English by Wilde's lover, Lord Alfred Douglas. Marcel Schwob, a young literary light and the secretary to Catulle Mendès, described Wilde in Paris in 1891:

A big man with a large pasty face, red cheeks, an ironic eye, bad and protrusive teeth, a vicious childlike mouth with lips soft with milk ready to suck some more. While he ate – and he ate little – he never stopped smoking opium-tainted Egyptian cigarettes. A terrible absinthe-drinker, through which he got his visions and desires.[35]

Wilde may have taken the inspiration for some of the themes of his children's stories from absinthe reveries, but his most enduring work is satirical, drawing-room comedy. From 1892 to early 1895 he was the most successful West End playwright, satirising the manners of the upper class in works such as *Lady Windermere's Fan* and *The Importance of Being Ernest*. This made him the most celebrated decadent but also the principal target and hate figure; his scorn gave his enemies no quarter and they would give him none.

The battle for the acceptance of advanced (meaning French) ideas in painting had been spearheaded by the New English Art Club, founded in 1886 'with a view to protesting against the narrowness of the Royal Academy and to obtaining fuller recognition for the work of English artists who had studied in France'.[36] It contained such leading figures of the 1890s as Aubrey Beardsley, Max Beerbohm, Charles Conder, Philip Wilson Steer, Walter Sickert and William Rothenstein. The influence of the Parisian schools was so evident that a name suggested for the club at its preliminary meeting was the Society of Anglo-French Painters.[37]

One of its members was Alfred Thornton, who had been brought up to be a civil servant but in 1890, at the age of 27, left the Foreign Office to go to France to paint and study art. He was in no doubt that there was a battle for modern art, and that in order to win it he and his New English Art Club colleagues must join in 'this constant search for new harmonies and new contrasts of colour that we had learnt from our contact with French work in Paris. We were some twenty years behind the French.'[38] They were defiant, self-conscious warriors on the artistic battlefield; Thornton remembered how his young colleagues would wipe their palette knives on their trousers so everyone would know that they were artists.

This desire to learn from French art was fiercely resisted by the bourgeoisie, who compounded new artistic techniques with immorality. In a paper titled *French Art and English Morals,* John Trevor, who is described as a writer on art, suggests that the trade and travel afforded by peace may not be such a good thing, for 'morality travels by steamboat, and immorality too, both first and second-class'.[39]

Trevor's aesthetic judgement is demonstrated by a visit to a gallery where Millais's paintings are on show, where he observes a picture of 'no modern Venus got up for the market but a pure-souled woman, who would make a noble wife and a happy home'. By contrast French art is 'deadly poison ... pernicious and venomous'; imbued with 'the spirit of license, of revolt against supremacy and restraint'. He wrote of the 'iniquitous realism' of French painting and of the need for 'that high principle and healthy vigour, which alone can prevent our Art from being infected by the disease of this French School'.[40]

The view that art should reflect or be contained by the morals of the middle class of society worked perfectly well when the only pictures which had to be considered were wholesome English ones, but now pictures were being imported along with dangerous French ideas about art. Impressionists had been criticised through-out the intervening period, but as an artistic 'craze' to be sneered at. The *Magazine of Art* in June 1888 ran a piece calling impressionism 'a far more dangerous craze' than 'the Pre-Raphaelitic...Born and bred in France, what is called "Impressionism" has tainted the art of this country.'[41]

A review of French literature over two volumes of the influential *Quarterly Review* by the Reverend F.W. Barry warned of 'not only the decadence but the end of civilisation' arising from the penmanship of such authors as Zola and Maupassant.[42]

Fear for the infection of English letters and art by the French was one part of an anti-French paranoia which at its most extreme saw the invasion of French art as a precursor to armed attack. The trigger for such a war, a genuine danger, was imperial rivalry in Africa; in West Africa rival British and French flags were being hoisted over large areas in the second half of the 1890s, leading to frequent danger of armed conflict. The Fashoda incident almost led to war in 1896, and for several months between 1898 and 1899 Britain and France stood on the brink of war over rival claims in the Upper Nile region.[43]

Popular books kept the threat of French arms alive, such as the 68-page novelette *The Siege of London*, with a lurid illustration of the Houses of Parliament amid billowing smoke, under bombardment from French guns. It remarks with febrile relish on 'the hereditary hatred of the French for the British,'[44] and sets a scene in the near future when

> For some years France had suffered from a colonising mania...
> success of the French arms seems to have filled the people with
> wild and Quixotic dreams, and they believed, and, in fact, openly
> proclaimed, that England's power was declining, and that France
> was destined to take England's place as a colonising nation.[45]

The conquest of Britain is described under such sub-headings as 'landing of French troops', 'Plymouth partly destroyed', 'splendid charge of the English who, however, are outnumbered', 'the march of the French on London', 'Sydenham seized by the French' and 'battle at Dulwich'. The mention of these comfortable suburbs, newly developed to accommodate the burgeoning middle class making money in London, struck a particularly chilling note.

The Siege of London is admittedly a prophetic novel. A virulent anti-French tract, *John Bull's Neighbour in Her True Light* was supposedly a representation of the present reality of France. It offered insights into aspects of French culture such as 'The deformed feet of the French...the torture in French prisons...the French habit of spitting in a tumbler at the dinner table'. It went through three editions and sold twenty thousand in the six weeks from first publication.[46]

Absinthe is described as 'the most villainous stuff that can be drunk. It maddens and kills quickly by bringing on softening of the brain, and it also produces a form of madness called in French *folie paralytique*.'[47] The reader is invited to

> Go into the poorer quarters of Paris; – peep into a low café, a buvette, a cabaret, a guingette, an estaminet, a brasserie; – look at the awful, bloated faces, sodden and distorted out of all semblance to God's image by absinthe and eau de vie; – look at the half-naked women and the young children soaking themselves with these cursed drinks.[48]

'Enormous quantities of absinthe and other filthy decoctions that are consumed must tend to sap vitality.'[49]

The twin images of France represented by *The Siege of London* and *John Bull's Neighbour in Her True Light* are reminiscent of the puerile propaganda of the Cold War, in which the enemy was presented as being both fiendishly poised for world domination and at the same time backward and incompetent. *Fin-de-siècle* England had a disgusted fascination with France, both a contempt for her supposed moral laxity and a prurient desire to see more of it. In artistic terms, the realism of Zola and Degas disgusted, while the decadence of Verlaine and Toulouse-Lautrec appalled bourgeois England; the best France had to offer was scorned.

The writer R.H. Sherard felt moved to write a book with the title *My Friends the French,* for the fact that he had French friends was in itself remarkable. Sherard, a good friend of both Wilde and Dowson, lived in Paris from 1883 to 1906, excepting a period in London for the last five years of the century. He supported himself mainly by writing journalism for British and American publications, and wrote some 33 books, mainly of hack work but with some exceptional investigations into poverty in Britain. His chief interest lies in his biographies of Wilde, Zola and Daudet, and his memoir of Dowson.

One of the most successful novels of the 1890s, Marie Corelli's *Wormwood: A Drama of Paris,* combined disgust at French decadence with a gloating fascination for absinthe. Corelli had developed the knack of taking a currently fashionable subject and making sensational fiction out of it, a technique that made her the most popular novelist of the 1890s.

She was born in Perth, Scotland in 1855, the illegitimate daughter of a minor writer, Charles McKay, best known for his work on panic and collective madness, *Extraordinary Popular Delusions and the Madness of Crowds.* Corelli changed her name and concealed details about her early life, doubtless with the intention of hiding the fact of her illegitimacy. Her close relationship with her lifelong companion, Bertha Vyver, has led to suggestions she was a lesbian, but there is nothing to substantiate this.

Corelli was advanced in many ways, for example in *Barabbas* making it clear that women are as wicked as men, thus transgressing a contemporary gender boundary, but in general her genius lay not in innovation but the bestseller's ability to catch the public mood. *A Romance of Two Worlds* exploited contemporary interest in religion, science and the occult. *The Mighty Atom* contrasted the claims on the soul of science and religion.

Early in life she had written, 'I have made up my mind to be "somebody" and I'll be as unlike anybody else as I can'.[50] While she was supposedly resolutely anti-decadent, this is the sort of statement which could easily have been made by Jarry or Rimbaud. Indeed, she shows explicit sympathy in her absinthe novel *Wormwood* for the genius of Charles Cros, 'whose distinctly great abilities were never encouraged or recognised in his lifetime'.[51]

Oscar Wilde asked her to write for *Woman's World,* of which he was editor in the late 1880s, and she sent a copy of *Wormwood* to the celebrator of decadence Arthur Symons. *Wormwood,* published in 1891, is dedicated to the *absintheurs* of Paris, 'who are the shame and the despair of their country'. The wretched narrator, Gaston Beauvais, the son of a wealthy banking family, looks back to the life which led him to 'the madness of absinthe, the wildest, most luxurious madness in the world'.[52]

Gaston is deranged when his betrothed, Pauline, is seduced by his friend Silvion, a trainee priest who has been having sex with Pauline while she was supposedly attending early morning mass. When this is revealed to him, Gaston walks around Paris in distress and chances to meet an old friend, André Gessonex, an impoverished artist who is a great talent but who will not compromise his principles: 'I am not to blame if these people who want to buy pictures have no taste ... Let me be poor – let me starve – but let me keep my artistic conscience!'[53] This stereotypical artist with his long hair and tattered clothes takes Gaston to a restaurant, where he orders an absinthe ('melted emeralds'), which is first nauseous to the narrator then 'new and indescribably delightful'.

His personality changes with 'the devil born of absinthe!' as he becomes selfish and immoral.[54] He cruelly denounces Pauline's infidelity at the altar and proceeds on an awful revenge, in which he murders Silvion and drives the now outcast Pauline to suicide by telling her of her lover's death. He leaves his family and lives in a series of ever-worsening lodgings, witnessing various horrors such as the retarded child of two *absintheurs*, the Paris morgue and the suicide in impoverished despair of his friend Gessonex – after which the painter is declared a great artist and a national treasure worthy of a state funeral.

Absinthe is described both as a physical poison and a moral contaminant. Gaston makes such declarations as, 'Civilisation is a curse, – Morality an enormous hindrance to freedom'; '*un vrai absintheur*, I enjoy a sneer at virtue'; 'What should I do with a home or home associations? – I, – an *absintheur*!'; 'Honesty is a mortal affront to an absintheur!'; 'the brain of a confirmed absintheur accepts the most fiendish ideas as both beautiful and just'.[55]

He develops a 'growing absinthe-mania', a shaking hand and absinthe pallor, and experiences nights of horror and ecstasy, hallucinating a leopard hunting him through the Paris streets. Finally, contemplating his own suicide, he is the complete *absintheur*,

> A thing more abject than the lowest beggar that crawls through Paris whining for a sou! – I am a slinking, shuffling beast, half monkey, half man, whose aspect is so vile, whose body is so shaken with delirium, whose eyes are so murderous, that if you met me by chance in the day-time you would probably shriek from sheer alarm.[56]

The book has the deficiencies of its genre: a histrionic tone and a melodramatic plot propelled by a succession of improbable meetings. The memorable characters are mainly stock: the inveigling priest seducing under the cloak of sanctity; the easily seduced, duplicitous French girl; the mad genius of an impoverished artist.

However, despite its failings, *Wormwood* is a more interesting novel than it is often given credit for, and Corelli a more interesting novelist. Perhaps unsurprisingly for a book written by a woman born illegitimate, it is as much a criticism of bourgeois morality as of absinthe. The pure, if illicit, love of Pauline and Silvion is necessarily contrasted with the narrator's sanctimonious preoccupation with the validity of the proposed marriage contract with a woman he may have never truly loved. For all his drinking of the bohemian elixir, Gaston's motivating preoccupation throughout the book is a bourgeois vindictiveness for a social transgression.

Corelli made a £400 advance on the book which sold out in ten days. She had become so irritated by negative criticism that she eventually forbade copies of her books to be sent to reviewers.

The critics who did look at the book sneered at it, but Corelli had included her response in the work itself:

> The Public itself is the Supreme Critic now, – its 'review' does not appear in print, but nevertheless its unwritten verdict declares itself with such an amazing weight of influence, that the ephemeral opinions of a few ill-paid journalists are the merest straws beating against the strong force of a whirlwind.[57]

She was correct: it went through 10 editions before the end of the century and was the defining literary work which told middle-brow Britons all they knew about absinthe.

It was in the atmosphere prepared by Corelli of moral degradation, vile tenements, degenerate children and absinthe mania that Degas's masterpiece was presented to the British public.

8 Anglo-Saxon Attitudes

IT WAS IN A CLIMATE OF HEIGHTENED AWARENESS of decadence, with its vile green lubricant, that Degas's painting, later called *L'Absinthe*, was placed before the British public in 1892–93. The outraged response to it is the more surprising because the painting had been in England for around 20 years, and had previously been exhibited without disturbance.

It was one of seven Degas pictures owned by Henry Hill of Marine Parade, Brighton, who was said to have the finest collection of Degas's work in Europe. Of all the impressionists, Degas enjoyed most appreciation in England, and he had many friends in artistic circles, including James Whistler, George Moore, Walter Sickert and Oscar Wilde. His work was widely shown in England and, generally, critically welcomed. The critic Frederick Wedmore in 1883 called Degas 'the master of the Impressionist School, the man of genius, the inspirer of the whole party'.[1]

Hill loaned the picture to the Third Annual Winter Exhibition of Modern Pictures in Brighton in September 1876, where it was exhibited as *A Sketch at a French Café*. The art critic of the *Brighton Gazette* wrote:

> The perfection of ugliness; undoubtedly a clever painting, though treated in a slap-dash manner, amounting to affectation. The colour is as repulsive as the figures: a brutal, sensual-looking French

workman and a sickly-looking grisette; a most unlovely couple.
The very disgusting novelty of the subject arrests attention. What
there is to admire in it is the skill of the artist, not the subject itself.[2]

This falls short of fulsome praise but, to reduce it to its essentials,
says merely that it is an unpleasant scene skilfully portrayed. There
is no suggestion that the subject matter is so offensive as to be
obscene, or that the picture would in itself be inclined to corrupt
the viewer. Most importantly in the present context, there is no
mention of absinthe. The poet and essayist Alice Meynell, writing
about Hill's collection in 1882, did not remark on the painting.

After Hill's death, Christie's were commissioned to sell his
collection, which they did at a sale held on 19 and 20 February 1892
at their gallery in King Street, Covent Garden; this was still called
their new gallery, as it had been opened only in 1885 to cater for
the increased interest in art among the moneyed classes.

Percy Colson, a writer and art lover, described the taste for over-
sugared English works in the late nineteenth century in his history
of Christie's:

> people of all classes wallowed in sentimentality. Songs about
> little choirboys who faded away in the third verse, and lost loves,
> were all the rage. The most banal of Tennyson's poems, such as
> the *Lord of Burleigh* or the *May Queen*, were far more popular than
> his really great work, and all England wept over Miss Marie
> Corelli's *Mighty Atom*. It was the same with pictures. 'Every
> picture told a story' – it had to! – so Marcus Stone's pretty pictures
> of true love in all its manifestations; Leighton's chocolate-box
> portraits of society women; Mr Leader's red sunsets, complete
> with pond, cattle and cottage children; Luke Fildes' *The Doctor*;
> Broughton's photographic art; and Alma Tadema's well-painted
> Greek boy, reclining elegantly on marble benches, reading a scroll,
> presumably Plato's latest thriller, or wondering if the water were
> warm enough to bathe in, roused the enthusiastic admiration of
> those rich and unsophisticated picture buyers.[3]

He continued to describe the atmosphere when pictures were presented to a public which so certainly knew what it liked. A painting

placed on the easel 'is received almost as a great tenor is received at the opera, and as one bidder caps the bid of another, often by a thousand guineas, the applause is renewed, and when the hammer falls the crowd roars its delight just as it does when the Derby favourite romps home'.

It was into this atmosphere on Saturday 20 February that Degas's *Au Café* was brought in by staff and placed on the easel beside the auctioneer. Instead of cheers and excited anticipation, a hush fell on the gallery, followed by low groans of disgust, then the sibilant sound of hissing anger. Arthur Kay, an experienced collector standing at the back of the room remarked, 'I believe disapproval of a great masterpiece, thus shown, must be almost unique'.[4]

The embarrassed auctioneer started the bidding, which proceeded sluggishly. Arthur Kay had already conceived an attraction to the picture and was standing where he could not be seen, in order to observe the dealer who would buy the picture. He recalled, 'I felt it would be wise to let him become buyer, and offer him a profit afterwards, rather than run him up at the auction. This policy worked; he bought the picture.'

A young art dealer from Glasgow, Alexander Reid, bought it for £180. He was clearly astute enough to realise any Degas was worth having, but apparently not sufficiently experienced to realise he should trust his instincts and ignore the crowd. Kay sought him out soon after and found the young man nonplussed at his purchase; he told Kay of the criticism he was receiving: 'many friends were chaffing and abusing him for buying such a work'. Reid thought he had made a mistake in buying it and was pleased at the price Kay offered, £200, giving him a moderate profit.

Kay took the picture home and said, 'It was hung in a position where I could see it constantly. Every day I grew to like it better.' He experienced a dual response to this painting, however, with requests to sell it from some visitors, contrasting with 'the questions of those incapable of understanding it'. He was clearly uneasy about it, as he exchanged the picture with a dealer in part payment for another, but it had not been gone for 48 hours before he could bear its absence no longer and went back to the dealer to buy it back, along with another Degas.[5]

He loaned the picture to the Grafton Gallery, a newly opened suite of galleries which was described as being 'half the length of the mews. There is wall-space enough to hold several hundreds of pictures; and it may be added that the fittings are as luxurious as those of the great private galleries in Paris.'[6] The gallery was clearly aiming at a comparison with Paris, and half the pictures came from France. Its exhibition opening on 13 February was announced as 'Paintings and Sculpture by British and Foreign Artists of the Present Day'.

The Grafton was attempting to rival the fame of the Grosvenor Gallery, whose exhibitions from 1877 to 1890 had created a social as well as an artistic stir. In this it was successful: because of Degas's picture, the gallery found itself part of the largest public storm in the art world since Whistler sued Ruskin twenty-five years before.

Whoever had catalogued the painting now called it *L'Absinthe*. Degas would not have given such a flamboyant title to the picture, a title which so clearly directed the viewer to one aspect of it. Degas's title, *Au Café*, simply describes the environment; the title *L'Absinthe* attracts attention on the drink as in some way the moving spirit of the scene. There are in fact three vessels in the picture: an empty decanter on an adjoining table, the absinthe in front of Andrée, and before Desboutin a cold black coffee in a tumbler – a drink known as a mazagran – but the absinthe was now the focus. The *Daily Chronicle* even referred to 'two victims of the maddening drug, seated in a restaurant'.[7]

Kay was shocked to find how it 'roused the roar of all good total abstainers, momentarily interested in art, against this picture, and it attracted also the attention of artists, serious critics and non-abstainers. The result was terrific. They abused each other in article after article in daily and weekly papers.'[8]

Early reviews were favourable. The *Times* critic said it 'appears as though, in conception, design, and execution it were the permanent and inevitable type of how a pair of topers in a cabaret must be painted'. Thus, this critic did not complain about the subject matter, but accepted both the subject and its treatment. The *Pall Mall Budget* critic said,

> It stands self-proclaimed and explained, the types are observed with a marvellous insight and the unflattering accuracy of genius. The big head of the man, a romantic, easy-going dreamer, is dashed in with a touch of instanteneity worthy of the greatest master. The woman, apathetic, heavy-lidded, and brutish, absolutely indifferent to all things external, nods to the warm langour of the poison. Her flat shuffling feet tell all the tale. Every tone and touch breathes the sentiment of absinthe.[9]

This last remark shows how the painting's subject matter and its newly acquired title had merged in the mind of the observer to create not a painting in a café in which a glass of absinthe was depicted, but a painting *about* absinthe.

D.S. MacColl, art critic of the *Spectator* since 1890, called *L'Absinthe*, 'the inexhaustible picture, the one that draws you back, and back again'.[10] Now the journalist John Alfred Spender, assistant editor of the *Pall Mall Gazette* from 1892 and a contributor to the *Westminster Gazette* under the unashamed pseudonym 'The Philistine', attacked MacColl for being 'not a critic so much as an advocate – the frankly partisan advocate for the young English imitators of French impressionists who call themselves the New English Art Club'. He is one of 'a band of critics teaching with great unanimity a theory of art which either denies that art is concerned with the beautiful or asserts that what a natural instinct calls "repulsive" is in reality the standard of beauty'. Of all that is abominable and served up by MacColl, *L'Absinthe* was the worst: '[If you] have been taught to think that dignity of subject and the endeavour to portray a thing of beauty are of the essence of art, you will never be induced to consider *L'Absinthe* a work of art'.[11]

The 'new criticism' was lambasted for lending itself to 'his rhapsody over a picture of two rather sodden people drinking in a café'. *L'Absinthe* was attacked as 'vulgar', 'boozy', 'sottish', 'loathsome', 'revolting', 'ugly', 'besotted', 'degraded', 'repulsive', 'humanity besotted by drink'.[12]

It is interesting that the detractors tended not to attack Degas, whose reputation was so considerable that it would have reflected badly on them; instead they attacked the painting itself or its defenders in the so-called new criticism. Harry Quilter, the art critic of the *Spectator* before MacColl, scorned the promoters of *L'Absinthe* for 'this denial of all forms of art save one, and that form as degraded as it is narrow, and as alien to all the ancient spirit of fine art as it is in close communion with the worst vices of our latter day civilisation'.[13]

The homosexually inclined *The Artist and Journal of Home Culture*, dedicated to high art and home improvement, supported *L'Absinthe*, which was, 'a bit of decoration made out of one of the tragic incidents of modern life; its beauty is the beauty of horror; it is a masterpiece assuredly but one of the most painful which has ever been produced'.[14]

Young artist Alfred Thornton was later to write in his memoirs that the painting's detractors and its defenders 'abused each other in article after article. Critics of backward and advanced art wrote against one another ... The stream of the New Art Criticism trickled from condensation of acrid vapour above a seething cauldron of absinthe, brandy, coffee and water.'[15]

Such sentiments ran directly into conflict with the hypertrophied bourgeois abhorrence of anything French. Baudelaire and his English disciple Swinburne, Zola and his Anglo-Irish counterpart George Moore (an art student in France before he took to literature) had been attacked, vilified and in some cases suffered prosecution. Henry Vizetelly was imprisoned in 1889 for the obscenity of publishing Zola in English translation. An explicit connection between Zola and Degas was made by a leading academician, Sir William Blake Richmond, who lambasted 'the very limited little picture under discussion ... *L'Absinthe* is a literary performance. It is not a painting at all. It is a novelette – a treatise against drink. Everything valuable about it could have been done, and has been done, by Zola.'[16]

Walter Crane called it 'a study of human degradation, male and female ... with all the devotion to the realisation (or idealisation) of squalid and sordid unloveliness, and the outward and visible signs of the corruption of society which are characteristic of the most modern modern painting'. He hated the thought of the public attending to the new criticism 'and drinking in "Absinthe"'.[17]

One of the things which shocked the public most was that it was the woman who was drinking absinthe, not the man. Even its defenders found it hard to contain their disgust: 'Heavens! – what a slut,' wrote Moore, 'a life of idleness and low vice is upon her face; we read there her whole life. The tale is not a pleasant one, but it is a lesson.'[18] Though a defender of the painting for its undoubted technical excellence, Moore still felt the urge to justify it on moral grounds, as if an attack on its supposed morality had any validity. While Moore is a radical, his comments here are within the range of the defiantly English John Trevor, who opined in *French Art and English Morals*, 'The limit of Art should be the limit of Morals. The sentiment of a picture should not transgress the sentiment of Society.'[19]

Marie-Claude Delahaye and Benoît Noël, in their book on absinthe and art, state that Degas 'seemed to have defined forever the state of absinthe: the drink of a despised but fascinating class, the potion of the bohemian untouchables'. They call the painting 'a national banner, typically a depiction of France, of Paris, of Montmartre ... Absinthe is essentially a French drink and Paris the capital of artistic and bohemian life. The strength of the picture is to have crystallised these gifts offered to the world.'[20]

This clearly must be the point: many in the English world wanted to throw the gift back over the Channel. As Arthur Thornton remarked, '"French" in painting, to the old-fashioned Briton, still connoted "lubricity", bloodshed and a pursuit of the "ugly"'.[21]

'Incredible as it seems, the attitude of the daily press had become more hostile and uncomprehending than before,' wrote Douglas Cooper in describing the climate for impressionism, which was treated as a foreign aberration, a craze that would soon pass and which therefore need not be treated too seriously.[22] It was a direct challenge to the Ruskinian model of art, which was morally up-lifting, dignified in its subject matter and beautiful in its treatment.

Under the anti-French onslaught, some retreated and even attempted to prove that they had never been supporters of French art in the first place. Walter Pater was the principal mentor of Wilde and a major influence on such decadents as Dowson and Gray. His principle of 'the love of art for its own sake' (often simplified to 'art for art's sake') was one of the main slogans of the decadence, with its defiance of the convention that art should relate to morality.[23] His work over the 30 years 1864–94 is littered with positive references to French literature, but he edited the later editions to delete references to the French, finding the climate as the century ended to be uncongenial.[24]

Kay had been 'abused from Budapest to Aberdeen' for having the temerity to own so despicable a painting as *L'Absinthe*.[25] Notwithstanding how he admired it, Kay was so embarrassed by the scandal that in April 1893 he sold the picture once again, to a Parisian dealer, so it left the shores of England, to offend no more the sensitivities of the bourgeoisie. It was sold to Count Isaac de Camondo for 21,000 francs, and was bequested to the Louvre, so it now hangs in the Musée d'Orsay.[26]

The artistic debate about *L'Absinthe* was about the artist's right to freedom of subject. The social outrage was about how this loosening of control over artistic subjects reflected a general loosening of morality, a decadence in art mirroring a decadence in society, and all symbolised by the hideous green glass of absinthe, the 'French poison'.

In the wake of the battle over *L'Absinthe,* some of the supporters of the new art met in a house in Sainte-Marguerite, just west of Dieppe. The house was rented by young artist Alfred Thornton and Henry Harland, an American journalist and short-story writer. They had met and joined forces, Thornton later wrote, 'because Harland was in revolt against the "old" fiction as we were against the "old" painting'.[27]

Joining them there were the critic MacColl, who was also a painter, and the romantic artist Charles Conder, who 'worked by fits and starts, his life punctuated by love affairs and too much absinthe'.[28] Beardsley, the supreme artist of the decadence, who was still only 20, was invited, but work commitments prevented his travelling, though his sister Mabel accepted the offer. These and other artists who met with them that summer discussed a new periodical of art and literature, perhaps at MacColl's suggestion, perhaps at Conder's – there was no shortage of people later willing to have had the idea for the *Yellow Book*.

Harland and Beardsley pursued the project with publisher John Lane, and the first volume of the quarterly *Yellow Book* appeared in April 1894. It was the most famous of the publications to which most of the decadents contributed, including Crackanthorpe, Le Gallienne, Johnson, Symons and Dowson, though it was scarcely decadent after the first four editions and some contributors could never have been called decadent. There was a common invocation of French art and literature in the *Yellow Book*, accompanied by a definite sense of combat against the establishment. Crackanthorpe remarked on it, 'during the past year things have been moving very rapidly...A sound, organised opinion of men of letters is being acquired; and in the little bouts with the bourgeois...no one has to fight single-handed.'[29]

Unsurprisingly, those who had excoriated *L'Absinthe* were incandescent at the advances the decadents were making into the mainstream. John Alfred Spender, who was to be editor of the *Westminster Gazette* from 1896, deprecated

> Degradation to suit a decadent civilisation; no longer does nobility of idea dictate subjects to authors; sex is over-emphasised; the peak of abomination has been reached by the *Yellow Book*, where a young man fresh from Oxford, named Max Beerbohm, dares to write 'In Defence of Cosmetics'. All this relates to the evil at work in the sister art of painting as expressed by the New English Art Club.[30]

A more vulgar criticism was that impressionist pictures (or post-impressionist, as the century turned) could be painted only by the deranged, that they had been driven mad by the decadent life. 'Cézanne and Matisse were dire victims of absinthe,' Thornton paraphrased.[31] An exhibition of paintings by patients at the Bethlem Royal Hospital was later used to show the similarity between the painting of mad people and that of modern artists in such articles as the *Daily Mirror's* 'when the insane paint: Strange Pictures by Lunatics Admired by Cubists and Futurists'.[32]

England had spluttered on and disgorged the decadents, then moved to eliminate them, a procedure rendered easy by Wilde's having walked into his enemies' hands. Wilde was not a proselytising homosexual, as his lover Douglas was. He need not have goaded the authorities into taking him to trial for homosexual behaviour under laws which had been rendered draconian only in 1885 (at a time when most countries were relaxing laws on sex).

However, Wilde was so imbued with the bourgeois spirit that when his lover's father the Marquis of Queensberry accused him, in writing, of posing as a sodomite, Wilde felt obliged to sue Queensberry for libel. The trial failed and, with some evidence of homosexuality forthcoming, the authorities pursued Wilde. Queensberry was barking mad, and his accusations could have easily been left unanswered, but after two further criminal trials of dubious integrity, Wilde was sent down for two years in May 1895.

With Wilde a pariah, it was open season on the decadents. The *Yellow Book's* windows were broken; its publisher removed all Beardsley's pictures from the edition then on the presses and sacked the artist. Harry Quilter, in *Contemporary Review* (also one of the main critics of *L'Absinthe*), felt the decadent school must be 'detected, exposed and destroyed'. Wilde's former friend W.E. Henley wrote, 'of the Decadents, of their hideous conceptions of the meaning of Art, of their worse than Eleusian mysteries, there must be an absolute end'.[33]

Spender published a book called *The New Fiction (A Protest Against Sex-Mania)* in 1895, largely compiled of pieces of journalism and replies from the correspondence columns, in which he lambasted new writing and painting under such headings as 'Progress or

Decadence' and 'The Defiant Man and the Revolting Woman'. Spender in his autobiography reports with what seems like satisfaction that 'The controversy has a modest place in the literary history of the 'nineties. John Lane told me in after years that it had killed the *Yellow Book* and spoilt the sales of some of his favourite writers.'[34]

The humorous magazine *Punch* made no attempt at humour when it declared, 'If such be "Artists", then may Philistines/ Arise, plain sturdy Britons as of yore,/ And sweep them off and purge the signs/ That England e'er such noxious offspring bore.'[35] What passed for criticism was by now mere abuse; Symons's new book of poems, *London Nights*, was dismissed by a reviewer (doubtless Spender himself) in the *Pall Mall Gazette* with, 'Mr Symons is a dirty little man and his mind is reflected in the puddle of his bad verses'.[36]

The decadents rallied and, with Leonard Smithers as publisher, Symons and Beardsley launched one last publication in the face of the hated bourgeoisie. Dowson was part of the editorial team which worked in the comparatively benign atmosphere of Dieppe to create the *Savoy*. The magazine was the last stand of the decadents; it contained work from Verlaine, Yeats and most of the remaining English decadents, as well as significant friends of the decadents such as Havelock Ellis and George Bernard Shaw.

It was to no avail: the *Savoy* published all through 1896, but it was a losing battle when such distributors as W.H. Smith refused to handle it and therefore denied the journal access to the marketplace. By the end of 1896 it was dead, and the decadents scattered around Europe, most to die young, such as Beardsley at 28 and Crackanthorpe at 26. Crackanthorpe, a leading figure in English letters, the bright hope of the decadents for a lasting contribution to the English novel, drowned himself in the Seine, his only significant work a book of stories titled *Wreckage*. The artist William Rothenstein, in his memoir of the period *Men and Memories*, said scornful contemporary criticism maintained Hubert's death was 'the judgement of God for adoring French idols'.[37]

Markets were harder to find – the mildly curious public had had their fill of the decadents; the word no longer had its lustre. The title of Symons's book (based on his earlier essay), which had been advertised as *The Decadent Movement in Literature*, was changed on publication to a safer *The Symbolist Movement in Literature*.

The recent suicide of Dowson's parents, his terminal illness and the impossibility of his relationship with Adelaide gave a personal dimension to the crisis of the decadents. Adelaide was 16 in 1894, and could now have married Dowson. His family problems made matrimony unlikely in that year, but the couple could certainly have set a date. The fact that they did not, and that Dowson stopped dining at Poland, suggests Adelaide herself knew this disturbed man was not marriage material.

Dowson was repeatedly being run in for being drunk and dis-orderly, and was neglecting his health and his appearance. He had been living in his office at the family dock (now doing very little business), but in 1895 he moved even from there and never again had anything which resembled a settled home.

He described a travelling companion as drinking and smoking nothing so he could afford two square meals a day, while 'I tighten my belt in order to allow myself a sufficiency of cigarettes and absinthe'.[38]

He made for France, which had provided a haven for artistic outlaws and even celebrated them: Paul Adam defended Wilde in an article in *La Revue Blanche* which Toulouse-Lautrec illustrated. Wilde's play *Salome*, banned in Britain, was performed in France, where Dowson went to see it.

Dowson was made welcome by the writers of bohemian Paris, and saw Verlaine, though the old poet was to die in January 1896, to be sent off with a long funeral cortege of literary France, in which Dowson took part. He soon left Paris for the cheaper location of Pont-Aven in Brittany, where Gauguin and Bernard had worked together on creating synthetism.

From his letters it is clear that Dowson was eating, if frugally, and his drinking was not limited to absinthe, as he mentions drinking rum and red wine, but when he was in need of a drink, only absinthe would do. He writes of being almost literally penniless but 'lo there was a letter and £1 and I went out with tears of gratitude in my eyes and had an absinthe and later breakfast'.[39]

He had some money forthcoming from writing ventures, and was translating French pornography for Leonard Smithers, the principal publisher of the decadents. Smithers published Dowson's first book of poems, *Verses*, which in the anti-decadent climate of 1896 was not well reviewed: 'confined to an entirely erotic and sentimental region', 'the wreck of all that is mouldy and unwholesome', 'nerveless effeminacy'.[40] Arthur Symons reviewed *Verses* in the *Savoy*, and found in it 'all the fever and turmoil and the unattained dreams of a life which has itself had much of the swift, disastrous and suicidal energy of genius'.[41]

The book was dedicated to Adelaide, 'to you, who are my verses'. Dowson was still writing devotedly to her, but whether he actually believed any more in the possibility of union is open to doubt. He said things such as that it would be better for their relationship if they were both away in another country, a condition for matrimony unlikely to be met. He had written that his heart was broken even before he returned to London and found she was going to be married. Adelaide, now 19, had chosen a German lodging with the family who worked as a tailor and sometimes helped out in the restaurant. Dowson wrote that he was 'suffering the torture of the damned', and after a brief visit soon left London again.

Wilde was released in 1897 and went into exile in France, near Dieppe, where Dowson visited him and the two broken men of letters had some last times of pleasure in each other's company. 'Ernest had an absinthe under the apple trees,' Wilde wrote, and he told Dowson to come for 'a morning meal of absinthe'. Someone asked Wilde why he tolerated such a drunk, to which he replied that it is not regrettable that a poet is drunk, but that more drunks aren't poets.[42]

Wilde himself drank brandy and absinthe in his later years, but as his means dwindled the cheaper absinthe predominated.

Oscar Wilde's last year, as reported by Frank Harris, was awash with absinthe. In a self-destructive parody of the absinthe stroll of the boulevards,

> Oscar stopped the carriage at almost the first café, got down and had an absinthe. Two or three hundred yards further on, he stopped the Victoria again to have another absinthe; at the stoppage a few minutes later Robert Ross ventured to remonstrate: 'You'll kill yourself, Oscar,' he cried, 'you know the doctors said absinthe was poison to you.'
>
> Oscar stopped on the sidewalk, 'And what have I to live for, Bobbie?' he asked gravely.[43]

He died three years after his release from prison, of an ear infection which spread to his brain and caused meningitis.

Dowson's behaviour too was on a downward spiral. His neglect of personal appearance was extreme and, as his contemporaries remarked, points to a deeper, psychological cause than mere poverty. In the same way his always choosing the hardest bed to lie on and getting into brawls where stronger men would beat him up suggests a need to punish himself.

R.H. Sherard, then living in Paris, found him slumped over a table 'sticky with absinthe' and took him home to the Boulevard Magenta. Sherard was fond of Dowson, 'the poor poet setting his little brilliancy and feeble verve against the pitiless forces of a cruel world'.[44] He reported that Dowson was frightened to go to his lodgings because he feared things in the room which would strangle him in his sleep. This could be a simple alcoholic paranoia, but there does seem to be a hallucinatory quality about it which may be attributable to absinthe. He was also subject to fits in 1899, not unusual for alcoholics in withdrawal.

Though only in his early thirties, Dowson was living out the dregs of his life, 'bitter as wormwood and salt as pain,' as he wrote. Dowson gave one of the best descriptions of an absinthe reverie in his prose poem 'Absinthea Taetra' – 'Hideous Absinthe'. In its entirety it reads:

Green changed to white, emerald to an opal: nothing was changed.

The man let the water trickle gently into his glass, and as the green clouded, a mist fell away from his mind.

Then he drank opaline.

Memories and terrors beset him. The past tore after him like a panther and through the blackness of the present he saw the luminous tiger eyes of the things to be.

But he drank opaline.

And that obscure night of the soul, and the valley of humiliation, through which he stumbled were forgotten. He saw blue vistas of undiscovered countries, high prospects and a quiet, caressing sea. The past shed its perfume over him, today held his hand as it were a little child, and tomorrow shone like a white star: nothing was changed.

He drank opaline.

The man had known the obscure night of the soul, and lay even now in the valley of humiliation; and the tiger menace of the things to be was red in the skies. But for a while he had forgotten.

Green changed to white, emerald to an opal: nothing was changed.

Dowson here sees absinthe first giving clarity as the ritual of mixing it with water plays out. The active ingredient in the drink first stimulates his brain so his consuming demons come to the fore, described as big cats – interestingly, in view of the use of the same metaphor by Marie Corelli in *Wormwood*. His pain and confusion die down as his mind is overtaken with a soothing vision of peace, perhaps in this case the effects of the alcohol taking hold. By the end of the poem the drink has given him an internal experience which has changed nothing but bestowed a period of oblivion.

Dowson's last years are well recorded, as many people who knew him, even slightly, wrote fascinated accounts of his following the bohemian trajectory towards self-destruction. He is known to have been still drinking wine and other drinks as well as absinthe. Notwithstanding his absinthe prose poem quoted above, nothing else seems to have been inspired directly by absinthe, and the facts of his life give ample reason for his general decline.

It was Sherard who saw out Dowson's last weeks in 1900, after having visited him in wretched lodgings on the Euston Road in London. Sherard invited the poet to return to the far-from-luxurious cottage in Catford, South London where he was currently living. With good food and only limited alcohol Dowson rallied and spoke of his plans for the future, but within weeks, less than two months into the new century, Dowson died at the age of 32. He had attended Verlaine's funeral, as Verlaine had attended Baudelaire's, but no such talents were present for his; Dowson was the last of the decadent poets.

The writer and critic Andrew Lang wrote a venomous piece all but applauding at the death of Dowson and disparaging his poetry. On Dowson's life and work, he wrote,

> If this kind of existence, if these sorts of productions, be decadent, surely even boys must see that decadence is rather a mistake. With all its faults, there is more to be said for muscular Christianity. However, on this head one need not preach to the Anglo-Saxon race, which is already converted.[45]

The 'race' had been assured by such poets as Robert Buchanan, now best remembered for condemning Swinburne and others in an essay as *The Fleshly School of Poetry*. Buchanan's own verse is all but forgotten to English letters, though he published six volumes of poetry to some acclaim (Dowson produced two, to critical neglect).

Buchanan wrote boldly of 'the City of absinthe and unbelief' which was Paris, whose inhabitants, noted for 'all the foulness and obsceneness/ Of dress and form, of face and look', were given to exclamations such as '"Vanity! Vanity! Love and Revel!"/ "Take a sip of absinthe, my dear!"/ "Religion's a bore but I like the Devil!"/ These are some of the words you hear.'[46]

Buchanan considers the French to have infected English fiction with the reptilian curse of ennui, 'the snake that grovels/ In a hoist of scrofulous novels,/ Leper even of the leprous/ Race of serpents vain and viprous,/ Bred of slimy eggs of evil,/ Sat on by the printer's devil,/ Last, to gladden absinthe-lovers,/ Born by broods in paper covers!'[47]

There was a good deal of posing around absinthe, with its self-consciously dangerous appeal, but serious writers, as in France, kept it as one symbol among many. Apart from the prose poem quoted above, Dowson does not mention it in his verse, using the more conventional reference to wine as a symbol of the search for oblivion, as in 'I cried for madder music and for stronger wine'.

The *fin-de-siècle* mood really did end with the century; the leading decadents were already dead or, like Wilde, Johnson, Harland and Conder, soon to die. The martial mood engendered by military disaster in the early weeks of the Boer War steeled the nation for something other than absinthe and affectation. As W.B. Yeats put it, 'in 1900 everybody got down off his stilts; henceforth nobody drank absinthe with his black coffee; nobody went mad; nobody joined the Catholic church; or if they did I have forgotten'.[48]

The disdainful attitude of English medical writers towards French attempts to define 'absinthism' as separate from alcoholism has been noted. By the beginning of the twentieth century, however, even the normally supercilious *Lancet* was heading an article 'The Absinthe Evil' and quoting work done at the Sorbonne by a Dr S.D. Lalou, who administered essences of absinthe and other drinks to dogs and other animals. The animals suffered agitation, restlessness, hallucinations, minor convulsions and then 'epileptiform seizure'. Alcohol alone produced agitation and coma.

This much was no more than had been done by Magnan more than 30 years previously – a high level of essences produces acute toxicity which shows itself in fits. Lalou went further, and administered not absinthe, which would have been the best tool, but essence of absinthe in small doses for long periods. In this case the dog lost weight and appetite, developed tremor and weakness and 'became stupid and ill-tempered'. This is hardly evidence of a model for 'absinthism' in man; if anything it suggests that acute poisoning by absinthe essence is a distinct phenomenon, and chronic poisoning is a quite different one.

The *Lancet* writer of 1903, however, finds this experiment to be convincing evidence that absinthe is 'a powerful nerve poison. That this was so has always been assumed by observant persons, medical and lay, but Dr Lalou's experiments prove the assumption.' Going outside his medical and experimental brief, the writer shows he thinks these experiments have a practical application: 'They may therefore become very valuable to the community, for their lessons can be used by the law as arguments upon which to base legal prevention of the grave physical and moral evils due to the drinking of absinthe'.[49]

The English predilection for moral panic might have led to a backlash against absinthe, but the fall of the decadents was so complete that there was no vestige of them remaining by the end of the century. The English had already had their panic about homosexuality and, by implication, other forms of sexual degeneracy which the decadents represented and which were symbolised by their diabolical green drink. There was no need of a show trial and execution of absinthe, though some endeavoured to stimulate an anti-absinthe tide. 'Why is England indifferent to the dangers of absinthe?' wrote one author, to which the obvious answer was that few were now drinking it.[50] In contrast to the situation in the 1890s, when Dowson and his friends could have an absinthe in every establishment they frequented, by 1907 a writer to the *Times* noted, 'absinthe is not unknown here, being sold in restaurants and hotels frequented by foreigners'.[51]

Paradoxically, being thus publicly damned in Britain saved absinthe from its fate on the continent of Europe. Absinthe became so unpopular, so associated with the decadents and with the hated French, that no government felt a need to take steps against it, and absinthe was never banned.

9   Absinthe Paranoia

AS THE NINETEENTH CENTURY drew to a close, absinthe came to symbolise everything the French right wing held in suspicion. Absinthe had played its part in making France the most culturally successful nation in the world and Paris the centre of world art. This was not to the taste of all. The decadence of French culture in the eyes of many, at a time of burgeoning German self-assurance, led French conservative thought to associate the symbolist artists with political anarchists.

This is not altogether fanciful, for some, such as the symbolist critic Félix Fénéon, a friend of Toulouse-Lautrec and editor of the *Revue Blanche*, were among the anarchists who were imprisoned in the wave of bombings and assassinations which followed government repression of strikers in 1891. Political anarchism and other radical approaches to society's needs often worked in alliance with the figuratively 'anarchistic' approach to art of Alfred Jarry and his like.

For French traditionalists, it was all too much happening too fast in the 1890s: the aristocratic dwarf who was a great painter; the laundress famous for showing her knickers who slept with the future King of England; the cafés where women in jackets and ties danced with one another; a government minister killed by a bomb in a café; the great French army challenged over the conviction of a

Jew; widespread drunkenness and the asylums filled with *absintheurs*. The liqueur was just one exotic factor in the *fin-de-siècle*, but unfortunately for its devotees, as society became jittery about the life of the cities, the pace of progress and rapid industrialisation, fears were projected onto absinthe as a very visible symbol of the descent of the French nation into the abyss of the modern. Absinthe became bottled madness, the green curse, the queen of poisons.

The genuine increase in alcoholism was certainly part of *fin-de-siècle* disintegration. Alcohol was believed to be eating away at the very fibre of the race. Writers looked to the effects of alcohol in order to explain France's failure to keep up with the population growth of the rest of Europe, others saw drink as weakening the productive capacities of French society.[1]

However, while this seems to concur with similar positions adopted by social reformers in temperance movements in Britain and America, there was an important difference: in France 'alcool' did not mean any alcohol, but only distilled spirits. Wine was a 'boisson hygiénique' – a 'healthy drink'. No health reformer was going to persuade France to relinquish wine, which had been an essential ingredient of French culture as long as there had been such a thing. If the modern malaise was going to be blamed on any drink, it had to be a modern drink.

Most doctors and temperance groups shared the belief that the consumption of wine was not a factor in the development of alcoholism. Alcoholism, it was maintained, had developed because wine shortages caused by the vine lice had led the French to turn from good, natural wine to vile, unnatural industrial alcohol in substances such as absinthe. Wine drinking was in fact prescribed as a means of curbing alcoholism, while temperance groups advised that one litre of wine a day was not dangerous for a hard-working adult man.[2] It was widely believed that the problem with alcohol was not the quantity consumed, but the quality. Even the drunkenness of alcohol, an 'ugly and squalid' drunkenness, was contrasted with the drunkenness of gaiety and fellow feeling, the Gallic drunkenness of wine ('ivresse gaie et bon enfant; l'ivresse gauloise').[3]

The definition of alcoholism in Dechambre's encyclopaedic medical dictionary of 1865 was 'By chronic alcoholism we understand a condition caused by prolonged use of spirits which develops slowly and progressively'. This authoritative pronouncement was written by Etienne Lancereaux, born in 1829, later to be president of the Académie and a significant figure in the anti-absinthe movement. He may even have been the first to use the term 'absinthism' in a scientific paper, though he was not a single-subject specialist, and published on a variety of topics.[4]

The debate around 'absinthism' was confused by its being said to be variously caused by the traditional ingredients of absinthe, by toxic additives, or by alcohol. It was in the interests of the large-scale producers of absinthe to blame any ill-effects of drinking the substance on ingredients added only by small manufacturers. It was strongly believed (and doubtless with some justification) that inferior absinthe was always contaminated with non-traditional additives. There were reports of copper salts (probably cupric acetate) being added to improve the tint and antimony trichloride to increase the creamy louche effect when water was added.[5] Edmond de Goncourt wrote in 1891 of 'an old society woman, an absintheuse who "puts away" twenty-two glasses of absinthe a day – that dreadful absinthe tinted with sulphate of zinc'.[6]

The *Lancet* in 1873 reported on a study at the French Conservatoire des Arts which found absinthe to contain a large proportion of antimony,

> a poison which cannot fail to add largely to the irritant effects necessarily produced on the alimentary canal and the liver by constant doses of a concentrated alcoholic liquid. As at present constituted therefore, and especially when drunk in the disastrous excess now common in Paris, and taken frequently upon an empty stomach, absinthe forms a chronic poison of almost unequalled virulence.[7]

Thus a poisonous effect of absinthe was conceded, but the poison was an added ingredient whose effect was exacerbated by its use with alcohol.

Not all observers, even those opposed to absinthe such as the English writer R.H. Sherard, accepted a qualitative difference between absinthe and other alcohol. He discussed the difference between

> those doctors who diagnose a special malady called absinthism as a result of the absinthe habit, as opposed to those who classify it with the hundred and one evil results of alcoholism. As a matter of fact, one has observed the usual results of absinthism, the hoarse, gutteral absinthe voice, the wandering, glazed absinthe eye, the cold and clammy hand, which seems to emerge from these swathing cloths, as well as all the accidents of which these symptoms are the forerunners, in people who have never drunk a glass of absinthe in their lives…Absinthe gets in its work more speedily, because it is the more insidious drink, and the absintheur consumes, therefore, a vastly larger quantity of alcohol than other drinkers.[8]

This may mean no more than that once people were alcoholics, they drank the most strongly alcoholic drink easily available, which was absinthe.

Ever the writer, however, once he has demonstrated that he is not taken in by the supposedly unique character of absinthe, cannot resist retelling a series of horror stories to describe the absinthe crisis:

> One reads every day of terrible things which have befallen absinthe drinkers…A few months ago the case of a man was reported who, whilst stirring his tenth 'blue' at a *marchand de vins* suddenly went blind, a case I took pains to authenticate. In a police station in Paris not very long ago there were brought in from the streets in one day six prisoners so demented from absinthe drinking that they had all to be sent to the lunatic asylum. Absintheurs drop down dead in the streets of apoplexy, cerebral congestion and heart failure, every day that dawns red over Paris.[9]

He goes on to tell the inevitable tale, a commonplace of city life, of a girl from a respectable family who gets into prostitution, drinks ten francs' worth of absinthe and throws herself in the Seine.[10]

Sherard's collection of absinthe tales concludes with an indication that not only the French can fall victim to the green plague:

> Last year at an inn in Normandy, where I had gone to watch the spring adorn the apple-trees, I saw an Englishman drink himself into epilepsy on absinthe. He took one month to effect this, and his drink bill fell just short of a five-pound note. Doubtless when he arrived at the inn he had previously undergone considerable alcoholic preparation, but that month's steady absinthing finished the work. It was just after luncheon one morning. 'I think I must have an absinthe,' he said. Then suddenly he gave a cry, grimaced and fell on the floor in a fit.[11]

Fits and madness had long been associated with absinthe. As far back as Henri Balesta's 1860 anti-absinthe tract *Absinthe et Absintheurs*, claims had been made that absinthe led to dementia, so that a tippler might imagine himself in 'a long cortege of idiotised absinthe drinkers, cretinised by abuse of the deleterious liqueur'.[12]

Valentin Magnan, the doctor who devoted his life to experiment on absinthe, characterised absinthism as being distinguished by sudden delirium, epileptic attacks, vertigo, hallucinatory delirium more active and impulsive than with alcohol alone, and sometimes unconsciousness.[13] Magnan was an advanced practitioner, one of the first to treat alcoholics as mentally ill and to look for psychological causes of the disease, though his contribution to the development of the field was undermined by his passionate conviction that alcohol was the prime cause of most mental disorders.

Magnan again tries to define the difference between alcoholism and absinthism, labouring the point in a manner which suggests he is arguing a case which his opponents have not completely conceded:

> In Absinthism the hallucination insanity is more active, more terrifying, sometimes provoking most dangerous reactions of extreme violence. It is accompanied by another symptom of great gravity; all at once the absinthe-drinker shouts out, grows pale, loses consciousness, and falls; the features contract, the jaws are clenched, the pupils dilate, the eyes turn upwards, the limbs

stiffen, urine is passed, gas and faeces are smartly expelled. At the end of some seconds he face is contorted, the limbs shake, the eyes are turned convulsively in all directions, the jaws are snapped, the tongue protruded between the teeth and severely bitten; a bloody saliva covers the lips; the face becomes injected, blue and puffy; the eyes become prominent and fill with tears, the breathing is stertorious; then the movements cease, the body becomes all relaxed, the sphincters lose their hold. A moment later the man raises his head, and looks about him with a dull stare. Coming to himself a little later, he has no recollection at all of what has happened; it is exactly like an attack of epilepsy.

This is a description, then, of an epileptic fit or a fit similar to those characteristic of epilepsy. Those in an advanced stage of alcoholism often suffer epileptiform fits, sometimes called 'rum fits' in the erroneous belief that rum was more likely to cause them than any other drink.

Magnan continues to describe the clinical symptoms he ascribes to absinthe-induced fits.

At other times the manifestation is less acute; the individual pales, some little twitches show at the corner of his lips, and for a moment he is completely ignorant of all that goes on around him; he has a vertigo. If these accidents recur, there may supervene an attack of delirium with great intensity, during which – contrary to what happens with the simple alcoholic, where a little lively inter-ference serves to stop the delirium for a moment – the patient is heedless of all interference, and gives himself over almost automatically to acts of the most violent character. Sometimes also another symptomatic difference distinguishes the drinker of absinthe from the ordinary alcoholic, and that is the unheralded appearance of delirium with hallucinations of great intensity without a single preceding tremor, or without his motor powers being markedly impaired. To sum up: to the credit of absinthe we must add the following symptoms; sudden delirium, epileptic attacks, vertigo, hallucinatory delirium more active and more impulsive than with alcohol, and sometimes very dangerous because unconscious.[14]

The claim that absinthe produces a more active and impulsive delirium than other forms of alcohol is clearly based on clinical observation which, though subjective, fits with the psychoactive nature of absinthe. This was, after all, what drinkers felt they could get from this drink and not others.

By the end of the century, Magnan's association between madness and absinthe was well established and his work on absinthism a classic text; this was substantially the attack on absinthe (referred to here in chapter 3) which Magnan established while in his twenties. The significant development in the 1890s is that now Magnan was connecting absinthe with the degeneration not of an individual but the entire race.

Magnan, born at Perpignan in 1835, did his doctoral thesis in Paris on general paralysis and madness in 1867, and that year became physician-in-chief of St Anne's Asylum. This was a senior post made all the more potent because from 1867 all the insane from Paris and the Seine department were placed under the central service of admission to St Anne's for assessment before being admitted or transferred to other asylums. Magnan's position, therefore, was effectively one of defining insanity in the most populous region of France and by implication in France itself.

In 1872 he published on alcoholic delirium as part of the continuing work he was doing on alcoholism, absinthism and heredity, including hereditary madness and hereditary criminality. With such works as *The Principal Clinical Signs of Absinthism* of 1890, he established what was perceived to be a solid clinical basis for attacks on absinthe. In 1893 he was elected a member of the Académie de Médecine.

His ideas caught hold and were given an alarming currency by the new public enthusiasm for statistics. An anonymous commentator explained,

> Lunacy has doubled and the expenses connected with it have more than doubled during the last thirty years. The asylums are full and, and new ones are needed, unless this measure [banning absinthe] is going to have an immediate effect upon the numbers

of the insane. Insanity exists chiefly where the consumption of this deadly spirit is highest and, what is worse, the descendants of absinthe-drinkers suffer for the sins of the father ... statistics fail to aid in estimating the number of half-insane from absinthe indulgence, for the majority go unrecorded until they call attention to themselves through the commission of some crime or become inmates of an asylum.[15]

A report for the public (and of no medical authority) noted that 'In the last thirty years the numbers of lunatics has increased threefold. In Paris, at the hospital where such cases are specially nursed, statistics show 9 out of 10 are due to absinthe poisoning.'[16]

Magnan himself is far more cautious, and his own records show over a more than 20-year period sufferers of 'absinthism' in single or the low double figures annually, while those judged to be suffering from 'chronic alcoholism' to be in three figures throughout the period. He presented this data but drew no conclusions from it for the benefit of his colleagues.[17] Others took to classifying absinthism into categories of acute, chronic and hereditary.[18]

The most obvious explanation for the observed connection between absinthe and mental disturbance, and confusion with alcohol is that high does of thujone could cause derangement (whether temporary or not, the research has not been carried out). This would fit with absinthe's mildly psychoactive effects caused by the thujone in the wormwood plant extract. However, only an alcoholic would be taking enough absinthe to ingest sufficient thujone to cause damage. There would be, therefore, only a qualified truth in the proposition that absinthe causes insanity, as it was only likely to injure people with already advanced stages of alcoholic disturbance.

Recorded insanity was on the increase in the 1890s and early years of the twentieth century, partly from improved diagnostic skills and ability to treat. Mainly the increase was because the multifarious pressures and uncertainties of modern life tipped borderline schizophrenics over, and cultivated the suffering of the neurotic and the depressed. It was, however, easier to blame a single factor for a condition than to understand its multi-factoral cause.

After 1887 Magnan had separate figures for those 'whose insanity was entirely due to excess of drink' and for 'all the psychopaths who are chiefly descendants of alcoholics'. He noted that where both parents are alcoholics there can be 'an hereditary alcoholic trait from both sides'.[19]

It was widely believed that acquired characteristics (such as brain damage from over-indulgence in a liqueur) could be passed on to children, a scientific fallacy called Lamarckism after its most celebrated exponent. Magnan maintained that the child of an absintheur would be born with a predisposition to insanity and serious disorders of the nervous system.

As Marie Corelli luridly put it in *Wormwood*:

> study our present absinthe-drinking generation, *absintheurs*, and children of *absintheurs*, – and then, – why then give glory to the English Darwin! For he was a wise man in his time, though in his ability to look back, he perhaps lost the power to foresee. He traced, or thought he could trace, man's *ascent* from the monkey, – but he could not calculate man's *descent* to the monkey again. He did not study the Parisians closely enough for that![20]

Anti-absinthe propagandists regularly printed pictures of the malformed and imbecilic offspring of absinthe drinkers. Foetal alcohol syndrome, caused by the poisoning of a foetus by alcohol consumed by an alcoholic mother while pregnant, is a well-described phenomenon. It has no relationship to absinthe or to genetic inheritance but is merely a form of tissue damage caused by an expectant mother's ingesting a poison. Moreover, temperance campaigners were claiming that the children of male absinthe drinkers were also so affected.

Magnan talked on alcoholism and degeneracy at the International Eugenics Conference in London in 1912, where he shared his categorisation of 'hereditary degenerates', who were, allotted such subjective categories as 'unbalanced', 'feeble-minded', 'imbecile' and 'idiot'. 'These poor wretches are born with the mark of their parentage on them,' he explained.[21] The conference, held at London University, was a prestigious affair, with delegates from as far afield as Japan and Australia. An inaugural dinner chaired by conference president Leonard Darwin was addressed by former prime minister A.J. Balfour.

The notion of civilisation reaching its climax and making a downturn had preoccupied the decadents, and it is unsurprising that a leading member of the decadent circle, the sexologist Havelock Ellis, attended the Eugenics Conference. Ellis had been Arthur Symons's friend, next-door neighbour and travelling companion to Paris to sample the decadent delights of the city. He contributed to the *Savoy*, and it was doubtless due to his influence that the April 1896 issue contained an essay by Cesare Lombroso, the Italian who had defined criminality in terms of physical characteristics.

Lombroso's eager pupil, Max Nordau, applied theories of degeneration more widely, to encompass art and political 'degeneracy' in his highly influential book *Degeneration* of 1895:

> Degenerates are not always criminals, prostitutes, anarchists and pronounced lunatics; they are often authors and artists. These, however, manifest the same mental characteristics, and for the most part the same somatic features, as the members of the above-mentioned anthropological family, who satisfy their unhealthy impulses with the knife of the assassin or the bomb of the dynamiter, instead of with pen and pencil.[22]

The prime example he chooses to illustrate this theory is Verlaine, with his peculiar physiognomy, eroticism, drunkenness and the lack of an obvious logic to his poetry. It was against this background that Magnan presented his evidence.

He remarked to the conference that of a thousand children of alcoholics, about a third 'disappear' (presumably he means they died) in the first two or three years.

> among the survivors are counted many idiots, epileptics and a large number of degenerates destitute of moral sense, instinctively perverted, impulsive, abnormal, miserable victims of their parents'

alcoholism ... a glance at the great group of mental degeneracies, the result of parental alcohol, was enough to convince one that alcohol provides men's quarters in the asylums of the Seine with three quarters of their population. The greater part of these unfortunate degenerates, with their physical, mental and moral defects, count alcoholics among their ascendants; to this root cause they owe their lack of mental balance, which is the root cause of all psychical mischief. That is one of the cruellest results of alcoholism, that it not only profoundly alters the individual, but transmits to his descendants defects which make of them invalids or criminals, of which the net result to society is a heavy surcharge and a serious danger.[23]

Magnan also believed that the parent's state of inebriation at the point of conception was a significant fact. He quoted approvingly a researcher studying 'hysterical, epileptic and idiot' children, who found that of a sample 'In 298 cases there was absolute certainty that the father or the mother was drunk at the moment of conception, and a probability in 122'.[24]

Epilepsy was considered to be a mental illness; posters showed a school-room, with a child falling from her desk in a fit, to the alarm of the teacher and other pupils. It was captioned 'parents absinthiques, enfants épileptiques'.[25]

A preoccupation with the health of children *en masse* was not merely a beneficent and general medical concern. Set against the political fears of the time, it reflected a social, collective anxiety. The defeat of 1870–71 had left France with a paranoid fear of low population growth compared to that of her bellicose neighbour, and a concern for the health of the population.

In 1821 France had a population of 30 million, against the 21 million of 'Germany' (the lands of the subsequent Reich). After the Franco–Prussian War France had 36 million against Germany's 41 million.[26] The bald fear was that the future France might simply have too few healthy soldiers to hold off a German offensive. The same American journal reporting 'facts' about madness added that 'The recruiting-boards are often obliged to reject conscripts from absinthe-ridden districts, because of mental deficiency and other signs of degeneracy. Thus absinthism makes mad those who suffer from it and weak-minded the next generation.'[27] An article martially entitled 'The War Against Absinthe' described how 'medical authorities are overwhelmed by this slow but sure poisoning of the population. The race is degenerating; the stature of men is lessening.' It was claimed that 'in some places soldiers up to the standard height are difficult to find; the minimum height in the army had to be lowered'. It was, of course, easier to blame the phenomenon of low-grade conscripts on personal failings such as absinthe drinking rather than the real cause: poor nutrition, physically crushing labour and disease, exacerbated by appalling living conditions. Britain, where absinthe was not an issue, also found great difficulty in recruiting healthy soldiers from its urban populations for the same reasons which prevailed in France.

A further reason for the fear of absinthe and its threat to the nation's future soldiers was the extent to which women were drinking it. These were not, as previously, only women of the demi-monde; now any woman could drink absinthe with, it was predicted, dire consequences. Sterling Heilig, Paris correspondent of the *Atlanta Constitution*, remarked,

> What doctors fear the most is from this ladies' drinking. Alcoholism
> in general (and absinthism in particular) is said to create a special
> race, both from the point of view of the intellectual facilities and
> physical characteristics. This race, the doctors say, may very well
> continue for a limited time, with all its physical deformities and
> vicious tendencies, even for several generations, but, exposed in
> every sort to accident and malady, given over to impotency and
> sterility, the race soon disappears. The family dies out.[28]

Other popular beliefs about absinthe which supposedly contributed to views on its role in a downward cycle of racial degeneration were that it was an abortifacient and that it rendered men sterile.[29]

'Absenthic children,' member of the Chamber of Deputies and pharmacist Henri Schmidt said,

> if they don't die a short time after birth, remain thin and under-
> developed; their resistance to infectious diseases is diminished,

they are predisposed to tuberculosis and are moreover subject to epileptic convulsions and grave mental problems…they often manifest criminal and vicious tendencies due to a profound depravity and a complete loss of moral sense.[30]

A declining birth rate is now seen as a concomitant of increasing wealth in the population in general, and a high level of education among women in particular. This was far from obvious in the late nineteenth century, when depopulation was seen as a decline in the nation's health which set a potentially catastrophic course for the future as the population dwindled towards supposedly unsupportable levels. For this, women were held primarily responsible.

In Saint-Sauveur, cabarets were built especially for emancipated women drinkers in the 1880s, and advertising posters showing women with a glass of absinthe demonstrate how acceptable it now was for women to drink in public.[31] Thus the winsome young cousin in a strapless dress looks back over her bare shoulder to offer a glass of Cousin Jeune absinthe; a well-built mature woman winks and encourages the viewer with an explicit sexuality, remarking that absinthe is one of her minor sins. A number of posters also showed Pierrot or some other stock character observing an unchaperoned courting couple drinking an absinthe by moonlight.

While male absinthe drinking was cause for legal restraint, nothing but an outright ban would do if women were drinking absinthe. As Lancereaux remarked, he thought formerly

that limitation of the number of cabarets and an increase of the duty on liqueurs would suffice to attract the progress of this evil, but since I learned better the attraction that this liqueur exercises on women even more than on men, on account of the essential oils which it contains, my conviction is that the only means of avoiding the danger is prohibition of the sale of this drink.[32]

The woman's drink of choice was often absinthe, and it was often drunk neat, it was suggested, because such a drink would not bloat their bodies uncomfortably inside their tight corsets. Another reason was women's low independent income compared to that of men, which meant the need for a drink which would last, and absinthe was an easy drink to sip slowly. Indeed, few could imbibe freely of unmixed absinthe, as the connoisseur of drinks George Saintsbury said, in neat absinthe 'the flavour is concentrated to repulsiveness; the spirit burns "like a torch-light procession"'.[33]

Heilig noted in 1894 that 'The ladies seem to have a special taste for these absinthes, vermouths and bitters. They rarely intoxicate themselves with wine (in Paris, practically no one does). But it must be acknowledged that, in Paris at least, the ladies of the high world, even the creatures of the demi-monde…and types from all the middle classes are too often victims of aperitifs.'[34]

The specific choice of absinthe by women is remarked on also in a report of the Académie de Médecine by Jean-Baptiste Vincent Laborde, who said,

> Women have a particular taste for absinthe and if they are rarely intoxicated with alcohol, it is necessary to notice that in Paris at least they are frequently affected by aperitifs and, without exaggeration, I would say that this intoxication has been, for several years, as common among women as men. It is possible to establish chronic absinthism clearly: after eight, ten months or a year, among young women or even young girls of eighteen or twenty.[35]

Another element in the mix of alcohol and national degeneration was a further stage in women's independence: not only were they drinking, smoking, riding bicycles and asserting personal independence in other ways, some were rejecting men altogether as sexual partners. This semi-public gender transgression was objectionable for its 'abnormality' but, more importantly, it was a form of relationship which denied France her yearned-for population growth, a further staging-post in the supposed national decline.

The Moulin Rouge's La Goulue was bisexual, and normally surrounded by a bevy of admiring women, which added to the frisson of her presence. She lived with La Môme Fromage, who famously teased her in public for denying that she was a lesbian, with, 'You don't mind it when you're eating me!'[36] The Rat Mort in the evening (opposite the Nouvelle Athènes in Place Pigalle) and

Le Hanneton in Rue Pigalle were known as lesbian cafés, as was La Souris, another lesbian bar near Toulouse-Lautrec's studio in Rue Caulaincourt. Toulouse-Lautrec frequented the bar, sometimes drawing pictures of lesbians caressing in their bedrooms.

Lesbian bars were first mentioned in a book for the general public in 1894, when Charles Virmaître identified them by name, saying they were hangouts for 'women who love each other with an ardent passion and in consequence detest men'. By the end of the century La Souris and Le Hanneton were included in what was billed as the 'Grand Dukes' Tour', a tour of Parisian nightspots for affluent tourists slumming, as legendary gathering places for lesbians, where sights were available for which 'we must dine in Lesbos to see,' as one commentator wrote.[37]

'Sexual inversion' was, for investigators such as Magnan – one of the first to write on the subject – like alcoholism, another congenital variant of degenerate heredity.[38] Lesbianism was, as Nicole Albert describes it, 'the proof and the consequence of an intrinsically corrupted and gangrenous civilisation'.[39]

Zola's *Nana,* with its orgies of food and drink, of desire and sordidness, describes this world, in which after a high life as a courtesan Nana lives with a brutal lover. As a respite from him she takes up with a lesbian lover, Satin. She takes Nana to a lesbian dining club in Rue des Martyrs and to a hotel on the Rue Laval which let rooms to lesbians, where they make love.

Satin never rouses herself until the gas is lit in the streets. In her apartment

> They were endlessly confidential, whilst Satin lay on her stomach in her nightgown, waving her legs above her head, and smoking cigarettes as she listened. Sometimes, on such afternoons as they had troubles to retail, they treated themselves to absinthe in order, as they termed it, 'to forget.' Satin did not go downstairs or put on a petticoat, but simply went and leant over the banisters, and shouted her order out to the concierge's little girl, a chit of ten, who when she brought up the absinthe in a glass would look furtively at the lady's bare legs.[40]

The theme of children being sent to buy absinthe was a common one – a cartoon in a popular magazine of 1906 shows a drunken mother sending a small girl out with the shouted words: 'six sous worth of absinthe and one sou worth of bread and don't break the bottle'.

It was rare for artists to depict women with absinthe until the last quarter of the nineteenth century; when they were depicted the paintings were often moralistic warnings of the danger of absinthe, associating the drink with promiscuous women or poverty. Picasso was more neutral in his approach when he painted four pictures of women drinking absinthe in 1901. At the time he was living in Paris, where he used to drink absinthe, though not to an exceptional degree. The only drug in which he indulged freely was tobacco – he liked to keep his creative energies free for work and sex. Born in Malaga, Spain in 1881, the son of an art teacher, Picasso demonstrated his gifts early, but impatiently left the Madrid Academy to find inspiration in the wider world. At the age of 18 in 1900 he went to Paris with a friend, Carlos Casagemas and, though constantly near starvation, found inspiration in the street life of Montmartre and the work of Toulouse-Lautrec and van Gogh. His favourite symbolist poet was Rimbaud, and he was fascinated by Jarry, who was convinced Picasso was the 'destroyer' who would come after him. Jarry had such confidence in Picasso's artistic mission that he gave the Spaniard his revolver.[41]

Early in 1901 Casagemas committed suicide in grief over a broken love affair, which affected Picasso deeply and propelled him into what has been described as his blue period, in which he painted scenes of loneliness, poverty and despair. His women drinking absinthe belong to this period.

As well as an inner isolation, Picasso's absinthe-drinking women look back to previous artists in a conscious recognition that the old days of absinthe and art are dying with the nineteenth century. Thus his first *Absinthe Drinker* is a gouache-and-crayon picture of a woman in a bar, elbow on the table and chin resting in a hand, staring into space over her glass, drawn in a manner reminiscent of Toulouse-Lautrec; the second, with the same title, shows a woman with her arms folded, looking intently ahead, with the bold lines and colour blocks strongly reminiscent of Gauguin.[42]

Another shows a dark-haired woman in profile leaning over a green glass of undiluted absinthe, one hand cupped around her ear as if she is trying to hear what the people on the other tables are saying. The fourth, of 1902, *Dozing Absinthe Drinker*, is an unhappy image typical of Picasso's blue period, with a woman in front of a small glass of unmixed absinthe, clutching a shawl or blanket around her thin body, her head bowed in sleep. Picasso also painted a poet friend, Cornuti, in front of his absinthe and absinthe spoon in 1903, and two cubist pictures in 1912 of posters advertising absinthe and a bottle of absinthe.

By this time it was a defiance of society to paint absinthe as anything but a social scourge, so in painting absinthe as a feature in a picture of a woman with no moral content Picasso, always a politically committed painter, was making a comment by default. As he said, 'One does not paint in order to decorate apartments. Painting is an instrument of offensive and defensive war against the enemy.'[43]

Through the early years of the twentieth century an increase in violent crimes and juvenile delinquency was blamed on absinthe. Absinthe was soon also being blamed not only for the diseases and vices of the poor, but for the militancy they expressed in protesting their condition: working-class political agitation and other mani-festations of the 'worker problem' were thus just a few more social problems which would be solved at a stroke with the prohibition of absinthe.

The association of absinthe with unruly workers by the right wing did not endear the aperitif to the left, however, for socialists denounced absinthe too as a capitalist poison which diverted the proletariat from their historic path. In 1905 *La Revue Socialiste* pub-lished an article warning of the alienating effects of absinthe, as did *L'Humanité*; and a socialist deputy such as Edouard Vaillant, a doctor, worked with conservatives and radicals in the anti-absinthe cause.

As Canadian historian Patricia Prestwich remarked of anti-absinthe campaigners, 'Armed with a seemingly comprehensive indictment of the drink as a serious factor in many of France's medical and social problems, they were able to create a popular image of absinthe as a poison that had to be eliminated from the social body of the nation'.[44]

Absinthe, then, contaminated the mind of the user, contaminated the genetic inheritance of future generations, led to sexual degeneracy and crime, and portended national catastrophe. One more horror was now thrown into the maelstrom of the French psyche of the *fin-de-siècle*: that of antisemitic agitation which saw absinthe as a Jewish poison in the heart of the French nation, an accusation which took its place among the usual mediaeval charges of deicide and ritual murder and exaggerated claims of Jewish influence in national life.

The focus for antisemitism was the Dreyfus affair, a bungled inquiry into the presence of a spy in the War Office which resulted in the only Jew in the place, Captain Dreyfus, being seized, convicted and imprisoned. The stages of the campaign of injustice against Dreyfus coincided with the years in which absinthe was most hotly contested: his conviction in 1894, the discovery of the evidence which showed him guiltless in 1896, his reconviction in 1899, and eventual exoneration in 1906.

The affair divided the art world as much as the rest of France, with Zola a notable defender of Dreyfus and Degas an antisemite who broke with such Jewish friends as the artist Pissarro and Count Isaac de Camondo, the collector who had saved many impressionists from penury.

In 1894, Arthur and Edmond Weil-Picard, who were half Jewish, had bought a controlling interest in Pernod Fils. Now the ubiquitous green liqueur found its place in antisemitic life, as Edouard Drumont, France's leading antisemitic intellectual denounced absinthe as 'a tool of the Jews'. Drumont was an immensely influential figure, founder of the French Antisemitic League, author of the bestselling two-volume book *La France juive* of 1886, and founding editor of

La Libre Parole (*The True Word*), with its slogan 'France for the French'.

Alphonse Daudet, always keen to see significance in the traditions of France and what he called 'her racial roots', was a close friend of Drumont.[45] He introduced the journalist to the publishers who took on *La France juive*, and he promoted its sales. Drumont taught Daudet's son Léon how to duel, and helped him on the path of antisemitic journalism. Léon took up the banner on behalf of the national drink to declare 'I am for wine – and against absinthe, as I am for tradition and against revolution'.[46]

Absinthe fought back. Its producers advertised it with slogans such as 'Patriotism' or 'Equality', and put tricolours on their labels. A manufacturer in the Doubs valley, Montbeliard, marketed a brand called Absinthe Anti-Juive (anti-Jewish), with the slogans 'superior quality' and 'France for the French'.[47]

The battle over absinthe had plumbed new lows of absurdity. It was in this heady mixture of fear and paranoia that absinthe was propelled into its final, terminal phase.

10 Twilight of the *Fée Verte*

IT WAS NOT UNTIL THE EARLY TWENTIETH CENTURY that anti-absinthe agitation resulted in prohibition of the drink in most countries where it was consumed. The forces against absinthe carried a formidable weight of prejudice, but had found themselves unable to mount a concerted attack. A temperance movement was set up in France in 1872 to sponsor educational programmes, scientific research and political action, but with no success. A group which inherited its limp baton in 1880, the Société française du tempérence, was Paris-orientated and enjoyed no popular following. It was not until the anti-absinthe scares of the 1890s that temperance really began to take off (half a century after similar agitations in England).

A new society was begun in 1891 by Dr Paul-Maurice Legrain, eventually to be called the Union française antialcoolique. It maintained several hundred sections through France, produced a monthly journal and a children's magazine, and succeeded in having a temperance message taught in all state schools. It is to this campaign that we owe the children's anti-absinthe poem which has the Green Fairy saying, with more passion than lyricism, 'Me, I kill the future and even in the family I destroy love of country, courage, honour'.[1] Other anti-absinthe verses included 'absinthe loses our sons', with its spirited refrain, 'Sing the De Profondis/ Because absinthe loses our sons' (with a pun on 'perd nos fils'/Pernod Fils).

By the end of the century the temperance movement had an estimated 40,000 members, but it was riven by internal schisms which prevented its taking concerted action. Some of these were reflected in the debate over absinthe, where some far-sighted temperance campaigners correctly surmised that the attention being given to absinthe's supposed unique qualities diverted efforts away from the genuine dangers of heavy alcohol consumption. Others, also correctly but with less vision, reasoned that absinthe was an easy target, and that once its abolition was achieved, they could go on to attack alcohol in its other manifestations. Yet others, with no vision at all, actually believed their own propaganda and considered absinthe a unique poison which had to be eliminated for the sake of social progress and national survival.

The concentration of their attack on absinthe left the French temperance movement in the paradoxical position of enjoying support from the main producers of alcoholic drinks in their country, the wine growers, who deduced that absinthe could easily be sacrificed, and that no serious attack on wine would take place. Thus the town council of Gabarnac debated a motion on 23 June 1907 that 'absinthe harms the health, ruins the family and destroys the race', but the strident prohibitionist tone was mitigated by its further complaint that 'the consumption of absinthe, still growing, is manifestly harmful to the consumption of natural wine'.[2] The crisis for wine growers was becoming acute because new methods of manufacture had allowed greater volumes of wine to be produced, but without a corresponding market to drink the produce. A major anti-absinthe rally in Paris in June 1907 assembled under such slogans as 'All for wine: against absinthe'. Despite this hysteria, absinthe never made up more than 3 per cent of the alcohol drunk in France, to wine's 72 per cent.[3] It is also worth remarking that wine and absinthe were not always thought to be inimical. Absinthe was said by some to intensify the power of wine, 'absinthe is the spark that explodes the gunpowder of wine'.[4]

A temperance observer was pessimistic, even in April 1907, writing,

> For a long time, at any rate, we cannot expect any active inter-
> vention of the French government. Public opinion, as a whole, is
> not yet stirred; the distilleries and publicans are still too powerful
> as electoral agents. The deputies and senators would not dare to
> touch the revenues of these 'honest traders'.[5]

Sherard was sceptical about both the French will and ability to ban
absinthe. He wrote,

> One is constantly reading in the papers that the French govern-
> ment is going to put a stop to the sale and manufacture of absinthe
> in France, but nobody who knows how governments are run is for
> one moment the dupe of these lying and hypocritical promises.
> The French tapster is the great political agent and his business
> must not be interfered with.[6]

Proposals to limit the number of *débitants* (retail outlets), some half a
million vendors which included anyone who sold alcohol, whether
a bar-keeper, pastry-shop owner or coal merchant, had been passed
by the National Assembly in 1903, but on the eve of the elections,
in 1906, the measure was rescinded. France also had a venerable
tradition of home distilling by the 'bouilleur de cru', of whom there
were a million in the early years of the twentieth century.

While the retailers formed a powerful electoral force against
the restriction of alcohol, they could not be relied upon to defend
absinthe if by sacrificing the green fairy they could keep their
privileges. They could always sell something else, and there was
evidence that the retailers' mark-up on absinthe was less than on
other drinks, as the small number of manufacturers maintained a
cartel in which competition by lowering prices was limited, and
they could control the retailer's percentage.

Large manufacturers were only too willing to sacrifice their local
rivals. Every small town had a liqueur resembling absinthe which
was marketed as a tonic and all-round panacea. These were made
by mixing plant essences, which were commercially available, with
industrial alcohol. An attack on these as inferior, adulterated
absinthes drew fire away from the large manufacturers while con-
ceding some part of the anti-absinthe movement's argument.

Much of the early debate on the road to abolition was not therefore about an absolute condemnation, but a comparative discussion about different kinds of drink and different kinds of absinthe. Confusion also existed because in French both the name of the drink and the name of one of its principal ingredients is the same: *absinthe*. So what was being condemned, the drink or one of its components? In English there is less confusion, as the drink is absinthe and the plant which contributes to it wormwood.

The campaign against absinthe was doomed to failure if it hit the target head on, so more surreptitious means had to be found to attack absinthe; the 'essences' debate gave an entry point. The essential oils are the odoriferous oils which can be extracted from plants. Concern about these essences in relation to 'absinthism' went back to the earliest medical work on the subject. By 1865, essences were sufficiently implicated in absinthism for the *Dictionnaire de Médecine* to describe it as a 'variety of alcoholism, acute or chronic, caused by the abuse of absinthe, and leading (more frequently than alcoholism) to mania and softening of the brain... due to the poisonous action of the essences which enter the composition of this dangerous liqueur'.[7]

This was unsupported by experimental work, which was then undertaken to reinforce the theory at a time when it was proving socially contentious. In the 1880s and 1890s a great deal of laboratory effort was expended in identifying the various essences in alcoholic drink and measuring their toxicity. The anti-absinthe doctor Laborde had, for example, in 1889 isolated anise as being the active – and destructive – ingredient and suggested the term 'anism' to replace 'absinthism'.[8] The modern biochemist Wilfred Niels Arnold remarks that the extensive essence research is 'considered of limited value today', though it received widespread (if not total) acceptance in the French scientific community at the time.

The socialist deputy and doctor Edouard Vaillant in 1900 took advantage of a debate on tax legislation to insert an amendment to forbid the circulation and sale of any essence recognised as dangerous by the Académie de Médecine. The government was not quick to act, but eventually asked the Académie to set up a commission to draw up a list of essences. It had seven members, including Drs Lancereaux, Magnan and Motet, who had made their reputations in the field of alcoholism, and absinthe in particular. Laborde was reporter to the commission, which in 1903 compiled a list of dangerous essences. In order to reduce the number of substances they must examine and (it must be assumed) to avoid the wrath of the powerful cognac manufacturers, the commission classified essences into two: as 'liqueurs naurelles', which were the products of the distillation of wine and traditional eaux-de-vie; and as 'les liqueurs artificielles', which were produced by the distillation of plants in alcohol. These were considered to be worthy of study, as they were said to be a part of the most dangerous drinks in common consumption. That is, the essences whose safety was to be tested were selected on the basis that the drinks in which they played a part were assumed to be dangerous, thus rather presupposing the outcome. Wormwood, hyssop and badiane, all constituents of absinthe, eventually came at the top of this list of highly toxic essences, and were recommended for prohibition.

The president of the Académie, Etienne Lancereaux, in February 1903 asserted a connection between absinthe, malnutrition and tuberculosis. He said, 'The phenomenon of malnutrition brought about by the abuse of drinks containing essences is remarkable. It starts with digestive troubles: nausea, vomiting, poor appetite, accompanied by a progressive weight loss and finally almost invariably by tuberculosis and death.' Men were likely to become tubercular 'more quickly and more frequently' drinking 'essences' such as those found in absinthe than simple alcohol. He also proclaimed, 'The picture of intoxication by drinks containing essential oils is clearly distinct from that owing to the action of purely alcoholic drinks. These last do not generally bring about paralysis or convulsions.'[9]

It took little time for the anti-absinthe lobby to learn to use essences for their own purposes. At temperance meetings, guinea pigs, rats and rabbits were injected with doses of essence of wormwood to die a convulsive death, supposedly for the edification of the audience. A description of one of these events, in this case put on to warn the soldiers of the 109th Infantry of the dangers of absinthe, was given by a captain in his memoirs. A guinea pig was injected with a quarter of a cubic centimetre of essence of absinthe (presumably wormwood essence).

> At first it seems thunderstruck. It remains fixed in one place as if stunned. At the end of two or three minutes there follow on this stupor the most frightening agonies. Suddenly it stiffens its paws, and then makes, all at once, a prodigious leap in the air. The poor little creature, ordinarily so harmless, takes on an entirely unexpected expression of ferocity. It resembles an hydrophobic [rabid] animal with its convulsed face, its twisted lips, covered with foam. In its eyes – wide open, haggard, convulsive, mad, one reads an impulse to kill.

This would be droll if it were not so unpleasant. The demonstrator presumably primed his audience to read into the animal's convulsions a simulacrum of alcoholic stupor, rage and then delirium. As the writer continues in this tale of anthropomorphic cruelty,

> It is now prey to hallucinations. Directly its spine curves in a half-circle. Its members and whole body are thrilled with shocks interrupted by plaintive cries. Then a brief moment of calm. The attack recommences, showing at each fresh crisis, signs of accumulated violence.

Eventually, after suffering for half an hour, the guinea pig dies.[10]

It did not take a keen scientific mind to detect the logical flaw in extrapolating to humans from tests on small mammals. The self-consciously bohemian poet and absinthe-lover Raoul Ponchon was inspired by a newspaper report that the deputy director of a municipal laboratory had 'injected ten cubic centimetres of absinthe in a guinea-pig, to demonstrate the mortal toxicity of the beverage'. Ponchon wrote a poem, 'Absinthe and the Guinea-pig':

> Ten centimetres: what a binge!
> But why not thirty?…
> But O expert (whom I respect)

you know well that I inject
relatively less. If I did it your way it would be as if,
rascal that I am,
I drank a litre at one sitting: no thanks!
For me, that ten centimetres cubed
of absinthe thrown down my throat:
I'll boldly take it
without putting a foot wrong,
but it's no marvel
that it breaks a guinea-pig.[11]

The economist Yves Guyot, invited to watch a guinea pig die in such circumstances in Laborde's laboratory, quickly worked out that the guinea pig had been given as much wormwood essence as could be found in ten litres of absinthe, and to give an average-sized man the same dose would mean he had drunk 730 litres of the drink.[12]

This was of course a repetition of the experiments Magnan and others did to show that essence of wormwood was toxic to experimental animals and that alcohol was less so. These experiments were dismissed as crude at the time, and inadequate to meet their objective. After a thorough modern review of the literature, Arnold reported that he had seen no studies on chronic administration of absinthe (or any of its constituents).[13] All the experiments were with acute doses, effectively the administration of a fast-acting poison. Tables of results were created to show the minimum dose of wormwood oil, thujone, camphor or other substances which could cause convulsions in cat, rat, rabbit, mouse and so on. But the condition of absinthism which this was supposed to mimic was a chronic condition consisting of daily administration over many years. There was, common sense could easily demonstrate, no connection between a large dose of a substance for a small animal administered intravenously, all at once, and a diluted form of the same substance taken orally by a human over what could easily be decades.

Not only was there a straightforward laboratory procedure for testing chronic consumption, it had been suggested to Magnan as early as 1869 in the supercilious piece 'Absinthe and Alcohol' in the British medical journal the *Lancet*:

> The question really before us is...of the comparative influence of repeated small *stomach* doses (reaching a high daily total) of an alcohol pure and simple, and of an alcohol flavoured with small quantities of wormwood, and, indeed, of half a dozen other flavouring matters besides.[14]

Magnan had to have read this – he himself wrote on absinthe in the *Lancet* in 1874, and it is standard procedure for scientists to read papers which review their own work. Yet such an assiduous researcher as Arnold cannot find reference to the advised experiments on chronic use of absinthe. Does this mean these obvious experiments were not done? There has to be the strong suspicion that they were conducted, perhaps many times, and that the results were 'disappointing'; that is, they failed to meet the experimenter's preconceived notion of what should happen, and they were therefore not published. One cannot prove a negative, so this line of inquiry can go no further, but in science the missing data is often the most valuable data: it may be missing for a reason.

The Académie skirted controversy by condemning all aperitifs because of their essences and high alcohol content – of course a condemnation of all was an effective condemnation of none, as there was no possibility of all liqueurs being banned. The Académie also recommended higher taxes, advice with which the government could happily concur. An increase in the tax on absinthe, moreover, made the drink more valuable to the state treasury and therefore less likely to be banned.

In a refinement of the tax laws, a super-tax was imposed in 1907 to eliminate cheap absinthe and protect the expensive. In a further step, in 1908, the manufacture, sale and possession of absinthe of less than 65 degrees was banned. The *Times* reported this under the headline 'Temperance measures', even though it enforced the sale of stronger alcohol in the place of weaker drinks. The apparent paradox of promoting as an anti-alcohol measure a law which increased the strength of alcoholic drinks available is explained by the *Times*'s writer that it was 'doing away with low-priced absinthe which is devastating both the urban and rural working classes'.[15] This law therefore pandered to the deep-seated belief that alcoholism was a disease of the poor.

This was a belief so profoundly felt that the one-act play *Absinthe,* by Charles Foley, caused a sensation in 1913. After a night of drinking absinthe, an aristocrat awakes to find blood and some red hair on his handkerchief; he gradually learns that he has strangled an exotic dancer in the night. Showing a crime committed by an aristocrat in an absinthe delirium challenged the assumption that the lives of only the poor were damaged by alcohol. It is interesting to compare this with Balesta's eagerness to demonstrate in his 1860 book *Absinthe et Absintheurs* that excessive use of absinthe is not only a problem for the rich, and that the poor can also suffer. In 50 years, conceptions about who drank absinthe had completely reversed.

Now fears were voiced that absinthe could tear through the ranks of the lower-middle class in the way it had those of the workers. A proposal for an anti-absinthe law in 1906 warned of the danger to 'Good, unsuspecting people who are deceived by impudent advertising and are perverted in their innocence' into drinking absinthe.[16] The condescending tone indicates that the writer was protecting his social inferiors, the bank clerks, provincial school-teachers and small shopkeepers, the conservative backbone of the Republic.

Absinthe campaigners fought back with promotion of the health benefits of absinthe, and pro-absinthe doctors in 1904 published a pamphlet called *Opinions scientifiques sur L'absinthe,* recommending it for gout, dropsy, worms, fever and as a general intellectual stimulant.

The supporters and critics of absinthe were evenly matched until one of those historical sparks which could pass virtually unnoticed outside the community in which it took place, were it not to fall on the dry tinder prepared by years of tireless work by propagandists. The anti-absinthe movement's boost of dramatic energy came, ironically, from Switzerland, the very birthplace of modern absinthe.

On 28 August 1905 in the village of Commugny in the Vaud canton of Switzerland, Jean Lanfray, a 31-year-old vineyard worker awoke at 4.30am and had his first drink of the day, absinthe with three parts water. Lanfray was a big man, French by birth, who had served in the army, where he acquired his absinthe habit. He lived with his wife, who was pregnant, and two children, four-year-old Rose and one-year-old Blanche, on the upper floor of a farmhouse. His parents and his brother lived downstairs.[17]

That day he told his wife to wax his boots, so he could go mushroom hunting in the woods the next morning. He tended to his cows and walked with his father and brother towards the vineyard where they worked. They passed an inn at 5.30am, and Lanfray had a crème de menthe and a cognac. He worked till 12, then ate lunch of bread, cheese and sausage with two or three glasses of his strong home-made red wine, called piquette. At 3pm he had a break for two gasses of wine and an hour or so later a neighbour gave him another glass. At 4.30 he stopped work and with his brother and father dropped in to a bar for a coffee and cognac.

Every day he drank between two and two-and-a-half litres of table wine and the same amount of piquette. He would also drink several brandies, cordials and one or two absinthes per day. At 5pm Lanfray and his father went home and each drank a litre of piquette. Lanfray's wife asked him to milk the family's 20 cows, at which he told her to milk them herself, which she did. He ordered her to give him coffee, then complained that it was not hot enough; then he noticed his boots, which had not been waxed, and began shouting at her. She shouted back, he told her to shut up, and she taunted him to make her. Lanfray went and got his old Vetterli repeating rifle, took aim, and shot her through the head. His father ran out of the building calling for help, his eldest daughter Rose ran in, to be shot in the chest by Lanfray, who then went to the cradle and shot the baby. He now tried to kill himself, but the barrel of the rifle was too long, so he tied a piece of string to the trigger and manoeuvred the weapon so he could shoot himself through the head, but the bullet missed his brain and lodged in his lower jaw.

Bleeding heavily, Lanfray picked up the corpse of the baby and carried it under his arm to the barn, where he lay down and fell asleep. He was found by the police, and taken to hospital in Nyon. Later he was taken to see his family in their coffins, where he said, 'It is not me who did this. Please tell me, Oh God, that I have not done this.'

The crime became headline news around the world. In the late twentieth century, cases of men killing their entire families became so common that they merited little expenditure of newsprint and would often make only local rather than national news. At the beginning of the century, however, such a crime was a horrendous event, to be compared in its monumental proportions only to Greek tragedy. Jean Lanfray was merely ahead of his time, but with no statistical background to demonstrate that, his awful crime had to have an immediate cause, and absinthe was primed for the role.

That Sunday, on 3 September, the villagers had a meeting, at which the culprit was named. 'Absinthe,' said the Mayor, 'is the principal cause of a series of bloody crimes in our country'. They got up a petition to ban absinthe in their canton of Vaud, within a few days obtaining 82,000 signatures.

Jean Lanfray had no fits, was not undernourished and he rarely drank more than two absinthes a day. This caused no problems for the opponents of absinthe, who now constructed an argument based on low intake. Albert Mahaim, a leading Swiss psychiatrist and a professor at the university of Geneva, examined Lanfray and said, 'without a doubt it is the absinthes he drank daily and for a long time that gave Lanfray the ferociousness of temper and blind rages that made him shoot his wife for nothing and his two poor children, whom he loved'.

Lanfray's trial started on 23 February 1906. His lawyers mounted an 'absinthe defence': that he had done it but was in a state of absinthe-induced delirium and was not therefore responsible for the murder. He was sentenced to life imprisonment, but three days later hanged himself in his cell.

At bottom this was the story of a man with a drink problem and a bad temper. Needless to say, Lanfray's total alcohol intake was not dwelt upon by the opponents of absinthe. A teetotal British Christian publication summarised, 'a drinker of absinthe had, in a fit of delirium tremens, killed his wife and children'.[18]

The Lanfray spark fell on tinder well prepared in Switzerland. The highly influential doctor Auguste Forel, now best known for his work on the cellular function of the brain, was a keen anti-alcohol campaigner. Born in 1848, he studied at Lausanne in Vaud and became Professor of Psychiatry at the University of Zurich Medical School in 1879. A complete abstainer, by way of example, he pioneered the treatment of alcoholism in the late 1880s, and like other anti-alcohol campaigners, based much of his message on eugenics and the supposed damage done to the race by alcohol. The medical approach to alcohol thus linked with social concerns which had produced an active campaign against absinthe that had been run since 1899 by the main abstinence society, the Blue Cross.

The canton of Vaud saw a vote on 10 May 1906 by the Grand Conseil of 126 to 44 for a law banning the sale of absinthe, though not its manufacture or consumption. A petition was got up to submit the law to a referendum, which took place on 27 September 1906. As a less than impartial observer noted, 'on the side of the public poisoners and on the side of the friends of the people great endeavours were made'.[19]

The defenders of absinthe said the new law was only the forerunner of prohibitive laws against wine. But the voters listened to the 'pastors, professors, doctors, surgeons and statesmen, who in great numbers spoke at public meetings, wrote in newspapers and endeavoured by all means to enlighten their fellow-citizens'. By 23,000 to 16,000 the law banning the sale of absinthe in Vaud was confirmed.

The way was now clear for a national ban. Fifty thousand signatures were required for a referendum, but by 31 January 1907 168,341 had been collected to revise article 32 of the constitution to forbid absinthe, more than had been collected for any referendum before, to 'free all honest Swiss citizens from the shame of seeing absinthe advertised all over the world with the white cross of the Confederation'.[20]

The vote, which took place on 5 July 1907, resulted in 236,232 in favour of a ban and 137,702 against. The distribution of votes was interesting in terms of the cultural make-up of Switzerland. Little absinthe was consumed in German-Swiss cantons, where the generally disdainful attitude of Germany towards absinthe prevailed. The ban would chiefly affect the French-Swiss, who both consumed absinthe and produced it. Understandably, in Neuchâtel, where 17 of the principal distilleries were situated, and in Geneva, where there were 11, there was a majority in favour of retaining absinthe. The law banning the production, sale and importation of absinthe came into force on 11 October 1910, with a payment of compensation of between £60,000 and £80,000 to the absinthe producers.[21]

Prohibition in Belgium was developed over the same period, though it was a matter of some dispute. In a heated debate in the upper house it was claimed that the bill had been sprung on the chamber at the end of the session (a common form of parliamentary ambush), and that some of the deputies who had sent it to the upper house admitted that they did not know what they were voting in.[22] Low consumption was given as a reason for the swiftness of the prohibition in Belgium, and the fact that there were no important commercial interests involved in the absinthe trade: Belgians drank less than 500 hectolitres a year, compared to France's consumption of more than 400 times that among a population of only six times the size.

The final vote took place on 23 February 1906, when absinthe was comprehensively banned, with a penalty of up to six months' imprisonment. The effectiveness of laws in changing deep-rooted drinking patterns remained to be demonstrated, however, as a writer to the *Times* noted in August 1907:

> the law prohibiting the sale of [absinthe] in Belgium appears to me to be a dead-letter. During the last few days I have had no difficulty in getting a 'Gernod' or a 'Verte Cusenier' whenever I

have asked for it. Taken in such a small quantity as, say, half an ounce, in plenty of iced water an hour before dinner, I have not found it poisonous.[23]

France now shared borders with two countries which had banned absinthe; the opposition was gaining ground. By 1906 a specific anti-absinthe campaign had been launched in France by the newly revivified temperance movement, which had resolved its internal problems and restructured as the Ligue nationale contre l'alcoolisme, now an effective campaigning body. Both houses of government, the Chamber and the Senate, had well-supported 'anti-alcohol' groups.

More than 400,000 French signatures were gathered on a 'petition against absinthe' declaring that

Absinthe renders people mad and criminal, provokes epilepsy and tuberculosis, and has killed thousands of French people. It makes a ferocious beast of man, a martyr of woman and a degenerate of the child. It disorganises and ruins the family and thus menaces the future of the country.[24]

In vain did such urbane characters as Adolphe Girod, deputy from Pontarlier remark to the chamber that he drank absinthe every day and felt no resemblance to a ferocious beast.

A debate which had been conducted at some level of knowledge in medical journals and newspapers was now in the cruder forum of political debate. In 1907, temperance groups decided to target mental illness, and made much of the increase in insanity, claiming that insanity diagnosed as being caused by alcoholism had increased by 37 per cent. With these statistics and the almost unchallenged assumption that absinthe causes insanity, a National Assembly deputy and temperance leader calculated that a person was 246 times more likely to go mad if they drank absinthe than if they drank wine. Henri Schmidt, a deputy, a pharmacist and temperance leader, told the Chamber of Deputies, 'The real characteristic of absinthe is that it leads straight to the madhouse or the courthouse. It is truly "madness in a bottle" and no habitual drinker can claim that he will not become a criminal.'[25]

When they went to the figures, anti-absinthe campaigners were often disappointed with the results. An inquiry into the cause of the illness of inmates of asylums found that out of 71,547, only 9994 were alcoholics. Of these, 1537 were described as suffering from absinthism. Some high absinthe-drinking regions had low rates of insanity and vice versa. The economist and former minister Yves Guyot attacked the faulty logic of the temperance campaign in his book *L'Absinthe et le délire persécuteur 'Absinthe and Paranoia'*. A Pontarlier state prosecutor, Edmond Couléru, analysed the results of the consumption of absinthe from 1871 to 1905 in a report to the Senate which was later a book, *Au Pays de l'absinthe (In Absinthe Country)*. He compared consumption rates with the rate of hospitalisation for insanity and with the level of violent criminality. He found, 'In this centre of absinthe manufacture, the pathological outbursts and disorders imputed to the action of that drink are less evident than in departments where large quantities of alcohol are consumed in other forms'. In fact, criminality in Pontarlier seemed to diminish over the period. Marie-Claude Delahaye has remarked that the proportion of entries to French psychiatric hospitals with alcoholism has remained high regardless of the consumption of absinthe.[26]

The situation was confused, however, as alcoholism was conflated with the argument over absinthe, so that drunks were described as absintheurs as a generic term, even if they never drank absinthe (rather like the American usage of referring to street alcoholics indiscriminately as 'winos' regardless of what they drank). This worked against the temperance campaigners' aim of using absinthe as a Trojan horse to enter the pro-alcohol camp, as whatever their precise intentions, absinthe was always taken as the target.

The National Anti-alcoholism League produced a poster announcing that 'each glass of absinthe is a step towards madness', but then diluted the message with another line: 'each bottle of alcohol leads to ruin'. So what was being attacked, alcohol or absinthe? Similarly, a poster of a tree showing in its branches various dire outcomes: prostitution, suicide, tuberculosis, and 'death of the race' are fed by the twin roots of absinthe and alcohol. The confusion was realised and attempts were made to address it, such as when temperance campaigners commissioned a painting in 1909 called *Alcohol Makes You Mad* (*L'Alcool rend fou*) from Philippe Zacharie. It showed a man with a pistol in one hand and a bottle in the other, looming over his murdered wife and child (the campaigns were never guilty of excessive subtlety). In common with other paintings touched by the green fairy, regardless of its title, it was always referred to as *L'Absinthe*.

There were annual attempts to ban absinthe from 1906 to 1909, which foundered more on financial than medical grounds. A ban on absinthe would cost the treasury both losses in tax revenue and in payments of compensation for the manufacturers who would lose their livelihoods. Parliamentarians were also accused of lacking personal motivation, as Sherard said: 'In the very buffet of the Chamber of Deputies whilst the absinthe habit and its ravages are being eloquently discussed from the benches, one can see many a parrot in the process of strangulation'.[27]

No temperance or legislative activity had any effect on actual consumption of absinthe, which in France which rose by 40 per cent between 1907 and 1911 despite the super-tax on it, in parallel with and outstripping a general increase in alcohol drinking.[28] 1913 was a bumper year for absinthe, with consumption reaching record levels, five-and-a-quarter million gallons consumed – though this represented a small proportion of the total alcohol intake.[29] Absinthe drinking was in fact concentrated along an axis from the mouth of the Seine to that of the Rhône, and along the course of these two rivers: some 13 administrative departments containing just over a quarter of the French population were responsible for 65 per cent of total absinthe consumption. It was Marseilles, not Paris, which had the highest rate, with an annual average consumption per inhabitant of three litres of absinthe.[30]

Laboratory work came to the aid of legislators with the isolation of thujone, the active ingredient of wormwood, by Dr Louis Duparc in 1908. A Senate committee had been set up in 1908 to investigate the absinthe question, though its report was not debated until June 1912, giving some idea of the urgency with which the matter was treated. The committee found absinthe was a poison, and recommended the banning of drinks containing thujone. This was an inspired solution which satisfied public-health requirements without, it was believed, destroying the absinthe industry, which could produce a highly alcoholic green drink without thujone.

Temperance campaigners argued bitterly that thujone was difficult to isolate, and there was no certainty that it was the only dangerous ingredient in absinthe, but it was to no avail. The campaigners had shot themselves in the foot by focusing on absinthe as a temperance measure; under the legislation now prepared, the alcohol content of absinthe could be retained along with most of its other constituents. The ban on drinks containing thujone was passed by the Senate and sent to the Chamber in 1912. It was referred to the hygiene commission, where nothing happened until the outbreak of war in August 1914.

The national emergency meant that while soldiers marched to the front, propagandists rushed to the presses, such as Léon Goulette, who wrote *L'Absinthe et l'alcool dans la défense nationale*, again considering absinthe and alcohol as separate, though he does describe absinthe as 'The most dangerous of all the alcoholic drinks', rather than considering it an entirely different entity.

Alfred Oulman in *Ruy Blas* expressed the feelings of many when he wrote that the war would cost them dear in money, but also in men: 'we have need tomorrow of a generation which is strong, vigorous and sane. It will not do for the men of tomorrow to still be able to find on each corner the horrible poison which kills then and renders them mad.'[31]

Tales were told of how absinthe was hindering national defence even as Germans were swarming into the *patrie*. Thus some days after the declaration of war, French soldiers arrived at a town to pass the night. The mayor of the unnamed town wrote to a newspaper, 'The cafés were taken by assault. More than sixty litres of absinthe were drunk. The next day, at reveille, a soldier, evidently alcoholic, got up hallucinating , seized a rifle and before anyone had the time to stop him, killed two horses and one of his comrades.' As soon as he heard of the incident, the mayor sent a letter to the cafés of his town forbidding the sale of absinthe to troops.[32]

The French general staff was banking on winning a short war through a decisive offensive in Lorraine. It launched such an attack over unsuitable terrain and gained a small patch of German-held territory. Meanwhile the German army was invading via neutral Belgium and occupying a swathe of northern France. The Germans came so close to Paris that the government was evacuated to Bordeaux before the Battle of the Marne, with its desperate image of troops being conveyed to the front in the capital's taxis, stalled the German advance. In the first four months of the war France lost 850,000 men dead, missing, wounded or prisoners, and yielded to German occupation one of its most important industrial and agricultural areas.

France's military failure in 1914 (and in 1870 and in 1940) pointed to a serious problem with her much-respected senior commanders, but no such challenge could be made at a time of calls to national unity. It was easier for the culprit to be one which had been clearly identified as the cause of national decline: absinthe.

On 16 August 1914 the Minister of the Interior called on prefects of departments to ban the sale of absinthe. This was a move to prepare civilians for the conflict and to reassure the nation that the government was in control and was taking resolute action. In fact the ban was administered in a haphazard way, with absinthe banned in retail outlets but still manufactured and circulated. Some prefects interpreted the ban to apply only to bars, so retailers could still sell it for home consumption, others were more stringent. There were widespread reports in newspapers of evasion of the ban and of the availability of absinthe.

Clearly a greater national sacrifice had to be made if the *Bosche* were to be kept at bay. As Finance Minister Ribot told the National Assembly, to vote for the bill to ban absinthe was an act of national defence.[33] The defenders of absinthe were reduced to patriotic appeals for generous compensation for the workers of the Doubs region, who had gone off to war and had their jobs legislated away in their absence. On 16 March 1915 absinthe was declared a toxic product, its manufacture and sale forbidden.[34]

To be fair to the French, their allies were acting in a similar fashion: an American cartoon of 1915 showed the anti-saloon campaigner Carrie Nation in the guise of Mars, having destroyed a house labelled 'French Absinthe' and another called 'Russian Vodka', now bearing down on 'Ye Olde English Inn'.[35] Italy had banned absinthe in 1913; alcoholism was such a serious cause of deficiencies in war production that the British in 1915 introduced licensing laws in an attempt to curtail drinking among armaments workers; Russia banned wines and spirits in 1914. The difference, as always in this tale, was that in France it was widely believed that banning one drink would solve the problem. At the same time legislation against absinthe was being enacted, the French high command was sending 1000-litre barrels of wine to the front to sustain troop morale.

Many of the artists associated with absinthe were now dead or scattered to other countries, and it fell to Picasso to make the bohemians' farewell to the green fairy. In 1913 he had become the first of the bohemians to move directly to commanding high prices for art without going through the Salons when his *The Family of Saltimbanques* sold for 11,500 gold francs. Despite outrage from the bourgeois press, it meant the avant garde had arrived at its destination.

In the climate of criticism of absinthe in spring 1914, he created six cubist bronze sculptures called *Absinthe Glasses*. Art critic Brooks Adams has remarked, 'Their celebration of the endangered absinthe was an emblem of his youth and of a whole era's excess – little bombs thrown in the face of high seriousness'.[36] Each is a different treat-ment of a goblet with a silver absinthe spoon and lump of sugar balanced on top. Picasso painted them all differently: one in stark black-and-white that 'alternately sticks out its tongue and makes a sign of the cross towards death', and the supposed fatality

Edgar Degas's *Au Café*, or *L'Absinthe* as it came to be called, 1876. Musée d'Orsay, Paris.

Vincent van Gogh with Absinthe, by his friend Henri de Toulouse-Lautrec. Vincent van Gogh Museum, Amsterdam.

The Absinthe Drinker, by Edouard Manet, 1859. Ny Carlsberg Glyptothek, Copenhagen.

The All Night Café, by Vincent van Gogh, 'a place where one can ruin oneself...'
Yale University Art Gallery, New Haven.

The same all-night café, painted by Paul Gauguin – Mme Ginoux drinks her
absinthe while behind her the postman sits with three prostitutes. Pushkin
Museum, Moscow.

The Green Muse, by Albert Maignan: the writer is seized with an absinthe inspiration.
Collection Marie-Claude Delahaye.

A. Bertrand's *Absinthe Drinker* of 1896 is closer to the reality than are the jolly girls in the posters. Musée de Pontarlier.

M. Boileau dans un café, by Toulouse-Lautrec. Cleveland Museum of Art: Hinman B. Hurlbut collection.

The Absinthe Drinker, by Picasso, 1901. Collection of Mrs Melville Hall.

The young cousin holds out the promise of fun and absinthe. Collection Marie-Claude Delahaye.

An advertising poster at the end of the nineteenth century becomes an art poster at the end of the twentieth. Collection Marie-Claude Delahaye.

The absinthe lobby protests the ban: the great days of the founding of the Swiss Confederation are contrasted with the murder of the green fairy by a ghoulish puritan. Collection Marie-Claude Delahaye.

Below
Louche twenty-first-century absinthe drinkers on the green promotional bus with the destination sign 'Oblivion'. Green Bohemia Limited.

of absinthe means 'all of Picasso's glasses qualify as sculptural memento mori'.[37] His father's recent death added poignancy to Picasso's reference to mortality.

One glass is coated with sand, another all black, recalling 'the satanic lull of absinthe taking effect', and black recurs through the six. Overall, Adams describes the rationale behind their creation:

> The edition's very existence as sculpture advocates absinthe's right to exist in 1914. By painting each sculpture differently, Picasso celebrates the individual's freedom of choice in matters of alcoholic consumption. The sculptures' open form suggests Picasso's open, political attitude about drug control. Legal restrictions on drugs repressed only the symptoms of workers' problems that were going to explode regardless.[38]

Ironically, the First World War, which sealed the fate of absinthe in France, also disproved the principal accusations against it. Conscription meant that doctors examined almost the entire adult male population and were obliged to accept that alcoholic damage to organs was as prevalent in those who drank 'hygienic' wines, beers and ciders as it was in the drinkers of spirits. Valentin Magnan died in 1916, the year after the ban, the culmination of his life's work of demonising absinthe which had begun in the 1860s.

Degas outlived his equals, on into the twentieth century, totally blind in one eye and almost so in the other, concentrating on sculpture so he could continue to work with his remaining senses until he lost his taste for sculpture too. He still cut a stately figure wandering around Paris in his Inverness cape, likened by some people to King Lear, oblivious of the events happening around him. 'Oh, that war?' he said when reminded of the conflict which had convulsed all of France.[39] He died in 1917, and his collection and his own works were auctioned to the distant sound of big guns.

11 Green in the USA

THE USA HAD SUCH MAJOR UPHEAVALS over alcohol in the first part of the twentieth century that absinthe was just a colourful marker bobbing about on a prohibitionist tide. Absinthe has maintained, however, a shadowy presence which became more distinct and enticing with the coming of the Internet in the late twentieth century.

Tour guides remark that when visiting New Orleans 'you absolutely must visit' the Old Absinthe House, the bar where the cocktail was said to have been invented.[1] Travellers have been so advised for the best part of two centuries. The Absinthe House has kept the name of absinthe alive in the USA, along with the memory of Louisiana's wild days of unrestricted drinking and prostitution.

Aleister Crowley, mystical poseur, wrote 'The Green Goddess' in the Absinthe House in 1916 while waiting for a woman friend.

> There is a corner of the United States which [time] has overlooked. It lies in New Orleans, between Canal Street and Esplanade Avenue; the Mississippi for its base. Thence it reaches northward to a most curious desert land, where is a cemetery lovely beyond dreams. Its walls low and whitewashed, within which straggles a wilderness of strange and fantastic tombs; and hard by is that great city of brothels which is so cynically mirthful a neighbour ... Art is the soul of life and the Old Absinthe House is heart and soul of the old quarter of New Orleans.[2]

Crowley, an eccentric and self-styled magician, was a link between the decadents of the 1890s and the writers of the twentieth century. His first book of poems, *White Stains*, was published by Leonard Smithers, the decadents' publisher. Crowley's use of absinthe was a minor feature in a life devoted to drug addiction and controlling other people by means of bogus supernatural powers. 'I have myself made extensive and elaborate studies of indulgence in stimulants and narcotics,' as he put it.[3]

'What is there in absinthe that makes it a separate cult?' he asked. 'The effects of its abuse are totally different from those of other stimulants. Even in ruin and in degradation it remains a thing apart: its victims wear a ghastly aureole all their own, and in their peculiar hell yet gloat with a sinister perversion of pride that they are not as other men.'[4] Crowley wrote much in the same vein, which showed how he missed his vocation, for he could have been a very fine writer but was too arrogant to subject himself to the discipline of the good editor he so obviously needed.

He travelled to New Orleans in 1916 and, as he said in his memoirs, 'took a room conveniently close to the Old Absinthe House, where one could get real absinthe prepared in fountains whose marble was worn by ninety years' continual dripping'.[5] This passage shows how the mystique of absinthe blended in with the personalities of the writers. There may well have been a limited amount of under-the-counter absinthe available, but by 1916 absinthe had been banned for four years and the fixed fountains (40 years old at most) would be used publicly only to drip water into anise drinks. Absinthe had never been prepared in fountains. The errors are interesting from the point of view of what the old fraudster Crowley thought his readers would swallow about absinthe by the time he was writing his memoirs in the 1920s.

New Orleans was by way of being a city of eternal decadence in the industrious America of the nineteenth century. The state of Louisiana owed its cultural appeal to the fact that it was held by the French until it was sold to the USA in 1803, retaining its French style and contacts, so such French specialities as absinthe were freely available. A drink called 'absynthe' was appearing in advertisements in 1837, though it was thought to be not much known in other parts of the country.[6]

The building later to be called the Old Absinthe House, on Bourbon Street and Bienville, was constructed in the middle of the eighteenth century, and in 1806 was established as an importing and commission house. Later it became a grocery store. Absinthe was imported and sold there at least from 1826 in what was described as the first established saloon in New Orleans. The role of absinthe seems to have been that of a variety of drinks available in a hard-drinking area. By 1836, with a population of 60,000, New Orleans had 543 licensed premises, with doubtless many unlicensed also; gambling houses and brothels added to the city's attractions.[7]

The best-known character in this environment, whose name is often associated with absinthe, is Edgar Allen Poe, who was born in Boston in 1809. Poe, whose work had so influenced Baudelaire (and thereby Verlaine) was a severe alcoholic binge drinker who inter-spersed long periods of sobriety with heavy drinking bouts which reinforced his reputation as a self-destructive genius. Poe's father, brother and sister were alcoholics, or at least very heavy drinkers.

Poe could not drink a glass of anything without going on to absolute drunkenness, as his lawyer friend Frederick W. Thomas said: 'His was one of those temperaments whose only safety is in total abstinence'.[8] Like any alcoholic, he would drink the strongest alcohol easily available, and the proposition that he might not have drunk absinthe is far more unlikely than the proposition that he did. A fellow student of his at the University of Virginia described him as drinking with a passion: 'It was not the taste of the beverage that influenced him; without a sip or smack he would seize a full glass, without water or sugar, and send it home at a single gulp'.[9] The drink could have been absinthe, which would explain the reference to sugar and water, but no further information is available.

Poe's publisher, John Sartain, was certainly an absinthe drinker, and when Poe and his friend Henry Beck Hirst would visit Philadelphia with him they drank a mixture of absinthe and brandy.

His work showed a taste for the macabre, for death, violence and mystery, and the love and death of beautiful women, 'much of Madness and more of Sin'. He foreshadowed Baudelaire and Rimbaud, over whom some absinthe influence can be argued, but also over such other American practitioners of the gothic as H.P. Lovecraft and Anne Rice, for whom absinthe has not been claimed to be a factor.

The brooding self-recrimination of his characters, such as the narrator who is guilty of horrible crimes in *The Black Cat*, bring to mind absinthe-induced reveries, but absinthe's role in the creation of nineteenth-century gothic horror seems more part of a scene than a motivating factor. Absinthe does not feature a single time in the concordances for Poe's poetry and prose. Biographers and contemporaries did not mention it as a remarkable aspect of Poe's alcoholism, and absinthe was an imported drink which had to come in from France and Switzerland; the perennially hard-up Poe would have got drunk more cheaply on brandy.

By the 1830s, when Poe was in his twenties, it was said that New Orleans had 'the most luxurious drinking palaces in the county... Drunkenness was very prevalent.'[10] The bar which became the Old Absinthe House was called Aleix's Coffee House in 1846. In the Civil War, with its devastating consequences for Louisiana, it became a rendezvous for army officers and others in the Confederate army.[11] In 1869, the owner, Jacinto Aleix, hired Cayetano Ferrer, who was to become a major figure in the history of alcohol in the USA, as 'principal drinks mixer'. Ferrer, from Barcelona, had learned his trade as barman at the Paris Opera House, and he introduced the Louisiana public to the dripped absinthe 'served in the Parisian manner'.

Ferrer leased the bar, which he called the Absinthe Room, and which made him, and absinthe, famous. In 1874 he produced a cocktail, absinthe frappé, comprising egg white, anisette and absinthe poured over cracked ice. The whole building came to be called the Absinthe House. Visitors to the city would not think their tour of the attractions complete until they had sampled Ferrer's absinthes.

In a book on famous New Orleans drinks, Stanley Clisby Arthur writes, 'What the customers came for chiefly was the emerald liquor into which, tiny drop by tiny drop, fell water from the brass faucets of the pair of fountains that decorated the long cypress bar'.[12] Ferrer was introducing the New Orleans public to the bourgeois refinements of drinking absinthe with elaborate water drippers, the paraphernalia adding to the cost of an already expensive drink. In the post-Civil War period of the 'gilded age', when everyone wanted to forget the misery of war and reconstruction and enjoy life again, absinthe was one of a number of refinements.

The Absinthe House was so proud of its tradition as a tourist attraction that it became a custom for visitors to tack their calling cards on the walls and ceilings, so the impression was given of a location to which people had flocked from all over the world. Indeed, New Orleans was a major destination; Degas, whose mother was a Creole from New Orleans, visited his two brothers, who were cotton merchants in the city in 1872 in the wake of the Franco–Prussian War and the commune.

Mark Twain, Walt Whitman, O. Henry and William Makepeace Thackeray were among other literary visitors, and Oscar Wilde drank in the Absinthe House in June 1882. Wilde had been commissioned by Richard D'Oyly Carte to undertake a lecture tour in the USA to promote aestheticism. D'Oyly Carte's Gilbert and Sullivan musical *Patience*, which satirised aesthetes, was performing in New York, and D'Oyly Carte had the inspired idea to promote its future success by bringing over a real aesthete at whom the American media could poke fun. Wilde, never one to miss an opportunity for self-promotion, consented immediately. This was Wilde's first public incarnation, as an aesthete – 'decadence' followed.

While it was a familiar drink in Louisiana at the end of the nineteenth century, knowledge of absinthe remained limited through the heydays of the Absinthe House, even on the sophisticated east coast. In August 1879 a Dr Richardson was quoted in the *New York Times* giving the most basic supposed facts about it:

The suggestion on offering absinthe is that it is an agreeable bitter, that it gives an appetite, and that it gives tone to weak digestions... it is coloured green with the leaves or the juice of smallage, spinach or nettles...The action of absinthe on those who become habituated to its use is most deleterious. The bitterness increases the craving or desire, and the confirmed habitué is soon unable to take food until he is duly primed for it by the daily provocative.

The piece finishes with a warning that 'In the worst cases of poisoning by absinthe the person becomes a confirmed epileptic'.[13]

Clearly the *New York Times* quickly became expert on the subject, as two months later, in October 1879, it was reporting with authority,

The dangerous, often deadly habit of drinking absinthe is said to be steadily growing in the country, not among foreigners merely, but among the native population. A good many deaths in different parts of the country, especially in large cities, are directly traceable to excessive use of absinthe. It is much more perilous, as well as more deleterious, than other forms of liquor. It is more seductive and treacherous; for at first there is very little reaction from it; it quickens the mental faculties, lends a glow to the health and spirits, and seems, to express it mathematically, to raise the mind to a higher power...A regular absinthe drinker seldom perceives that he is dominated by its baleful influence until it is too late...All of a sudden he breaks down, his nervous system is destroyed; his brain is inoperative; his will is paralysed; he is a mere wreck; there is no hope of his recovery. Victims of intemperance of the common sort frequently reform, but the absinthe drinker, after he has gone to a certain length, vary rarely does or can throw off the fatal fascination. The more intellectual a man is, the more readily the habit fastens itself upon him. Some of the most brilliant authors and artists of Paris have killed themselves with absinthe and many more are doing so. Only a few years since, absinthe could not easily be got in this country, save in big cities; now it can be had almost everywhere, and is called for with alarming frequency.[14]

Absinthe easily fitted in with the prohibitionist message, which was being forged into legislative power in the USA. A report of 1880 gave an abbreviated version of the downward path of the absinthe drinker: 'The habitual drinker becomes at first dull, languid; is soon completely brutalised and then goes raving mad. He is at last wholly or partially paralysed, unless, as often happens, disordered liver and stomach brings a quicker end.' The writer warns of the dangers to the unwary:

> Many people have been induced to take absinthe for indigestion, and have thus gradually fallen under its baleful influence ... The earliest symptoms of ailment lead to an examination, and to the knowledge that his entire system is deranged, usually beyond restoration. His first illness is apt to be his last, and death is a welcome relief.[15]

Clearly no amount of absinthe is safe, even a small amount for medicinal purposes, only total prohibition can save the unwary from the effects of 'this most alluring poison'.

By 1884 *New York Times* readers were accustomed to the horrors of absinthe, when a triple-decker headline announced, 'The Charms of Absinthe ... The Allurements it Holds Out to its Victims ... And the Sting That Comes Afterward.'

The tale is of a cynical, sophisticated Frenchman drinking absinthe at a bar in New York and apparently corrupting a 'thoughtful and dudesque' young American who had been trying to look 'dissipated and rakish'. The sallow-faced Frenchman tells his story to the youth: he was once a medical student, aged 24, successful at his studies but melancholy and unpopular, until he took an absinthe to relieve his unhappiness. Soon he 'took it regularly night and morning. I grew to crave for it.' Finally, he confesses, 'I just escaped a lunatic asylum'. Now he drinks absinthe in moderation.

What appears, therefore, as if it will be a Henry James story of cynical Europe corrupting a naive American 'anxious to receive new impressions' is in fact a temperance warning. The young man vows never to touch absinthe, 'in tones of awe, forgetting to be dissipated'.[16]

In a similarly, though even more, lurid vein, short-story writer W.C. Morrow writes of Arthur Kimberlin, a stranger in San Francisco, starving and with nothing left to pawn, in a story called *Over an*

Absinthe Bottle, published in 1897. Taking shelter from the rain in a bar doorway, a man invites Kimberlin in to have a drink. They sit in a private booth and the man sends for a bottle of absinthe, a pitcher of water and some glasses. 'Ain't goin' to drink all o' that, are you?' asks the barman, already lending a sense of foreboding to the drinking session.[17] The man gives Kimberlin some money, and then plays dice with him for its return. It is a melodramatic piece with a jerky plot, its interest in the fact that absinthe is felt to be the drink of men of mystery like the desperate, dying gambler and the starving adventurer who both die over the dice and the absinthe bottle.

A writer in the New York magazine *Harper's Weekly* in 1907, at a time when an absinthe ban was in force in Belgium and under active discussion in Switzerland and France, was concerned at 'the growing consumption in America of absinthe, the "green curse of France"'. There was no scepticism about the report, which asserted with no supporting evidence that absinthe was 'recognised as being almost as fatal as cocaine in its blasting effects on the human body'. It described the effect of continued use as being 'a deep melancholy, followed by homicidal tendencies'.

The writer blamed absinthe's popularity on a song, 'Absinthe Frappé', written in 1904 by the lyricist Glenn MacDonough. It celebrated the hangover cure which had been developed by Cayetano Ferrer at the Absinthe House. The lyric ran:

It will free you first from the burning thirst
That is born of a night of the bowl,
Like a sun 'twill rise through the inky skies
That so heavily hang o'er your soul.
At the first cool sip on your fevered lip
You determine to live through the day,
Life's again worth while as with dawning smile
You imbibe your absinthe frappé.[18]

The procedure for making absinthe frappé was later described: 'To a split of cool champagne in a tall highball glass you add one jigger of absinthe shaken vigorously in cracked ice'.[19]

Before 'Absinthe Frappé' was sung, the *Harper's* writer noted, absinthe 'was little known and less indulged in among the general public, but the catchy air served to familiarise it'.[20] MacDonough had already written some of the lyrics for the hit stage musical *The Wizard of Oz* in 1903 for Victor Herbert, an Irish-American who incidentally was the first composer to write film music.

The *Harper's* writer noted that absinthe had attracted the attention of the Department of Agriculture, where an investigation had been ordered to determine to what extent absinthe was being manufactured. Wormwood was widely available in the eastern USA, it 'grows wild upon almost every farm'. Wormwood was cultivated in order to produce oil of wormwood for medical purposes (demonstrating the continued use of this folk remedy in the twentieth century). The oil was also used for horse and cattle remedies in the USA, and was exported for the European market, which took as much oil of wormwood as the USA supplied. The writer assumed that government action would be taken to check the development of an absinthe industry, but not prevent the manufacture of medicinal wormwood oil.

The Pure Food Board of the Department of Agriculture in December 1911 decided that the import of absinthe should be banned. Dr Wiley, head of the board, said 'absinthe is one of the worst enemies of man, and if we can keep the people of the United States from becoming slaves to this demon we will do it'. This statement rather lacked temperance, as little, if any, evidence had been brought forward to support the claim that any damage had been done by absinthe in the USA.

The banning of absinthe was, however, in keeping with a trend towards prohibition throughout the Western world. Countries which banned absinthe before the USA, as well as those already mentioned, were Brazil, Holland, Canada, Argentina and Germany.

This was also a period of the increasing legislative control of mind-altering drugs, indicating that what was happening over absinthe was not a reaction to its uniquely dangerous effect, but a manifestation of an increasing government interest in policing the public use of recreational drugs. The same meeting which banned absinthe announced a series of measures to restrict the import of morphine, opium and cocaine.[21] The Harrison (Narcotic) Act of 1914 banned the use of drugs off-prescription, and provided the model for drug prohibition legislation throughout the Western world. In the UK, for example, the import of cocaine and opium was banned in July 1916. There were other crossovers in the new field of addiction studies: Magnan, who had done so much work on 'absinthism', was also interested in cocaine to such an extent that one of the withdrawal symptoms of the habitual cocaine user, the feeling of a foreign body under the skin, is still called 'Magnan's sign' after him.

Food Inspection Decision 147 in 1912 banned the import of absinthe into the USA and its sale in inter-state commerce. This was officially a 'pure food' decision made with reference not to facts garnered in the USA but to decisions made in other parts of the world. The statement said, 'it is generally recognised that this beverage is dangerous to health'. The use of the term 'generally' is generally an indication that the writer has not checked but has accepted the conventional view.[22]

Newspapers covered attempts at shipping absinthe into the USA, but the absinthe story was subsumed into the bigger picture of teetotal agitation and prohibition.[23] Absinthe was a very minor issue in US national debate, if it were mentioned at all. Newspaper coverage of legal action against absinthe was in small pieces, indicating the comparative lack of importance accorded it compared to the actions of the Anti-Saloon League and successive state votes on prohibition. Georgia was in the lead of the national drive against alcohol, having agreed state-wide prohibition in 1907. Banning the use of minor drugs was reaching ridiculous proportions in the USA at this time: in New York City the Sullivan Ordinance of 1907 banned women from smoking cigarettes in public.

Alcohol prohibition measures were already enforced in other countries: spirits and other strong drinks were banned in Iceland between 1908 and 1934, Russia 1914–24 and Finland 1916–27. In this context the prohibition era in the USA from 1920 to 1933 seems less of a bizarre anomaly. Prohibition was passed in 1919 by the Eighteenth Amendment and enforced by that October's Volstead Act. Such absinthe substitutes as Pernod and Herbsaint had been used to keep an alcoholic drink with an aniseed flavour in circulation, but by 1920 liquor sellers had more on their minds than maintaining a taste for absinthe.

Prohibition did not succeed in its primary aim, to prevent the drinking of alcohol; its main achievement, by criminalising a widely practised activity, was a multiplication in the number of criminals. New Orleans was a major centre for the import of illegal alcohol, with smugglers running drinks in via the Mississippi. Most restaurants and cafés in New Orleans served alcohol during prohibition, but made efforts to conceal it from the general view. The surreptitious nature of drinking in the prohibition era – waiters serving alcohol from hip flasks, barmen squirting a syringe of pure alcohol into soft drinks they were serving – was not conducive to absinthe, which was a drink of display and provocation. Moreover, as a specialist drink, it was even less easily available than wine, beer or whiskey.

For some, the extra illegality of absinthe made it a special challenge at a time when breaking a foolish law was an expression of individual independence. Elizabeth Anderson, wife of short-story writer Sherwood Anderson and part of the literary scene in New Orleans, wrote in a memoir,

> There was a great deal of drinking among us but little drunkenness. We all seemed to feel that Prohibition was a personal affront and that we had a moral duty to undermine it. The great drink of the day was absinthe, which was even more illegal than whiskey because of the wormwood in it. Bill Spratling [who worked at Tulane University] had bought ten jugs of it from some woman whose bootlegger husband had died, and he shared his booty liberally with his friends. It was served over crushed ice, and since it did not have much of the taste of alcohol that way, it was consumed in quantities.

Anderson gives some indication of her husband's character, and the expectation of male American drinking, when she writes,

> Sherwood drank absinthe, but never cared what he drank or if he drank at all. He had the natural kind of high spirits that carried everyone along on the crest of his enthusiasms. But he thought of himself as a hard, two-fisted drinker because that is what he believed men should be.

When she met a woman reporter in the Absinthe House, by this time a speakeasy, both sipped absinthes, and the reporter, filled with the need to share her taste of forbidden fruit, announced in her pages, 'Miss Elizabeth spends her days sipping absinthe in a popular New Orleans bistro'.[24] New Orleans was so blatant in its continued drinking that it was described as the 'liquor capital of America', and inevitably attracted attention from federal agents, who raided the city in their hundreds in 1925. The Absinthe House was closed under 'padlock proceedings' for violation of prohibition in 1925 and again in 1926. A newspaper article noted that

> The place has been identified with some of the most colourful meetings in the history of New Orleans. The military of the old Spanish regime and then of the French rubbed shoulders there with actors, artists and noted men of all professions. The marble font bears deep fissures worn by the constant dripping of soda in the preparation of the milky concoction from which the place drew its name.[25]

The Absinthe House was to celebrate 100 years of doing business in 1926, but as the *New Orleans Picayune* noted: '[the] doors of the historic old Absinthe House were closed on its hundredth anniversary Saturday when the United States marshal nailed them together following a padlock injunction of the United States Court'.[26]

After the doors were nailed shut, many of the fittings were sold to a Pierre Cazebon, including the cash register, the pictures on the walls, the old fountain to drip water onto absinthe, and the marble-topped bar. He moved them down Bourbon Street to open another bar, later to be called the Old Absinthe Bar, which also came under attack from the authorities in October 1929, when 'deputy United States marshals descended on the old bar, placed the proprietor, Pierre Cazebon, and the bartender, Sam Mitchell, under arrest and clamped a padlock on the door'.[27]

Prohibition was finally lifted in 1933, but as absinthe had been banned for eight years before prohibition, its use had declined, and by 1933 few felt moved to revive it. It was the North American expatriates and travellers Robert Service, Harry Crosby and Ernest Hemingway, following on the earlier travels of Jack London, who now made the most of absinthe – the green fairy was now part of the thrills of travel, enticingly illegal in their own country. It was not now the drink of effete intellectuals and poets, it was a man's drink for sailors, war correspondents and other manifestations of the tough guy in world literature.

Jack London was born in 1876 in San Francisco, and grew up in poor circumstances. He tried his luck working in a factory, as an oyster pirate, hoodlum and seaman, finally got his grades and started to study. He then went to Alaska as a gold digger, lived for months in the London slums, and travelled the world drinking heavily, as he reported in his memoir of his relationship with drink, *John Barleycorn* of 1913. He recounted how he went to the south sea islands in 1907 (where, incidentally, Gauguin had died four years previously).

A crewman's error had left a water tap open, which drained their 1000-gallon drinking-water tank, leaving only a precious 10 gallons in another container, so they were limited to two pints of water per person. London remarks, 'So it was that I reached the Marquesas the possessor of a real man's size thirst. And in the Marquesas were several white men, a lot of sickly natives, much magnificent scenery, plenty of trade rum, an immense quantity of absinthe, but neither whisky nor gin.' London drank absinthe, seemingly without enthusiasm, 'The trouble with the stuff was that I had to take such inordinate quantities in order to feel the slightest effect'. This may have been inferior absinthe, therefore, or a peculiarity of London's constitution, for of all the complaints which have been levelled against absinthe its weakness as an alcoholic drink has not featured. London sailed on 'with sufficient absinthe in ballast to last me to Tahiti, where I outfitted with Scotch and American whisky'.

London died of kidney failure at his ranch in 1916 at the age of 40; whether or not this was a suicide by overdose of morphine is disputed. His use of absinthe is very much that of the adventurer-traveller, seeking new experiences and writing about exotic lands for a highly literate public still linked to the daily grind but with a taste for vicarious thrills.

From the same stable was the poet Robert Service, who was born in England in 1874, brought up in Scotland and trained as a bank clerk, then emigrated to Canada at the age of 21. He worked as a ranch-hand, then returned to banking, and it was in this capacity in 1904 that he was sent to the Yukon, where the Klondike gold-rush had recently taken place. Here he wrote the popular thumping ballads of outdoor life that were to make him famous, of such characters as Dan McGrew and Sam McGee. He was celebrated by others as 'the Canadian Kipling', though he represented himself as a Scot.

He worked as a newspaper correspondent, covering the Balkans War of 1912–13, and then settled in Paris, in an attic on the Quai Voltaire (though he could afford a higher class of accommodation), where he created the character of the Bohemian for another book of verse, *Ballads of a Bohemian*.

This book presents Service as the same bard of the boulevards as he had been of the Yukon, 'I'm a reckless painter chap who loves a jamboree,' as one character says.[28] His persona is a man who 'kicked over an office stool and came to Paris thinking to make a living by my pen', meaning he would starve in a garret in a world full of tarts, thugs, cabaret singers, and mysterious meetings with artists and eccentrics. He meets such characters as the absinthe drinker, who has sat for 20 years in the Café de la Paix nursing a hatred for a rival in love, with his hand on a revolver in case the enemy should appear.[29]

The Bohemian dreams of: 'Oh Wilde, Verlaine and Baudelaire, their lips were wet with wine;/ Oh poseur, pimp and libertine! Oh cynic, sot and swine!/ Oh votaries of velvet vice! ... Oh gods of light divine.' He prays for his art: 'Before I drink myself to death./ God, let me finish up my Book! ... Rare absinthe! Oh it gives me strength/ To write and write.'[30]

In the First World War, Service was a war correspondent for the *Toronto Star*, then joined an ambulance corps set up by young Americans in Paris who wanted to be involved before the USA entered the war. The Bohemian also joins up, his life becoming a war story and his verse war poetry. This tale, of the bohemian life turning into life on the Western Front, is one which has every appearance of being the truth, rather close to the lives of many bohemians.

Another adventurer who landed on the shores of bohemia was Harry Crosby, born in 1898 to a wealthy Boston banking family, and able to devote his entire life to cultivating a bohemian image. He was influenced by Baudelaire and the French symbolists, and by the English decadents, particularly Wilde, whose *Picture of Dorian Gray* he took as an instruction manual on how to live the decadent life. He was another whose life was touched by the First World War, again as an ambulance driver, in which role he was nearly killed at Verdun, leaving him with a sense that he had been preserved for some special role.

He lived the life of hedonistic excess which was available to those who inherited wealth, and was aped by other more impoverished Americans who went to Europe in the inter-war period. His wife Caresse found Crosby 'electric with rebellion' for his wild indulgences.[31]

Absinthe was a deliciously dangerous forbidden fruit, though opium was far more his drug of choice, and absinthe may have been no more a major drug for him that cocaine or hashish. His diaries are full of the boyish fun of minor transgression, as if he feels the need to proclaim, as much to himself as to the world, that he is the sort of chap who takes opium, drinks absinthe, meets aristocrats and engages in adventurous sex.

> 15 March 1925 Jasper invented Enosinthe, half-absinthe, half Eno's
> Fruit Salts…29 November 1925 we met the count and he came
> to tea and five glasses of absinthe…12 June 1928 I went and pro-
> cured in a bookshop a bottle of very old absinthe (it was a choice
> between this or an erotic book with pictures of girls making
> love)…17 November 1928 [on re-entering the USA] I go through
> the customs my pockets stuffed with opium pills, flasks of
> absinthe and the little Hindu Love Books.[32]

He was a poet, though one of those better known for their lifestyle
than their verse. His wealth and literary aspirations meant he was
able to help authors, so the Black Sun Press, set up to publish his
poetry, was also used for the publication of D.H. Lawrence's *The
Sun* and James Joyce's *Work in Progress*.

Obsessed with death, Crosby talked of suicide for years, and
evaluated suicide techniques: jumping from a plane, poison, leaping
into a volcano. On 9 December 1929, his lover Josephine Bigelow
sent him a poem ending 'Death is our marriage'. She got her wish.
On 10 December he and Bigelow took off their shoes in a borrowed
New York apartment and lay on the bed together, fully clothed.
Crosby put a .25 automatic pistol to her head and pulled the
trigger. Some time later, without moving from the bed, he shot himself.[33] The last words he wrote were, 'There is only one happiness/
it is to love and to be loved,' a bold statement which was used as
the motif for the 2001 film *Moulin Rouge*.[34]

One of his expatriate friends, who Crosby met three years before
his death, was Ernest Hemingway, born to a comfortable family
in Illinois in 1899. He became a reporter, like Service and Crosby,
served in the First World War driving ambulances, and was wounded on the Austro–Italian front.

Hemingway was based in Paris in the 1920s, where he met such
American writers as F. Scott Fitzgerald and Gertrude Stein, and
began to write stories about frightened gangsters and boxers down
on their luck, and ageing bullfighters like the one in *Death in the
Afternoon*, who needs to drink three or four absinthes to get into the
bullring. Hemingway invented a champagne-and-absinthe cocktail

that he also gave the name 'death in the afternoon'. Absinthe also features in Hemingway's tale of the 'lost generation' of post-World War One American writers who stayed in Europe, *The Sun Also Rises*.

He had a passion for wars, going to observe the Japanese invasion of China and the Second World War as a correspondent, though it is the Spanish Civil War with which he is most associated. Spain had never banned absinthe, which was one of its attractions for Hemingway. Indeed, Pernod moved production to Tarragona in Spain after the French ban.

In Hemingway's *For Whom the Bell Tolls*, the protagonist, Robert Jordan, is an American volunteer fighting for the democratic government against the fascists. At one point he takes out his hip flask of absinthe and is asked what it is; he replies that it is medicine. But what is the medicine for?

'"For everything," Robert Jordan said. "It cures everything. If you have anything wrong this will cure it."'

He lets his companion have some, but hopes he will not take too much, as

> there was very little left and one cup of it took the place of the evening papers, of all the old evenings in cafés, of all the chestnut trees that would be in bloom now in this month, of the great slow horses of the outer boulevards, of book shops, and kiosks, and of galleries, of the Parc Montsouris, of the Stade Buffalo, and of the Butte Chaumont, of the Guaranty Trust Company and the Ile de la Cité, of Foyet's old hotel, and of being able to relax and read in the evening; of all the things he had enjoyed and forgotten and that came back to him when he tasted that opaque, bitter, tongue-numbing, brain-warming, stomach-warming, idea-changing liquid alchemy.

Jordan explains, 'It is supposed to rot your brain out but I don't believe it. It only changes your ideas.' His companion, however, makes a face and remarks that 'It is better to be sick than have that medicine'.[35]

Hemingway had first been to Paris in 1918, and had lived there in the 1920s; he had never been there when absinthe was freely available. The memories he gives Robert Jordan are not his own but already, by the time they were written in 1940, relate to an absinthe-scented Paris of the mind.

Hemingway went sea fishing and big-game hunting, married four times and settled in Cuba, where he could obtain absinthe, and in Florida. 'Got tight last night on absinthe and did knife tricks,' he wrote to a friend in 1931, 'Great success shooting the knife underhand into the piano'.[36]

Hemingway was awarded the Nobel Prize in 1954, but his mental and creative powers were failing, not improved by electro-convulsive therapy; in 1961 he committed suicide with a shotgun. It is difficult not to see these men as living out the dregs of a bohemian dream in Europe between the wars. If absinthe contributed to their art it was in a very minor way.

In the inter-war years in Europe absinthe was a dead issue; it was rare to find any mention of it. An exception was a writer in the *Lancet,* who warned of the continued use of absinthe in England by the smart set in 1930. He wrote of being informed 'by a member of an exclusive London club that when a cocktail is ordered it is customary to inquire whether a "spot" shall be added – that "spot" being absinthe'. Another informant told him of a cocktail 'with a kick in it' being ordered 'by the more hardened cocktail drinker', and that the 'kick' is often obtained by adding absinthe. He was alarmed that absinthe was still used when it had been so widely banned, and was unconcerned that consumption was still very low, noting that in seven years between 1885 and 1892 absinthe use increased by almost 125 per cent in France, and 'there is no reason to suppose that a similar increase would not occur in England if fashion and folly should so ordain it'.[37]

Evelyn Waugh and his brother Alec drank absinthe in London, but rather self-consciously, as Alec wrote many years later: 'Not many people alive today have drunk it. I did in the Domino Room at the Café Royal. I took it with appropriate reverence, in memory of Dowson and Arthur Symons, Verlaine, Toulouse-Lautrec and the Nouvelle Athènes … I only drank it once for I loathed the taste of it.'[38]

It is significant that even these records are of a socially rarefied, high-society absinthe use, the sort of cocktail-set people with whom Harry Crosby would have felt at home. By the middle year of the twentieth century absinthe had become a historical curiosity, hardly worthy of comment.

The hedonistic 1970s led to renewed interest in forbidden fruits and new forms of personal expression. In this atmosphere Maurice Zolotow wrote a lengthy feature on the social history of absinthe in *Playboy* magazine. *Playboy* featured quality writing alongside pictures of naked women, put together with an anti-establishment stance which placed *Playboy* against the Vietnam War and sexual censorship, and tolerant of soft drugs.

Zolotow wittily remarks that a guilty conscience is that part of the human being that is soluble in absinthe; he tells its story and gives a recipe for an absinthe cocktail, a 'Suissesse', and also tells a personal anecdote of a time when he had sex with a women after drinking absinthe which she had supplied.[39] Absinthe was making tentative steps into the counter-culture, the most energetic ideology in the 1970s.

The counter-culture mobilised over Vietnam, women's issues, civil rights, rock music and drugs, all of which were an assault on the old order. The use of drugs as an act of social defiance and personal liberation received the official response of more stringent enforcement measures.

The greater restriction of absinthe was a small part of this. While the import and sale of absinthe had been banned in 1912, now thujone was banned as a food additive according to Section 801A of the Federal Food, Drug, and Cosmetic Act of August 1972. Wormwood was included on a list of unsafe herbs which the Food and Drug Administration released in 1975. An incipient absinthe revival was quickly terminated.

The English writer Wendy Perriam uses absinthe in her frothy 1980 novel *Absinthe for Elevenses,* in which the drink is a symbol of the dangerous, exotic lifestyle of flashy psychoanalyst Caldos de Roche, whose girlfriends have 'absinthe for elevenses instead of ginger nuts', the fare of the novel's suburban heroine who falls in love with the dastardly seducer.

Absinthe continued to be available in Spain and some parts of eastern Europe, but it was the end of the Cold War in the late 1980s and early 1990s US tourism to Prague which brought the absinthe boom of the 1990s; in bars where young Americans would soak up the atmosphere of this new bohemia and dream of writing the Great American Novel.

Their experiences were often similar to those of Chuck Taggart, a writer on New Orleans cuisine who confided to the worldwide web that on his 1996 trip to the Czechoslovakia he called at the Globe Coffeehouse and Bookstore in Prague and sampled the elusive liqueur.

> I was quite curious, and in the interests of taking a dip into New Orleans history, I ordered some. It was emerald-green, and was served neat – not in the old traditional manner, with an absinthe spoon and sugar cube. I don't think tradition would have helped. It was ... rather vile, actually. It had a powerful kick, due to its high alcohol content, and my travelling companion opined that it smelled to him rather like turpentine. Unfortunately, its flavour resembled turpentine as well, and was nothing like the Herbsaint pastis that I had come to enjoy so much. I didn't notice any particular effect from the thujone content, and if I had to drink copious amounts of this swill to get any effect, I declined to find out if the effect was forthcoming.[40]

As absinthe entered the global information age, the green fairy presented her last secret: why did the experience of absinthe in the twenty-first century so miserably fail to match up to descriptions of it in the nineteenth?

12 Pop Goes the Fairy

ABSINTHE SUFFERED ITS WIDESPREAD BANS at the beginning of the twentieth century, at a time when other drugs were also being banned or restricted, including opiates, cannabis and tobacco. It was appropriate therefore that absinthe was making a return in the last years of the twentieth and the first years of the twenty-first century, when attitudes towards recreational drugs were again relaxing.

The revival of commercial absinthe began in Czechoslovakia, where the drink had never been outlawed. It became popular during the Second World War, when a rationing system was put into effect by the Nazi regime based on volume of liquid rather than strength. People soon realised that a drink with little liquid but a high alcohol content gave better value for money; they could buy absinthe, water it down and still have a strongly alcoholic drink.

After the war the new communist regime confiscated the distilleries, along with other businesses in private hands. Among those who lost out were the Hill family, whose distillery making absinthe and other drinks was taken from them. Famously, Radomil Hill memorised his father's recipes and saved a book of other original recipes from that period. Absinthe was not officially produced after 1948, and Hill worked in state-owned distilleries and liqueur companies, but he never used or divulged his own recipes. After the 'Velvet Revolution' of 1989, Hill started to rebuild the family business, so that in 1992 a new plant was acquired in the southern Bohemian town of Jindrichuv Hradec.

Following the fall of the Berlin Wall and the collapse of the Soviet Empire, young Europeans and Americans flooded into historic Prague to enjoy the experience of newly liberated eastern Europe. Not surprisingly, given the two-minute culture of the twentieth century *fin-de-siècle*, the bohemian avant garde in the 1990s comprised not authors and painters but popular musicians and magazine writers, several of whom can claim the rediscovery of absinthe. The rock band the Sugar Cubes, best known for their lead singer Björk, visited Prague as a promotional gesture, as the city was said to be the place where the first sugar cube was made. An obvious local photo opportunity was to picture the band with the traditional Czech method of drinking absinthe: dipping a cube of sugar on a spoon into the undiluted absinthe, setting it alight then stirring it into the absinthe in the glass while adding just enough water to douse the flames. The Sugar Cubes took the drink to the thriving club culture of Iceland, where it was recognised as a fascinating new trend by the many British young people who visited the scene in Reykjavik.

Another musician, John Moore of the Jesus and Mary Chain, tried absinthe after a performance in Prague, and in 1997 wrote about it in a fashionable London magazine, the *Idler*. He introduced the *Idler*'s founder Tom Hodgkinson and art director Gavin Pretor-Pinney to absinthe and they, together with a businessman called George Rowley, set up Green Bohemia to import absinthe to Britain for the celebrations of the millennium. They brokered a deal with the Czech firm headed by 81-year-old Radomil Hill.[1]

The launch in December 1998 emphasised the drink's colourful and even dangerous history, and the artist absinthe drinkers of the past. An advertisement for Hill's, 'Tonight we're gonna party like it's 1899', cleverly combined a sense of history with fun in the present. Absinthe was promoted as 'the spirit of freedom', with a warning to licensees not to sell anyone more than two shots of it: a brilliant marketing ploy which also protected the distributors from claims of irresponsibility in selling a dangerous product. Press coverage predictably ranged from amused fascination to outrage, depending on the sophistication of the newspaper.

For the young creatives working in the advertising industry or on the fringes of the music business, drinking in trendy Soho bars amid chrome and blond wood, to be sitting before a glass of absinthe was to have the glamour of a transient world bottled and on display. The green fairy had once again become what was socially expected of her. Buoyed up on expectation and the taste of forbidden fruit, the young trend-setters duly experienced heightened perceptions. As a club critic put it,

> Giovanni and I drank six or seven of these preparations and stumbled off in the early evening to The Player Club, which was just being built at the time. The place had just been decorated and the totally kitsch P insignia carpet had just been laid. The two of us sat there gawking at it for hours. Man! that thing was wriggling around in front of us like a bucket of eels.[2]

Inevitably, such harmless fun provoked official reaction. In late 1990s Britain absinthe was also a daring and dangerous luxury in a culture becoming dismally homogenised. Repeated warnings and restrictions on soft drugs, diet and smoking had already caused a reaction, so that for example smoking was on the increase among the young as a pleasing gesture of defiance to authority. Absinthe fitted this mood precisely, as Tom Hodgkinson said: 'For me, one of the principal attractions of absinthe is that by drinking it, one is cocking a snook at New Labour's nanny culture. This is a government that seems to enjoy banning things.'[3]

This was prophetic. On the eve of the Green Bohemia operation in December 1998, the member of parliament for Bolton South East, Brian Iddon, asked Home Office Minster George Howarth what assessments he had made for policy regarding the availability of narcotics, considering Green Bohemia's intention to sell absinthe.

'I have identified no such implications,' he replied. 'Absinthe does not come within the scope either of domestic legislation on the misuse of drugs or of the international conventions on the control of narcotic or psychotropic substances.'[4] Clearly someone thought again, as two weeks later the government was said to be ready to ban imports of absinthe 'amid fears that drinking the hallucinogenic green concoction is becoming a dangerous new craze'. Howarth said the reappearance of absinthe was a 'cause for deep concern'. He said he would consider referring the issue to the government's Advisory Council on the Misuse of Drugs, saying, 'We shall be keeping a very close eye on this to see if sales take off'.[5]

This approach provoked the withering contempt of journalist Michael Bywater, who wrote,

> It's not banned yet, but little Mr Blair has let it be known that he is keeping a close eye on the matter and if it becomes popular he will ban it... [that] remark tells us more than we might wish to know about little Mr Blair's 'government'...the urge to invade private behaviour is a pestilential infection among the political class.[6]

There was clearly some scratching of heads in Whitehall, and the government backed away from absinthe. Whatever the individual feelings of ministers, a ban would be difficult to achieve in a climate of liberalising drug use where mere possession of cannabis is often no longer prosecuted, and ecstasy may be redesignated to reduce prosecutions. The moves on recreational drug use, taken reluctantly as an effective admission of the failure of prohibitory drug laws, would sit badly with proposals for fresh bans.

The legal position is that thujone is controlled, in common with many other active substances. European Union regulations stipulate that no more than 10 parts per million of thujone should be sold in alcoholic drinks containing more than 25 per cent alcohol. Where a national ban existed, as it did in France, these regulations had no effect; they were to permit safe levels of use in countries which had no ban.

New interest in absinthe spawned a multifarious sub-culture, which flourished in the glowing, unregulated world of Internet sites. 'The Emerald Quest', run by art historian Alex Goluszko, is an illustrated log of travels, experiences and research related to absinthe describing how various individuals have travelled to sample new absinthes and visit old distilleries. It is advertised as 'a sort of scrapbook of memories and curiosities. It hopes to one day become a knowledgebase of hard to find information for the absinthe-ignorant masses.'[7]

In keeping with the fascination about absinthe as a cultural phenomenon, Marie-Claude Delahaye opened an absinthe museum in 1994 in Auvers-sur-Oise, the town where van Gogh killed himself. Her interest had long preceded the fashionable revival of interest in absinthe, however – she had first become interested in the drink when she found an absinthe spoon in an antique market in 1981, and resolved to discover all she could about it. The museum contains an original collection of art and books featuring absinthe, lithographs, satirical drawings and absinthe impedimenta such as decorative spoons and water fountains, and has a life-sized model of an 1890s bar.

The town museum in Pontarlier has two rooms well stocked with items recalling the heady days of absinthe production in the town, and such events as the great absinthe fire of 1901, when the Pernod factory was hit by lightning. In the ensuing blaze, a quick-witted warehouseman opened the safety valves to allow the highly inflammable alcohol to flow into the river Doubs, which therefore ran with absinthe, allowing townspeople to dip a cup into it to drink, a vision of paradise or hell depending on one's point of view.

Pierre Guy and Les Fils d'Emile Pernod, two distilleries in Pontarlier still producing liqueurs, do a good trade in showing visitors the great copper alembics where absinthe was once made and selling bottles of their current product, which does not include absinthe. The green fairy had changed again in France, from destroyer of the nation to a curiosity for coach-loads of tourists in the great national theme park.

Countries which maintained a ban, such as the USA, found absinthe endlessly fascinating. A hard rock band from Boston, Massachusetts took the name Absinthe, and the goth sub-culture revelled in the heady, illicit atmosphere of absinthe with some, such as Absinthe Notuk of Oklahoma, taking the name of the forbidden nectar.[8]

D.J. Levien found absinthe a rich metaphor of bitterness for his 1999 satire on Hollywood, *Wormwood,* in which the hero Nathan Pitch is a story editor at a studio (notably, therefore, he is presented as not himself creative but leeching on the creativity of others). He becomes addicted to absinthe and suffers insomnia, nightmares and bad sex in a world where 'true talent was a lagging second to good hype'.[9]

Absinthe was once again a handy metaphor for decadence and wickedness, but this time civilisation was not considered to be threatened. A world which had witnessed the horrors of the twentieth century was not going to be unduly alarmed by a green drink, in marked contrast to the world of the 1890s, where peace and progress had reigned for generations. Now absinthe's temptations were entertainment, as in Francis Ford Coppola's 1992 film *Bram Stoker's Dracula* and Albert and Allen Hughes's 2001 *From Hell,* on the theme of Jack the Ripper.

In keeping with the new image of absinthe, Baz Luhrmann's *Moulin Rouge* used popular signer Kylie Minogue to represent the green fairy of absinthe and, with deliberate anachronism, had characters singing the words of late-twentieth-century pop songs. The absinthe culture of the twenty-first century was that of popular music, though the artistic haven of nineteenth-century Paris remained as a lingering worldwide myth with absinthe as its enduring symbol.

A search for absinthe in mid-2002 found more than 94,000 mentions on websites, doubtless most of them trivial. Many were recipes for cocktails, there were advertisements for the sale of absinthe or absinthe impedimenta and homely advice on do-it-yourself absinthe. There was no shortage of people eager to put their experiences at the service of the worldwide web, though these experiences tended to involve an urge to talk, poetic inspiration and difficulty in walking, all of which could be accounted for by drinking strong alcohol. They revealed themselves on such sites as 'The Vaults of Erowid', where a college student enthused, 'My roommate had explained that people from America's past had raved about this drug until it was outlawed, so I decided the trip must be somewhat enjoyable. However I was wrong. This stuff tasted like liquid dog shit! I could barely drink a two ounce bottle without gagging uncontrollably.'[10]

Many website reports found absinthe literally undrinkable, but gave advice to persevere, such as: 'absinthe may be nasty, but you'll find the more you drink the less you'll care'; 'try to get through your first glass within ten minutes'; and 'ignore your taste buds. They are your worst enemy'.[11]

Fear Heiple, who runs an absinthe bar at the hedonistic Burning Man festival, contributed a recipe for do-it-yourself absinthe, which involves infusing an ounce of dried wormwood in 750ml of vodka for 10 days, then adding angelica, hyssop, coriander, caraway, cardamon and fennel, and leaving for another four days.[12]

Inevitably, some do-it-yourself practitioners discovered why absinthe has a reputation as a dangerous substance. The *New England Journal of Medicine* in 1997 carried a report titled 'poison on line – acute renal failure caused by oil of wormwood purchased through the internet'. It described the case of a 31-year-old man who was found at home by his father in an agitated, incoherent and disorientated state. He was taken to hospital, where in the emergency room he was lethargic but belligerent. His mental status improved after treatment with haloperidol, and he reported finding a description of absinthe on the Internet. Finding another site offering essential oils used in aromatherapy, the man purchased a 10ml bottle of oil of wormwood and drank it, on the assumption that oil of wormwood was the same as absinthe when in fact it is a concentrated form of one of the drink's ingredients.

His incoherent state when he was found by his father was due to acute renal failure, which is commonly caused by injury, seizures, infections and drugs. The man recovered after eight days in the hospital, and was clear of the toxic effects of his encounter with wormwood after 17 days.[13]

Not all appreciated the new openness about absinthe. The US military newspaper *Stars and Stripes* ran two articles on absinthe in February 2001 with a strapline 'Hot trend – although illegal in many places, absinthe is regaining popularity among the young'. A service person from Okinawa immediately wrote to the *Stars and Stripes* ombudsman to say, 'The person who wrote it disregarded responsible journalism and the long-term potential effects by popularising an illegal substance … How many young people will now look into this? Hope none read it.'[14]

For those who did get hold of absinthe from eastern Europe in the first wave of the absinthe revival, there were several problems: it stayed green with water and did not louche; it was by all accounts to be drunk in shots, not a palatable drink to be sipped on boulevards as it was in the green hour; it did not taste or smell strongly of aniseed; it did not give rise to hallucinations, or even very different mental activity. The reason for the failure of this absinthe to measure up to the experience of the nineteenth century was that the Czech product was not the absinthe drunk by Verlaine, Toulouse-Lautrec and van Gogh. Czech absinthe is very highly alcoholic, at 70 per cent proof, but with little further similarity to French absinthe of the past. Hill's, for example, has 1.8 parts per million of thujone, well below the legal limit of 10 parts per million; it is not made with anise, and does not have essential oils held in alcohol which louche on contact with water.

Purists protested to Green Bohemia that they should not be marketing the eastern European product as if it were French absinthe. Among them was Marie-Claude Delahaye, who then co-operated with the company in launching a French-style absinthe, La Fée Verte, made to a nineteenth-century recipe containing wormwood, anise, lemon balm and hyssop among other herbs. It was legal for it to be made in France, but not sold there. It contains 68 per cent alcohol, an undisclosed 'respectable but legal dose' of thujone, and louches with water.[15] Keeping the popular-music theme established with their Czech product, its symbol is an eye modelled by singer Sarah Nixey of Black Box Recorder.

After a time on mail order, Fée Verte went on sale in Britain in February 2002 at a cost of £36 per bottle (at a time when a pint of beer would cost £2–2.50 in a public house, a bottle of moderate table wine £4 in a supermarket). Over the same period, 1998–2002, a dizzying range of other absinthes from France, Bulgaria, the Czech Republic and Spain came on the market. The 'Angelfire' website boasts 'old absinthes have returned', and a variety of sites discuss the varieties and colours of louche and quantity of thujone in each brand.[16] A good deal of vitriolic criticism is directed on enthusiasts' websites at the makers of supposedly inferior brands for their deficiencies of taste and failure to include sufficient thujone in the mixture.

Mysteries remain, however, as the new absinthes obstinately failed to deliver the promised artistic inspiration. One of the best informed of the modern aficionados of absinthe, Alex Goluszko, wrote of the aperitif's supposed hallucinogenic qualities,

> the absintheurs of today – those who've sipped on vintage and contemporary brews alike – discern none of the 'effects' perpetuated in myth. Other than the obvious influence of high proof alcohol, the Green Fairy's spell lies in a sense of lucidity, which tends to render the ethanol intoxication less burdensome – even then, this peculiar wakefulness is fleeting and even completely unnoticed by some.[17]

The main reason for the disparity between the experience of absinthe past and present is the different levels of wormwood. Phil Baker gives a helpful clue when he remarks that in the nineteenth century absinthe was generally served with sugar, but he has never had a modern absinthe in need of sugaring.[18] As the bitterness is a product of wormwood, it is reasonable to conclude that twenty-first century absinthe contains less *Artemisia absinthium* than the nineteenth-century drink, and that consequently the thujone content is lower.

As absinthe was produced from a variety of recipes by large commercial and small independent distillers, it is impossible to say what level of thujone was present in the nineteenth-century product, which anyway could doubtless vary widely between one batch and another.

One figure sometimes quoted is 260 parts per million, but as this comes from an 1855 paper which was self-published, it must be treated with scepticism as regards both the sensitivity of the assay and the lack of scrutiny of the method used.[19] It does, however, accord with Arnold's estimate that nineteenth-century absinthe could contain 260 parts per million, though that is based not on an analysis of the drink but an assessment based on the percentages of thujone in the dried ingredients which were known from old recipes to be included in absinthe. This assumes that the percentages of thujone in the plants will manifest themselves in the same percentages in the drink as bottled.[20]

An estimation of 152 parts per million for old absinthe has also been printed, and between 60 and 90.[21]

Detailed research was carried out in 2002 by Ian Hutton, who scorns the high figures for thujone, noting that analytical techniques available in the nineteenth century were not capable of separating thujone from the related compounds present in the essential oils used to make absinthe. Hutton, of the company Liqueurs of France, subjected samples of old and new absinthes to gas chromatography to analyse their chemical make-up. He took vintage Pernod fils from 1900, a sample of absinthe made from an illicit still in Switzerland, and two modern commercial products. The vintage absinthe had six parts per million of thujone, the commercial products eight and ten. The illicit Swiss absinthe had 25 parts per million. Hutton remarked that 'even at the highest concentrations found in any of the samples tested, the effects of alcohol would far outweigh those of the thujone'.[22] He supports the view, always held by absinthe industry experts in the nineteenth century, that the health problems experienced by chronic users were likely to have been caused by adulterants in inferior brands.

Research has also been done on the way absinthe works to produce a unique effect. Karin M. Höld and colleagues at the University of California and Northwestern University Medical School in Illinois in 2000 produced a lengthy and detailed paper based on meticulous research work on thujone and the brain.

The object of the study was to examine thujone in relationship to chemicals which inhibit brain activity called Gamma-aminobutyric acid (GABA).

When sites for its action are unobstructed, GABA inhibits or moderates the activity of neurones – that is it quietens down mental activity. Höld and colleagues compared the action of thujone with picrotoxinin, a known blocker of GABA receptors, to find it similar. They examined thujone's activity in fruit flies and mice, and in brain tissues from mice and rats. They found, based on four different tests, that thujone blocks the GABA receptors, 'thereby providing a reasonable explanation for some of the actions of absinthe other than those caused by ethanol'.[23]

To simplify: thujone blocks neural inhibition activity, allowing the brain's chemistry to fire off too easily and randomly, giving an explanation for the unusual thoughts said to be stimulated by absinthe. Moreover, as GABA inhibits uncontrolled brain activity, it follows that too much suppression of the GABA receptors leads to convulsions, always said to be a concomitant of 'absinthism'.

Richard W. Olsen from University of California School of Medicine later reviewed recent work to state that thujone does not, contrary to previous suspicions, behave in a similar way to cannabis, though it does share a low affinity to the receptor binding sites of the active ingredient of cannabis. 'Cannabinoids,' he says, 'are central-nervous-system depressants, like a sleeping pill', while thujone excites the brain.

It is unsurprising to him that thujone produces mood elevation and anti-depressant effects, but he warns of too simple a conclusion: 'do not forget, however, that in absinthe one is balancing the effect of thujone with the intoxicating, disinhibitory and depressant effects of ethanol'.[24]

Similarly, in a timely article titled 'What's Your Poison?' in the *British Medical Journal* for December 1999, the authors reminded a partying public that whatever potential damage could be done by small levels of thujone in modern absinthe,

there is a grave danger of demonising a particular drink and thereby missing the wider importance of alcohol related harm...As our
knowledge of multiple organ damage, neurotoxicity, and diverse
psychiatric sequelae of excessive alcohol use has increased, the
possibility emerges that much of the syndrome of absinthism was
actually acute alcohol intoxication, withdrawal, dependence and
other neuropsychiatric complications: major health and social
problems, but not unique to absinthe.[25]

The BMJ's advice is a model of good sense which fits in with the
liberal, tolerant guidance expected by the educated public in today's
Britain. Any scientific fact is ductile and plays to the gallery of
contemporary concerns, so that scientific knowledge is mediated
by the cultural milieu.

In the 1850s and 1860s, when French artistic society was
seemingly going crazy with new ideas, to the discomfort of the
bourgeoisie, absinthe was scientifically demonstrated to make
people mad. After 1870, when societal concerns were that the
French population was too small to withstand a perceived German
military threat, scientists were on hand to demonstrate that
absinthe causes not just individual madness but the degeneration
of the entire race. In the 1970s, scientists were excited by recreational drugs and worked to demonstrate that absinthe had a
similar action to cannabis. In the late 1990s, scientists working with
molecular technology and clinical detachment were eager to
demonstrate that absinthe caused its effects because of chemical
reactions in the brain. Science today thus shows a state-of-the-art
approach to the cultural scene, as it always has done.

In terms of absinthe use, as the excitement of forbidden fruit
wears off, absinthe will find itself one of a number of similar drinks
with unusual properties. For example, there are many other drinks
which contain oils suspended in alcohol, such as ouzo and
Jägermeister. Jägermeister, a 'cult product made of fifty-six herb
products and fruits' is a 70 per cent proof liqueur which is drunk
ice cold.[26] Ouzo is made from anise and alcohol distilled from raisins
and louches when ice is added. It also has an important cultural

meaning in Greece, such that bars serving little else, called ouzeries, were once to be found in every town, and where men would sit for hours talking and fiddling with worry beads. As a high-alcohol drink available in the Mediterranean heat, ouzo can be dangerous for the unwary tourist who, lured by its attractive taste, drinks far more than they normally would and becomes, literally, blind drunk. For the same reason it was a problem for British troops stationed in Greece in the Second World War, who were forbidden to drink it after excess led to damage. However, there is no suggestion that Greece should ban ouzo, which poses no danger when used sensibly. Similarly, tequila, fermented and distilled sap from the pina (core) of the blue agave cactus, is claimed to have mildly hallucinogenic effects. Agave juice was long used as a herbal remedy, and Aztecs are said to have believed it came from the gods. Any of these could have filled the role occupied by absinthe in the nineteenth century.

Absinthe, as developed in Switzerland and mass produced in France at the beginning of the nineteenth century, was the right product at the right time. It had sufficient alcohol to be the major alcoholic drink at a time when social dislocation and a vine blight led to an increase in alcohol consumption. Its physical properties of changing colour with water and attractive aroma made it adaptable for use by those with refined tastes when they were in the ascendant. It had sufficient psychoactive properties for it to be a favoured drink of the creative when social change, available money and national movement made for the development of centres of artistic excellence. Its unique properties were vastly exaggerated by both its supporters and its detractors to suit their own requirements.

As for the present, absinthe is a high-alcohol, mildly psycho-active substance. Particularly with current restrictions on the levels of thujone, only an alcoholic would drink enough of it to cause serious mental disturbance; by that time the damage done by the alcohol would be grossly apparent. Drunk to excess, absinthe is a social evil, but then, as the experience of eighteenth-century England showed, so is gin.

Excessive use may bring on incipient mental illness, but this is both unproven and makes it no more of a problem than many other substances. Treated with no more than usual caution, absinthe is not dangerous. Some people will abuse it, but this will be because of their tendency to abuse substances, not because of inherent qualities in the drink itself.

Its position is well summed up by the sophisticated *bon viveur* and bibliophile George Saintsbury: 'I suppose (though I cannot say that it ever did me any) that absinthe has done a good deal of harm'.[27]

Appendix: 'Lendemain'

Avec les fleurs, avec les femmes
Avec l'absinthe, avec le feu
On peut se divertir un peu,
Jouer son rôle en quelques drames.

L'absinthe bue un soir d'hiver
Eclaire en vert l'âme enfumée
Et les fleurs sur la bien-aimée
Embaument devant le feu clair

Puis les baisers perdent leurs charmes
Ayant duré quelques saisons
Les réciproques trahisons
Font qu'on se quitte un jour sans larmes

On brûle lettres et bouquets
Puis le feu se met à l'alcôve
Et si la triste vie est sauve
Reste l'absinthe et ses hoquets.

Les portraits sont mangés des flammes
Les doigts crispés sont tremblotants
On meurt d'avoir dormi longtemps
Avec les fleurs, avec les femmes.

Charles Cros

An English translation of 'Lendemain' is on page 43.

Notes on the Text

Works are referenced in full the first time they occur in any chapter.

Introduction: The Devil Made Liquid

1   It should be said that, as it is not sweet, absinthe is not technically a
    liqueur. It is so frequently referred to as such, however, that this fine
    distinction is also ignored here.
2   Balesta, Henri, *Absinthe et Absintheurs*, Paris, 1860, p.62.
3   Marrus, Michael R., 'Social Drinking in the Belle Epoque', *Journal of
    Social History*, vol. 7 no 4, Winter 1974, p.122.
4   Trevor, John, *French Art and English Morals*, Liverpool, 1886, p.8.
5   Prestwich, P.E., 'Temperance in France: The Curious Case of Absinthe',
    Historical Reflections (Canada), vol. 6 no 2, Winter 1979, p.303.
6   Delahaye, Marie-Claude: *L'Absinthe, histoire de la Fée verte*, Paris, 1983;
    L'Absinthe, muse des peintres (with Benoît Noël), Paris, 1999; *L'Absinthe,
    muse des poètes*, Auvers-sur-Oise, 2000; *L'Absinthe, son histoire*, Auvers-sur-
    Oise, 2002. Other Delahaye works, not referred to in *Hideous Absinthe*,
    include *L'Absinthe, art et histoire*, Paris, 1990; *L'Absinthe, les cuillères*,
    Auvers-sur-Oise, 2001 and *L'Absinthe, les affiches*, Auvers-sur-Oise, 2002.
7   Prestwich, op. cit., p.319.
8   Sournia, Jean-Charles, *A History of Alcoholism*, Oxford, 1990, p.77.
9   Arnold, Wilfred Niels: 'Absinthe', *Scientific American*, vol. 260, June 1989,
    pp.86-91; 'Vincent van Gogh and the Thujone Connection', *Journal of
    the American Medical Association*, vol. 260 no 20, 25 November 1988,
    p.3042; *Vincent van Gogh: Chemicals Crises and Creativity*, Boston, 1992.
10 Lanier, Doris, *Absinthe: The Cocaine of the Nineteenth Century*, Jefferson,
    1994, p.vii.
11 Ibid., p.156.

12 Conrad, Barnaby, *Absinthe: History in a Bottle*, San Francisco, 1988, p.xi.
13 Baker, Phil, *The Dedalus Book of Absinthe*, London, 2001, p.11.

Chapter 1: Bitter Beginnings

1   Revelation 8:10–11.
2   Proverbs 5:4.
3   Jeremiah 9:15; Lamentations 3:15.
4   Plinius Secundus, C., trans. Philomen Holland, *Historia Naturalis*, London, vol. II, 1601, p.276. Pliny does not here claim, as is frequently remarked, that the charioteer receives the wormwood as a reminder that victory can also be bitter.
5   Kightly, Charles, *The Perpetual Almanack of Folklore*, London, 1987, entry for October 18 (no page numbers).
6   Culpeper, N., *The Complete Herbal and English Physician, Enlarged of 1653*, London, 1995, pp.274–75.
7   Delahaye, Marie-Claude and Noël, Benoît, *L'Absinthe, muse des peintres*, Paris, 1999, p.14.
8   Shakespeare, W., *Romeo and Juliet*, 1:iii, 30–32.
9   Sieur Martin in *Aphorismes et Conseils de l'Ecole de Salerne*, quoted in Delahaye, Marie-Claude, *L'Absinthe, muse des poètes*, Auvers-sur-Oise 2000, p.17.
10 Zolotow, Maurice, 'Absinthe', *Playboy*, June 1971, p.174.
11 Podlech, D., *Herbs and Healing Plants of Britain and Europe*, London, 1996, p.70.
12 *Oxford English Dictonary*, 'Wormwood', 5.
13 *Notes and Queries*, 13 September 1851, p.193.
14 *Times*, 26 April 1872, p.10.
15 Arnold, Wilfred Niels, 'Absinthe', *Scientific American*, vol. 260, June 1989, p.86.
16 Early local historians who told this tale were Alphone Pierrepont, in his 1871 *Un demi-siècle de l'histoire de Neuchâtel 1791–1848* and Edmond Quartier-La-Tente in a review of Neuchâtel history in 1893. Both sources are discussed in Delahaye, Marie-Claude, *L'Absinthe, son histoire*, Auvers-sur-Oise, 2002, pp.29–30 and refs.
17 Ibid., p.30.
18 Zolotow, op. cit., p.174.

19 Delahaye, Marie-Claude, *L'Absinthe, histoire de la Fée verte*, Paris, 1983;
    and L'Absinthe à Pontarlier website.
20 Arnold, op. cit., p.89.
21 From a display in the Absinthe Museum, Auvers-sur-Oise.

Chapter 2: The Green Hour and the New Art

1   Goncourt, Edmond and Jules de, *Pages from the Goncourt Journal*, London,
    1984, p.15. He also prayed that his urine should be less cloudy and for
    little flies to stop stinging his backside.
2   Millot, Maurice, in Delahaye, Marie-Claude, *L'Absinthe, muse des poètes*,
    Auvers-sur-Oise, 2000, p.36.
3   Anon., 'The House of Absinthe', *Once a Week*, 11 July 1868, p.29.
4   Balesta, Henri, *Absinthe et Absintheurs*, Paris, 1860, pp.12–13.
5   Delahaye, *L'Absinthe, muse des poètes*, op. cit., pp.22–23.
6   Decroos, P., *La réglementation légale de l'absinthe*, Paris, 1910, p.250. Quoted
    in Delahaye, Marie-Claude, *L'Absinthe, histoire de la Fée verte*, Paris, 1983
    p.76.
7   Delahaye, *L'Absinthe, muse des poètes*, op. cit., pp.51–52.
8   Goncourt, op. cit., p.392.
9   *New York Times*, 14 October 1879, p.4.
10 Dumas, Alexandre, *A Dictionary of Cuisine*, London, 1958, pp.38–39.
11 Bourgeois, Edmond, 'A Musset', in Delahaye, *L'Absinthe, muse des poètes*,
    op. cit., p.61.
12 More, Julian, *Impressionist Paris*, London, 1998, p.39.
13 *Times*, 4 May 1868, quoting *Pall Mall Gazette*.
14 Ponchon, Raoul, 'La mort de Pelloquet', in Delahaye, *L'Absinthe, muse
    des poètes*, op. cit., p.28.
15 Goncourt, op. cit., p.57.
16 Hamilton, George Heard, *Manet and His Critics*, New Haven, 1954,
    pp.30–31.
17 Hartley, Anthony, *Introduction to French Verse III: The Nineteenth Century*,
    London, 1957, p.xxvii.
18 I am grateful to Professor Simon Harvey, in a personal conversation,
    for this insight.
19 Delahaye, *L'Absinthe, muse des poètes*, op. cit., p.62.
20 Hamilton, op. cit., pp.21–22.

21   Stuckey, Charles F., 'Manet Revised: Whodunnit?', *Art in America*, 71, November 1983, pp.162–63; Delahaye, Marie-Claude and Noël, Benoît, *L'Absinthe, muse des peintres*, Paris, 1999, pp.45–46. The lack of consistency in translating the titles of French paintings is deliberate, aimed at making clear distinctions between paintings with very similar titles. The title Manet gave this picture was *Le Buveur d'absinthe*.

22   Moreau-Nélaton, Etienne, *Manet raconte par lui-même*, Paris, 1926, p.26; Hamilton, op. cit., p.22.

23   Proust, Antonin, *Edouard Manet: Souvenirs*, Paris, 1913, p.33.

24   Moore, George, *Confessions of a Young Man*, Montreal, 1972, pp.102–5.

25   Marie-Claude Delahaye was responsible for the insight that absinthe drinking was seen as a sign of women's emancipation. Personal communication, 23 December 2002.

26   'Brutal Saxon', *John Bull's Neighbour in Her True Light*, London, 1884, p.35.

27   Balesta, op. cit., p.46.

28   Delahaye and Noël, op. cit., p.52.

29   Ibid., p.49.

30   Quoted in Delahaye, *L'Absinthe, muse des poètes*, op. cit., p.187.

31   Delahaye, Marie-Claude, *L'Absinthe, son histoire*, Auvers-sur-Oise, 2002, p.128.

32   Ibid., p.170.

33   Delahaye, *L'Absinthe, muse des poètes*, op. cit., p.229.

34   Sherard, R.H., *Twenty Years in Paris*, London, 1905, p.382.

35   Delahaye, *L'Absinthe, muse des poètes*, op. cit., p.150.

36   McMullen, Roy, *Degas: His Life, Times and Work*, London, 1985, p.165.

37   Delahaye, *L'Absinthe, muse des poètes*, op. cit., p.140.

Chapter 3: Absinthe for the People

1   Sherard, R.H., *My Friends the French*, London, 1909, p.42. Sherard lived in Paris only after 1883 so is not referring to the situation in the late 1850s, but there is no reason to suppose that drinks for the poor were less adulterated than previously.

2   Delahaye, Marie-Claude, *L'Absinthe, muse des poètes*, Auvers-sur-Oise, 2000, p.220.

3   Marrus, Michael R., 'Social Drinking in the Belle Epoque', *Journal of Social History*, vol. 7 no 4, Winter 1974, p.124.

4   Balesta, Henri, *Absinthe et Absintheurs*, Paris, 1860, p.62.

5   Ibid., p.28.

6   Ibid., p.76.

7   Sherard, op. cit., p.40.

8   Dumas, Alexandre, *A Dictionary of Cuisine*, London, 1958, p.38.

9   Balesta, op. cit., p.54.

10   Sherard, op. cit., p.40.

11   Balesta, op. cit., pp.56–57.

12   Prestwich, P.E., 'Temperance in France: The Curious Case of Absinthe', *Historical Reflections* (Canada), vol. 6 no 2, Winter 1979, p.302.

13   Hooper, Lucy H., 'Parisian Maniacs and Madhouses', *Lippincott's Magazine*, June 1878, p.764.

14   McMullen, Roy, *Degas: His Life, Times and Work*, London, 1985, p.202.

15   Schneider, Pierre, *The World of Manet*, New York, 1968, p.21.

16   McMullen, op. cit., p.139.

17   Bouret, Jean, *Degas*, London, 1965, p.239.

18   Pickvance, Ronald, 'L'Absinthe in England', *Apollo*, 15 May 1963, p.395.

19   McMullen, op. cit., p.86.

20   Bouret, op. cit., p.91.

21   McMullen, op. cit., pp.252–53.

22   Delahaye, Marie-Claude, *L'Absinthe, histoire de la Fée verte*, Paris, 1983, p.79.

23   Marrus, op. cit., p.117.

24   Balesta, op. cit., p.87.

25   Ibid., p.89.

26   Beck, J. and T., *Elements of Medical Jurisprudence*, London, 1842, p.580.

27   Nickell, Joe and Fischer, John F., *The Skeptical Inquirer*, vol. 11 no 4, Summer 1987, pp.352–57.

28   Balesta, op. cit., p.89.

29   Hooper, op. cit., p.764.

30   Sournia, Jean-Charles, *A History of Alcoholism*, Oxford, 1990, p.81.

31   Marcé, L., 'Sur l'action toxique de l'essence d'absinthe', *Comptes rendues hebdomadaires des Scéances de l'Académie des Sciences*, vol. 58, 1864, pp.628–29, quoted in Arnold, Wilfred Niels, *Vincent van Gogh: Chemicals, Crises and Creativity*, Boston, 1992, p.104.

32   Anon., 'Absinthe and Alcohol', *Lancet*, 6 March 1869, p.334.

33   Anon., 'New Researches on the Properties of Absinthe', *Lancet*, 7 September 1872, p.341.

34 Magnan, V., 'On the comparative action of alcohol and absinthe', *Lancet*, 19 September 1874, p.410.

35 Ibid., p.412.

36 Dupuy, B., *Absinthe: Ses propriétés et ses dangers*, Brussels, 1875, p.44.

37 *Pêle-Mêle*, 1902 and *La Vie Pour Rire*, 1900, quoted in Delahaye, *L'Absinthe, muse des poètes*, op. cit., pp.286, 287.

38 Balesta, op. cit., pp.65–66.

39 Vogt, Donald D., 'Absinthium: a nineteenth-century drug of abuse', *Journal of Ethnopharmacology*, 4, 1981, p.338.

40 'Absinthe', *American Journal of Pharmacy*, 40, 1868, pp.356–60, quoted in Vogt, op. cit.

41 Goncourt, Edmond and Jules de, *Pages from the Goncourt Journal*, London, 1984, p.42. Jules wrote the journal, sometimes to his brother's dictation, until Jules's death in 1870. It is not clear whose experience is being described at any particular time.

42 Del Castillo, J. et.al., 'Marijuana, absinthe and the central nervous system', *Nature*, no 253, 31 January 1975, pp.365–66.

43 Vogt, Donald D. and Montagne, Michael, 'Absinthe: Behind the Emerald Mask', *International Journal of the Addictions*, vol. 17, 1982, pp.1025–26.

44 Meschler, J.P. et al., 'Thujone Exhibits Low Affinity for Cannabinoid Receptors but Fails to Evoke Cannabimimetic Responses', *Pharmacology, Biochemistry and Behaviour*, vol. 62 no 3, 1999, pp.473–80.

45 Max, B. 'This and That', *Trends in the Pharmacological Sciences*, 11, February 1990, pp.58–60.

46 Fothergill, John, *My Three Inns*, London, 1949, p.139.

47 Ellmann, Richard, *Oscar Wilde*, London, 1987, p.441.

Chapter 4: Poets Breaking the Rules

1 Sherard, R.H., *My Friends the French*, London, 1909, p.39.

2 There is a detailed examination of absinthe spoons and their manufacturers in Delahaye, Marie-Claude, *L'Absinthe, histoire de la Fée verte*, Paris, 1983 and in her *L'Absinthe, les cuillères*, Auvers-sur-Oise, 2001.

3 Pagnol, Marcel, *Le Temps des Secrets*, Paris, 1960, pp.141–42.

4 Richardson, Joanna, *Verlaine*, London, 1971, p.26.

5 Delahaye, Marie-Claude, *L'Absinthe, muse des poètes*, Auvers-sur-Oise, 2000, p.88.

6 Verlaine, Paul, *Confessions of a Poet*, London, 1950, p.105.
7 Richardson, op. cit., p.37.
8 Verlaine, op. cit., pp.106–7.
9 Ibid., p.113.
10 Ober, William B., 'All the Colours of the Rimbaud', in *Bottoms Up!*, London, 1990, p.224.
11 Miller, Henry, *The Time of the Assassins*, London, 1956, p.146.
12 Richardson, op. cit., p.81.
13 Ibid., p.88.
14 Goncourt, Edmond and Jules de, *Pages from the Goncourt Journal*, London, 1984, pp.253–54. Chien as applied to a woman was not insulting but suggestive of attractiveness and courage.
15 Ober, op. cit., p.254.
16 Miller, op. cit., p.vi.
17 Delahaye, *L'Absinthe, muse des poètes*, op. cit., p.112.
18 Coulon, Marcel, *Poet Under Saturn: The Tragedy of Verlaine*, New York, 1970, pp.94–96.
19 Delahaye, *L'Absinthe, muse des poètes*, op. cit., p.92.
20 Applegate, Bergen, *Verlaine: His Absinthe-Tinted Song*, Chicago, 1916, p.12.
21 Corelli, Marie, *Wormwood*, London, 1913, p.68.
22 Kington, Miles, *The World of Alphonse Allais*, London, 1976, p.11.
23 Delahaye, *L'Absinthe, muse des poètes*, op. cit., pp.159–61.
24 Ibid., p.7.
25 Kington, op. cit., p.37.
26 Harvey, Sir Paul and Heseltine, J.E., 'Le Symbolisme', in *The Oxford Companion to French Literature*, Oxford, 1959, p.691.
27 Delahaye, *L'Absinthe, muse des poètes*, op. cit., p.139–40.
28 Harvey, Sir Paul and Heseltine, J.E., 'L'Esprit décadent', in *The Oxford Companion to French Literature*, Oxford, 1959, p.255.
29 Delahaye, *L'Absinthe, muse des poètes*, op. cit., p.106.
30 Thompson, Vance, *French Portraits*, Boston, 1900, p.3, quoted in Richardson, op. cit., p.252.
31 Delahaye, *L'Absinthe, muse des poètes*, op. cit., p.102.
32 Moore, George, *A Great Poet in Impressions and Opinions*, London, 1913, pp.85–88.
33 Applegate, op. cit.
34 Delahaye, *L'Absinthe, histoire de la Fée verte*, op. cit., p.77.
35 Quoted in Richardson, op. cit., p.306.

36 Richler, Jean, *Paul Verlaine*, Paris, 1975, p.84.

37 Verlaine, op. cit., p.112.

38 Lepelletier, Edmond, *Paul Verlaine: His Life, His Work*, London, 1909, pp.10–11.

39 Fosca, François, *Histoire des Cafés de Paris*, Paris, 1934, quoted in Richardson, op. cit., p.245.

40 Lyndon, Howard, 'The Poet of Absinthe', *The Bookman*, New York, 1898–99, vol. 8, p.441.

41 Michaud, Guy, *Message poétique du symbolisme*, 1947, p.215, quoted in Richardson, op. cit., p.245.

Chapter 5: Madmen of Art

1 Arnold, Wilfred Niels, 'Absinthe', *Scientific American*, vol. 260, June 1989, p.90.

2 Sherard, R.H., *My Friends the French*, London, 1909, p.4.

3 Wallace, Robert, *The World of Van Gogh*, London, 1969, p.51.

4 Sweetman, David, *The Love of Many Things*, 1990, p.277.

5 Cabanne, Pierre, *Van Gogh*, London, 1963, p.96.

6 Arnold, op. cit., p.88.

7 Cabanne, op. cit., p.110.

8 Ibid., p.105.

9 Nagera, Humberto, *Vincent van Gogh: A Psychological Study*, New York, 1967, pp.105–6, quoted in Lanier, Doris, *Absinthe: The Cocaine of the Nineteenth Century*, Jefferson, 1994, p.81.

10 Lubin, Alfred J., *Stranger on the Earth*, St Albans, 1975, p.219.

11 Van Gogh, Vincent, *Complete Letters*, London, vol. 2, 1999, p.534.

12 Cabanne, op. cit., p.124.

13 Van Gogh, op. cit., vol. 3, p.31.

14 Ibid., vol. 3, p.482.

15 Ibid., vol. 3, p.494.

16 Delahaye, Marie-Claude and Noël, Benoît, *L'Absinthe, muse des peintres*, Paris, 1999, p.93.

17 Conrad, Barnaby, *Absinthe: History in a Bottle*, San Francisco, 1988, p.62.

18 Delahaye and Noël, op. cit., p.83.

19 Van Gogh, op. cit., vol. 3, p.76.

20 Ibid., vol. 3, p.160.

21 Alauzen, André M. and Ripert, Pierre, *Monticelli, Sa vie et son oeuvre*, Paris, 1969, p.166; Isnard, Guy, *Monticelli sans sa légende*, Geneva, 1967, p.37.

22 Delahaye and Noël, op. cit., p.96.

23 Sweetman, op. cit., 289.

24 Report of a forthcoming book from Rita Wildegans in *Sunday Times*, London, 25 July 2001, p.4.

25 Sweetman, op. cit., p.296.

26 Ibid., p.299.

27 Ibid., p.302.

28 Ibid., p.305.

29 Trevor-Roper, Patrick, *The World Through Blunted Sight*, London, 1988, pp.73–74; Arnold, Wilfred Niels, 'Vincent van Gogh and the Thujone Connection', *Journal of the American Medical Association*, vol. 260 no 20, 25 November 1988, p.3042; Arnold, Wilfred Niels, *Vincent van Gogh: Chemicals, Crises and Creativity*, Boston, 1992; Lubin, Alfred J., *Stranger on the Earth*, St Albans, 1975, pp.218–19.

30 Van Gogh, op. cit., vol. 3, p.298.

31 Arnold, Wilfred Niels, 'Vincent van Gogh and the Thujone Connection', *Journal of the American Medical Association*, vol. 260 no 20, 25 November 1988, p.3042.

32 Arnold, Wilfred Niels, 'Absinthe', *Scientific American*, vol. 260, June 1989, p.91.

33 Van Gogh, op. cit., p.116.

34 Bonkovsky, Herbert L. et al., 'Porphyrogenic Properties of the Terpenes Camphor, Pinene and Thujone', *Biochemical Pharmacology*, vol. 43 no 11, 1992, pp.2359–68.

35 Danielsson, Bengt, *Gauguin in the South Seas*, London, 1965, p.182.

36 Letter to Daniel de Monfreid, November 1895, quoted in Littlewood, Ian, *Sultry Climates: Travel and Sex since the Grand Tour*, London, 2001, p.164.

37 Danielsson, op. cit., p.191.

38 Wallace, op. cit., p.121.

39 Danielsson, op. cit., p.228.

40 Ibid., p.93.

41 Meyer, Michael, *Strindberg: A Biography*, Oxford, 1987, pp.315–16.

42 Heller, Reinhold, *Munch: His Life and Work*, London, 1984, p.107; Wood, Mara-Helen, *Edvard Munch: The Frieze of Life*, London, 1993, p.32.

43 Meyer, op. cit., p.267; Norseng, Mary Kay, *Dagny: The Woman and the Myth*, Seattle, 1991, p.17.

44 Hodin, J.P., *Edvard Munch*, London, 1972, p.66.

45 Gibbons, Fiachra, *Guardian*, 2 September 1999, p.9.

46 Norseng, op. cit., p.8, though Norseng questions some of the Dagny 'myth'.

47 Ibid., p.23.

48 Meyer, op. cit., p.269.

49 Ibid., p.278.

50 Ibid., p.340.

51 Hodin, op. cit., p.66.

52 Norseng, op. cit., p.66.

53 Ibid., p.63.

54 Cavanaugh, Jan, *Out Looking In: Early Modern Polish Art 1890–1918*, Berkeley, 2000, p.55.

55 Wood, op. cit., p.123.

56 Heller, op. cit., p.197.

57 Meyer, op. cit., pp.149, 356.

58 Ibid., pp.164, 238.

59 Ibid., p.169.

60 Ibid., p.356.

61 Anderson, E.A. 'Strindberg's Illness', *Psychological Medicine*, vol. 1, 1971, p.111.

62 Ibid.

63 Meyer, op. cit., p.330.

64 Ibid., p.336.

65 Ibid., p.372.

66 Anderson, op. cit., p.114.

67 Meyer, op. cit., p.385.

Chapter 6: The Absinthe Binge

1 Marrus, Michael R., 'Social Drinking in the Belle Epoque', *Journal of Social History*, vol. 7 no 4, Winter 1974, p.122.

2 Arnold, Wilfred Niels, *Vincent van Gogh: Chemicals, Crises and Creativity*, Boston, 1992, p.103.

3 Conrad, Barnaby, *Absinthe: History in a Bottle*, San Francisco, 1988, p.22; Heilig, Sterling, *Atlanta Constitution*, 19 August 1894, p.6, in Lanier, Doris, *Absinthe: The Cocaine of the Nineteenth Century*, Jefferson, 1994.

4   Delahaye, Marie-Claude and Noël, Benoît, *L'Absinthe, muse des peintres*, Paris, 1999, p.71.

5   Ibid., p.73.

6   Moffett, Charles S., *The New Painting: Impressionism 1874–1886*, Oxford, 1986, p.303.

7   Bouret, Jean, *Toulouse-Lautrec*, London, 1965, pp.243–44, quoting a theory of Dr Pierre Devoisins.

8   Frey, Julia, *Toulouse-Lautrec: A Life*, London, 1994, p.145.

9   Coolus quoted in Frey, op. cit., p.357; Moreau quoted in Conrad, op. cit., p.55.

10   Bouret, op. cit., p.61.

11   Guilbert, Yvette, *La Chanson de ma vie: Mes Mémoires*, Paris, 1927, p.77.

12   Gauzi, François, *Lautrec et son Temps*, Paris, 1954, quoted in Frey, op. cit., p.241.

13   Bouret, op. cit., p.103.

14   Frey, op. cit., p.274.

15   Hugh, H.P., 'The Two Montmartres', *Paris* magazine, June, 1899, quoted in Littlewood, Ian, *Paris: A Literary Companion*, London, 1987, p.194.

16   Wallace, Robert, *The World of Van Gogh*, London, 1969, p.54.

17   Balesta, Henri, *Absinthe et Absintheurs*, Paris, 1860, p.22.

18   Beaumont, Alfred, *Alfred Jarry*, Leicester, 1984, p.1.

19   Ibid., p.125.

20   Ibid., p.270.

21   Frey, op. cit., p.333.

22   Wallace, op. cit., p.56.

23   Delahaye, Marie-Claude, *L'Absinthe, muse des poètes*, Auvers-sur-Oise, 2000, pp.118–30.

Chapter 7: English Decadence and French Morals

1   Corelli, Marie, *The Master Christian*, London, 1900, p.89.

2   Plarr, Victor, *Ernest Dowson 1888–1897*, New York, 1914, p.16.

3   Maugham, Somerset, *Of Human Bondage*, vol. 1, 1960, pp.286, 319.

4   Le Gallienne, Richard, *The Romantic '90s*, London, 1993, p.112.

5   Kernahan, Coulson, 'Two Absinthe-Minded Beggars', *Chambers Journal*, June 1930, p.451. Richard Le Gallienne's memoir is suspect in other ways also: in it he remarks on absinthe as being Lionel Johnson's

'favourite' drink when there are more recollections of his drinking whisky, and Le Gallienne's account of his death is wrong.

6 'Brutal Saxon', *John Bull's Neighbour in Her True Light*, London, 1884, p.40.

7 *New York Times*, 3 August 1879, p.3.

8 *Times*, 19 September 1889, p.6.

9 *New York Times*, 30 July 1882, p.9, quoting the *British Medical Journal*.

10 Sturgis, Matthew, *Passionate Attitudes*, London, 1995, p.3.

11 Plarr, op. cit., p.22.

12 Moore, George, *Confessions of a Young Man*, Montreal, 1972, p.109.

13 Flower, Desmond (ed.), *New Letters of Ernest Dowson*, Andoversford, Gloucestershire, 1984, letter of late April 1889.

14 Flower, Desmond and Maas, Henry (eds), *The Letters of Ernest Dowson*, London, 1967, 30 June 1891, p.205.

15 Adams, Jad, *Madder Music, Stronger Wine: The Life of Ernest Dowson*, London, 2000, p.43.

16 Ibid., p.4.

17 Flower and Maas, op. cit., c.15 February 1889, p.35.

18 Ibid., 16 October 1889, p.107.

19 Ibid., July 1894, p.307.

20 Adams, op. cit., p.81.

21 Quoted by Montgomery Hyde, H., *An Introduction to The Romantic Nineties*, London, 1993, p.xxii.

22 Yeats, W.B., *The Grey Rock in Yeats's Poems*, London, 1989, p.200.

23 Adams, op. cit., p.50.

24 Corelli, Marie, *Wormwood*, London, 1913, p.176.

25 Adams, op. cit., p.70.

26 Flower and Maas, op. cit., c.28 November 1893, p.299.

27 Hichens, Robert, *The Green Carnation*, London, 1961, pp.22–23.

28 Pearson, Hesketh, *The Life of Oscar Wilde*, London, 1954, p.147.

29 Ellmann, Richard, *Oscar Wilde*, London, 1987, p.528.

30 Wilde, Oscar, *Pen, Pencil and Poison in the Works of Oscar Wilde*, London, 1963.

31 Ellmann, op. cit., p.528.

32 Harris, Frank, *Oscar Wilde*, New York, 1959, p.86.

33 Ellmann, op. cit., p.441.

34 Fothergill, John, *My Three Inns*, London, 1949, p.139.

35 Ellmann, op. cit., p.327.

36 Laidlay, W.J., *The Origin and First Two Years of the New English Art Club*, London, 1907, p.3.

37 Thornton, Alfred, *Fifty Years of the New English Art Club 1886–1935*, London, 1935, p.3.

38 Ibid., p.9.

39 Trevor, John, *French Art and English Morals*, Liverpool, 1886, p.7.

40 Ibid., pp.19, 22, 46, 43.

41 Denvir, Bernard, *The Chronicle of Impressionism*, London, 2000, p.166.

42 Barry, Rev. W.F., *Quarterly Review*, July 1890, p.90.

43 These disputes were resolved by the Anglo-French Conventions of June 1898 and March 1899, though, as in the Cold War, the facts of diplomacy and military conflict are less important than the perception of danger.

44 'Posteritas', *The Siege of London*, London, 1885, p.52.

45 Ibid., p.23.

46 'Brutal Saxon', *John Bull's Neighbour in Her True Light*, London, 1884, p.vi.

47 Ibid., p.68.

48 Ibid., p.69.

49 Ibid., p.104.

50 Ransom, Teresa, *The Mysterious Miss Marie Corelli*, Gloucester, 1999, p.1.

51 Corelli, Marie, *Wormwood*, London, 1913, p.67.

52 Ibid., p.12.

53 Ibid., p.142.

54 Ibid., p.193.

55 Ibid., pp.286, 235, 323, 331, 410.

56 Ibid., pp.207, 448.

57 Ibid., p.295. Publication facts from Bertha Vyver, memoirs, quoted in Ransom, op. cit.

Chapter 8: Anglo-Saxon Attitudes

1 Pickvance, Ronald, 'L'Absinthe in England', *Apollo*, 15 May 1963, p.395.

2 Ibid., p.396.

3 Colson, Percy, *A Story of Christie's*, London, 1950, p.62.

4 Kay, Arthur, *Treasure Trove in Art*, Edinburgh, 1939, p.27.

5 Cooper, Douglas, *The Courtauld Collection*, London, 1954, p.42.

6   *Times*, 20 February, 1893, p.8.

7   *Daily Chronicle*, 17 February, 1893, p.3.

8   Kay, op. cit., p.28.

9   Pickvance, op. cit., p.396.

10 MacColl, D.S., *Spectator*, 25 February 1893, pp.256.

11 'The Philistine', *Westminster Gazette*, 9 March 1893, pp.1–2.

12 Kay, op. cit., p.28.

13 Quilter, Harry, 'The New Art Criticism', *Westminster Gazette*, 15 March 1893, p.3.

14 Hiatt, Charles J., 'The Grafton Gallery', *The Artist and Journal of Home Culture*, 1 March 1893, p.86.

15 Thornton, Alfred, *The Diary of an Art Student of the Nineties*, London, 1938, p.31.

16 Richmond, W.B., 'The New Art Criticism', *Westminster Gazette*, 20 March 1893, p.2; 16 March 1893, p.2.

17 Crane, Walter, 'The New Art Criticism', *Westminster Gazette*, 20 March 1893, p.2.

18 Moore, George, 'The Grafton Gallery', *The Speaker*, 25 February 1893, p.216. As *L'Absinthe* became a *cause célèbre*, Moore felt the need to apologise for this sentiment: *The Speaker*, 25 March 1893, p.342.

19 Trevor, John, *French Art and English Morals*, Liverpool, 1886, p.9.

20 Delahaye, Marie-Claude and Noël, Benoît, *L'Absinthe, muse des peintres*, Paris, 1999, p.60.

21 Thornton, Alfred, *Fifty Years of the New English Art Club 1886–1935*, London, 1935, p.6.

22 Cooper, op. cit., p.43.

23 Pater, Walter, *Studies in Art and Poetry*, Berkeley, 1980, p.190.

24 Brake, Laurel, *Print in Transition 1850–1910*, London, 2001, p.275.

25 Thornton, *Fifty Years of the New English Art Club 1886–1935*, op. cit., p.9.

26 Denvir, Bernard, *The Chronicle of Impressionism*, London, 2000, p.190.

27 Thornton, *The Diary of an Art Student of the Nineties*, op. cit., p.44.

28 Ibid., p.39.

29 Crackanthorpe, Hubert, 'Reticence in Literature: Some Roundabout Remarks', The Yellow Book, vol. II, July 1894, p.262.

30 Thornton, *The Diary of an Art Student of the Nineties*, op. cit., p.36.

31 Ibid., p.44.

32 *Daily Mirror*, 9 August 1913, pp.1, 5.

33 Adams, Jad, *Madder Music, Stronger Wine: The Life of Ernest Dowson*, London, 2000, p.99.

34 Spender, J.A., *Life, Journalism and Politics*, London, 1927, p.58.

35 Sturgis, Matthew, *Passionate Attitudes*, London, 1995, p.233.

36 Ibid., p.252.

37 Crackanthorpe, David, *Hubert Crackanthorpe and English Realism in the 1890s*, Columbia, Missouri, 1977, p.141.

38 Flower, Desmond and Maas, Henry (eds), *The Letters of Ernest Dowson*, London, 1967, p.317, 15 October 1895.

39 Ibid., 11 December 1895, p.326.

40 Adams, op. cit., pp.130–32.

41 Ibid., p.132.

42 Ibid., pp.144–45.

43 Harris, Frank, *Oscar Wilde*, New York, 1959, p.332.

44 Sherard, R.H., *My Friends the French*, London, 1909, p.273.

45 Lang, Andrew, 'Decadence', *The Critic*, August 1900, p.173.

46 Buchanan, Robert, *Complete Poetical Works*, vol. II, London, 1901, pp.390, 391, 393, in verses disparaging Zola, Heine, de Musset, Verlaine, Wilde and many others.

47 I am grateful to Phil Baker, without whose work for *The Dedalus Book of Absinthe* these rhymes would have continued to enjoy a well-deserved obscurity.

48 Yeats, W.B. (ed.), *The Oxford Book of Modern Verse*, Oxford, 1936, p.xi.

49 Anon., 'The Absinthe Evil', *Lancet*, 29 August 1903, p.620.

50 Brasher, C.W.J., 'Absinthe and Absinthe Drinking in England', *Lancet*, 26 April 1930, p.945.

51 Soltau, W., 'The Drinking of Absinthe', *Times*, 12 August 1907.

Chapter 9: Absinthe Paranoia

1 Marrus, Michael R., 'Social Drinking in the Belle Epoque', *Journal of Social History*, vol. 7 no 4, Winter 1974, p.118.

2 Prestwich, P.E., 'Temperance in France: The Curious Case of Absinthe', *Historical Reflections* (Canada), vol. 6 no 2, Winter 1979, p.304.

3 Marrus, op. cit., p.118.

4 Sournia, Jean-Charles, *A History of Alcoholism*, Oxford, 1990, p.70; Use of 'absinthism': *Bulletin de l'Académie de Médecine*, 19, 1888, p.885.

5 Arnold, Wilfred Niels, 'Absinthe', *Scientific American*, 260, June 1989, p.89.
6 Goncourt, Edmond and Jules de, *Pages from the Goncourt Journal*, London, 1984, p.382.
7 Anon., 'Absinthism', *Lancet*, 4 January 1873, p.22.
8 Sherard, R.H., *My Friends the French*, London, 1909, p.41.
9 Ibid., p.43.
10 Ibid., p.45.
11 Ibid., p.44.
12 Balesta, Henri, *Absinthe et Absintheurs*, Paris, 1860, p.21.
13 Adumbrated in Arnold, Wilfred Niels, *Vincent van Gogh: Chemicals, Crises and Creativity*, Boston, 1992, p.105.
14 Magnan, V., and Fillassier, A., 'Alcoholism and Degeneracy', *Problems in Eugenics: Papers Communicated to the First International Eugenics Conference*, London, 1912, p.371.
15 Anon., 'France Banishing Absinthe', *Literary Digest*, 8 May 1915, p.1084.
16 Anet, H., 'The War Against Absinthe on the Continent', *Economic Review*, 17, April 1907, p.192.
17 Magnan and Fillassier, op. cit., p.373.
18 Heilig, Sterling, *Atlanta Constitution*, 19 August 1894, p.8.
19 Magnan and Fillassier, op. cit., pp.368–69.
20 Corelli, Marie, *Wormwood*, London, 1913, p.197.
21 Magnan and Fillassier, op. cit., p.377.
22 Nordau, Max, *Degeneration*, London, 1913, p.viii.
23 Ibid., p.374.
24 Ibid., p 374.
25 Delahaye, Marie-Claude, *L'Absinthe, son histoire*, Auvers-sur-Oise, 2002, p.249.
26 Ensor, R.C.K., *England 1870–1914*, Oxford, 1936, p.102.
27 Anon., 'France Banishing Absinthe', *Literary Digest*, 8 May 1915, p.1084.
28 Heilig, op. cit., p.8.
29 Fillaut, Thierry, 'Fée verte et poison social: L'absinthe en France au XIXe siècle', *Psychotropes*, vol. 2 no 3, Autumn 1985, p.30.
30 Ibid.
31 Marrus, op. cit., p.126.
32 Quoted in Brasher, C.W.J., 'Absinthe and Absinthe Drinking in England', *Lancet*, 26 April 1930, p.945.
33 Saintsbury, George, *Notes on a Cellar-Book*, London, 1921, p.143.
34 Heilig, op. cit., p.8.

35 Delahaye, Marie-Claude, *L'Absinthe, histoire de la Fée verte*, Paris, 1983, p.81.

36 Guilbert, Yvette, *La Chanson de ma vie: Mes Mémoires*, Paris, 1927, p.78.

37 Quoted in Choquette, Leslie, 'Homosexuals in the City: Representations of Lesbian and Gay Space in Nineteenth Century Paris', *Journal of Homosexuality*, vol. 41 no 3-4, 2001, pp.149–67.

38 Charcot, Jean-Martin and Magnan, Valentin, 'Inversion du sens génital', *Archives de neurologie*, vol. 3, 1882, pp.54–56.

39 Albert, Nicole, 'Sappho Mythified, Sappho Mystified or the Metamorphosis of Sappho in Fin de Siècle France', *Journal of Homosexuality*, vol. 25 no 1/2, 1993, p.95.

40 Zola, Emile, *Nana*, London, 1962, p.223.

41 Huffington, Ariana Stassinopoulos, 'Creater and Destroyer', *The Atlantic*, June 1988, p.46.

42 The gouache-and-crayon picture is also known as *Girl in a Café* and was once incorrectly dated to 1903. The second picture of the same name is sometimes called *Girl with Folded Arms* and is sometimes confused with *L'Aperitif* of the same year, which shows a woman with her elbows on a table in front of a glass and a soda siphon – not, therefore, a glass of absinthe. Daix, Pierre and Boudaille, Georges, *Picasso: The Blue and Rose Periods*, London, 1967, pp.188, 201.

43 Picasso, Pablo, *Encyclopaedia Britannica*, Chicago, vol. 14, 1977, p.443.

44 Prestwich, op. cit., p.303.

45 Byrnes, Robert F., *Antisemitism in Modern France*, New York, 1969, p.149. Pierre Birnbaum, in *Anti-Semitism in France* (Oxford, 1992), discusses the mythology of wine in the context of antisemitism, pp.133–46.

46 Zolotow, Maurice, 'Absinthe', *Playboy*, June, 1971, p.178.

47 Delahaye, *L'Absinthe, histoire de la Fée verte*, op. cit., p.177 pictures them.

Chapter 10: Twilight of the Fée Verte

1 Delahaye, Marie-Claude, *L'Absinthe, histoire de la Fée verte*, Paris, 1983, p.151.

2 Ibid., p.161.

3 Ibid., p.61.

4 Zolotow, Maurice, 'Absinthe', *Playboy*, June 1971, p.172.

5 Anet, H., 'The War Against Absinthe on the Continent', *Economic Review*, 17 April 1907, p.192.

6   Sherard, R.H., *My Friends the French*, London, 1909, p.39.

7   Arnold, Wilfred Niels, *Vincent van Gogh: Chemicals Crises and Creativity*, Boston, 1992, p.104.

8   Conrad, Barnaby, *Absinthe: History in a Bottle*, San Francisco, 1988, p.105.

9   Lancereaux, Etienne, 'Discussion sur les liqueurs à l'essences', *Bulletin de l'Académie de Médecine*, 49, 1903, pp.220–44, quoted in Delahaye, Marie-Claude: *L'Absinthe, son histoire*, Auvers-sur-Oise, 2002, pp.204–5; *L'Absinthe, histoire de la Fée verte*, Paris, 1983, p.131.

10 Conrad, op. cit., p.128.

11 Delahaye, Marie-Claude, *L'Absinthe, muse des poètes*, Auvers-sur-Oise, 2000, p.263.

12 Delahaye, *L'Absinthe, histoire de la Fée verte*, op. cit., p.106.

13 Arnold, op. cit., p.131. It may be that a doctor L. Camus in 1906 did such experiments, giving dogs the equivalent of six absinthes a day for a man of average weight. Well-nourished dogs showed no symptoms of 'absinthism', but poorly fed ones died. Cited in Delahaye, *L'Absinthe, son histoire*, op. cit., pp.228–29.

14 Anon., 'Absinthe and Alcohol', *Lancet*, 6 March 1869, p.334.

15 *Times*, 4 December 1908, p.19.

16 Fillaut, Thierry, 'Fée verte et poison social: L'absinthe en France au XIXe siècle', *Psychotropes*, vol. 2 no 3, Autumn 1985, p.31.

17 Zolotow, Maurice, 'Absinthe', *Playboy*, June 1971, pp.169–74. All quotes and information about Lanfray are taken from this piece.

18 Anet, op. cit., p.190.

19 Ibid., p.190.

20 Ibid., p.191.

21 *Times*, 11 October 1910, p.7.

22 *Times*, 9 December 1905, p.17.

23 Whin-Hurst (letter), *Times*, 17 August 1907, p.13.

24 Delahaye, *L'Absinthe, histoire de la Fée verte*, op. cit., p.156; Fillaut, op. cit., p.31.

25 Senate, 18 May 1911, quoted in Prestwich, P.E., 'Temperance in France: The Curious Case of Absinthe', *Historical Reflections* (Canada), vol. 6 no 2, Winter 1979, p.308.

26 Couléru, E., *Au pays de l'absinthe y est-on plus fou ou plus criminel qu'ailleurs?*, Paris, 1908, p.246, quoted in Delahaye, *L'Absinthe, histoire de la Fée verte*, op. cit., p.140.

27 Sherard, op. cit., p.43.

28 Anon., 'The Consumption of Alcohol in France', *Lancet*, 14 September 1912, p.794.

29 Sournia, Jean-Charles, *A History of Alcoholism*, Oxford, 1990, p.76.

30 Fillaut, op. cit., p.28; Delahaye, *L'Absinthe, histoire de la Fée verte*, op. cit., p.65, where it is additionally mentioned that the inhabitants of Marseilles had an annual consumption of 3 litres of absinthe per year.

31 Quoted in Goulette, Léon, *L'Absinthe et l'alcool dans la défense nationale*, Paris, 1915, p.8.

32 Ibid., p.20.

33 Chamber debate for 12 February 1915, quoted in Prestwich, op. cit., p.317.

34 The law also banned *similaires* – products similar to absinthe with which manufacturers hoped to replace absinthe. In 1922 these were permitted and have become popular under such names as Pernod and Ricard.

35 *Harper's Weekly*, 1 May 1915, pp.420–21.

36 Adams, Brooks, 'Six Drinks to the End of an Era', *Artforum*, April 1980, p.31.

37 Ibid., p.32.

38 Ibid., p.33.

39 Bouret, Jean, *Degas*, London, 1965, p.260.

Chapter 11: Green in the USA

1 www.neworleans.travelape.com. The notion that the cocktail was 'invented' at the Absinthe House is a fanciful one which dates from the time of the Absinthe House's success as a fashionable bar in the 1870s. The word 'cocktail' long predates that; for example Dickens uses it in his 1844 novel *Martin Chuzzlewit*.

2 Crowley, Aleister, 'The Green Goddess', *The International*, New York, 1918, consulted at www.erowid.org.

3 Crowley, Aleister, *The Confessions of Aleister Crowley*, London, 1969, p.490.

4 Crowley, 'The Green Goddess', op. cit.

5 Crowley, *The Confessions of Aleister Crowley*, op. cit., p.817.

6 Lanier, Doris, *Absinthe: The Cocaine of the Nineteenth Century*, Jefferson, 1994, p.124.

7 Sinclair, Harry, *The Port of New Orleans*, New York, 1942, quoted by Lanier, op. cit., p.127.

8   Quinn, Arthur Hobson, *Edgar Allan Poe: A Critical Biography*, New York, 1998, p.381.

9   Thomas, Dwight and Jackson, David K., *The Poe Log: A Documentary Life of Edgar Allen Poe 1809–1849*, Boston, 1987, p.xxxvii.

10 Fossier, Albert E., *New Orleans, the Glamour Period 1800-1840*, New Orleans, 1957, p.381, quoted in Lanier, op. cit., p.126.

11 *New York Times*, 31 October 1902, p.9.

12 Arthur, Stanley Clisby, *Famous New Orleans Drinks and How to Mix 'Em*, Gretna, Louisiana, 1977, p.36, quoted in Lanier, op. cit., p.132.

13 *New York Times*, 3 August 1879, p.3.

14 *New York Times*, 14 October 1879, p.4.

15 *New York Times*, 12 December 1880, p.6.

16 *New York Times*, 19 October 1884, p.5.

17 Morrow, W.C., 'Over an Absinthe Bottle', in *The Ape, the Idiot and Other People*, Philadelphia, 1897, p.94.

18 Zolotow, Maurice, 'Absinthe', *Playboy*, June 1971, p.176. Slight differences in wording exist in other versions.

19 Ibid.

20 *Harper's Weekly*, 13 July 1907, p.1035.

21 *New York Times*, 15 December 1911, p.2.

22 *New York Times*, 13 July 1912, p.2.

23 Lanier has researched San Francisco newspapers in this period: op. cit., pp.150–51.

24 Anderson, Elizabeth and Kelly, Gerald R., *Miss Elizabeth: A Memoir*, Boston, 1969, pp.90–91.

25 Quoted in Lanier, op. cit., p.140.

26 *New Orleans Picayune*, 21 November 1926.

27 *Morning Tribune*, 3 October 1929, quoted in Lanier, op. cit., p.141.

28 Service, Robert, *Complete Poems*, New York, 1934, p.20.

29 Ibid., p.25.

30 Ibid., pp.84, 121.

31 Crosby, Harry, *The Journals of Harry Crosby*, ed. Edward Germain, Santa Barbara, 1977, p.149.

32 Ibid., pp.48, 91, 192, 211.

33 Ibid., p.7.

34 Ibid., p.287. The repeated refrain in the film is 'The greatest thing you'll ever learn is just to love and be loved in return'.

35 Hemingway, Ernest, *For Whom the Bell Tolls*, London, 1967, p.53.

36 Conrad, Barnaby, *Absinthe: History in a Bottle*, San Francisco, 1988, p.137.
37 Brasher, C.W.J., 'Absinthe and Absinthe Drinking in England', *Lancet*, 26 April 1930, pp.944–46.
38 Waugh, Alec, *In Praise of Wine*, London, 1959, p.180.
39 Zolotow, op. cit., p.176.
40 www.gumbopages.com/absinthe.

Chapter 12: Pop Goes the Fairy

Directions to websites containing recipes are for information only and do not imply the author or publisher's endorsement for any product or practice. All websites are as at Winter 2002.

1   Green Bohemia website (www.eabsinthe.com) and Baker, Phil, *The Dedalus Book of Absinthe*, London, 2001, pp.161–62.
2   Bradsell, Dick in *Class* – 'the magazine of bar culture' – on eabsinthe.com. To be fair to Bradsell, he recognises that any untoward effects are as likely to have been caused by high levels of alcohol as by absinthe's other ingredients.
3   *Daily Telegraph*, 3 December 1998.
4   *Hansard*, 7 December 1998, p.20.
5   *Sunday Telegraph*, 27 December 1998.
6   Bywater, Michael, 'Why Government is Bad for You', *Daily Telegraph*, 25 February 1999.
7   www.beautyandruin.com.
8   www.netgoth.org.uk.
9   *Daily Telegraph*, 11 September 1999.
10 www.erowid.org/experiences.
11 www.newspeakdictionary.com.
12 www.rain.org/~philfear.
13 Weisbord, S.D., Soule, J.B. and Kimmel, P.L., 'Poison On Line: Acute Renal Failure Caused by Oil of Wormwood Purchased through the Internet', *New England Journal of Medicine*, 337, pp.825–27, 18 September 1997.
14 *Stars and Stripes*, 11 and 19 February 2001.
15 www.eabsinthe.com.

16 www.angelfire.com/tv/absinthe.

17 Goluszko, Alex, 'Absinthe: The Misunderstood Muse', on eabsinthe.com, noted as originally in *The Sentimentalist*.

18 Baker, op. cit., p.197.

19 Strang, John, Arnold, Wilfred N. and Peters, Timothy, 'Absinthe: What's Your Poison?' *British Medical Journal*, 18 December 1999, p.1591.

20 Arnold, Wilfred Niels, *Vincent van Gogh: Chemicals, Crises and Creativity*, Boston, 1992, p.120.

21 Meschler, J.P. et al., 'Thujone Exhibits Low Affinity for Cannabinoid Receptors but Fails to Evoke Cannabimimetic Responses', *Pharmacology, Biochemistry and Behaviour*, vol. 62 no 3, 1999, p.479 (where the concentration is given as 2.4 mM); Baker, op. cit., p.197.

22 Hutton, Ian, 'Myth, Reality and Absinthe', *Current Drug Discovery*, September 2002, p.63.

23 Höld, Karin M. et al., 'Alpha-thujone (the active component of absinthe): Gamma-Aminobutyric acid type A receptor modulation and metabolic detoxification', *Proceedings of the National Academy of Sciences USA*, vol. 97 issue 8, 11 April 2000, pp.3826–31.

24 Olsen, Richard W., 'Absinthe and Gamma-aminobutyric acid receptors', *Proceedings of the National Academy of Sciences USA*, vol. 97 issue 9, 25 April 2000, p.4417.

25 Strang et al., op. cit., p.1591.

26 www.jager.com.

27 Saintsbury, George, *Notes on a Cellar-Book*, London, 1921, p.142.

Select Bibliography

Books and Journal articles

Adams, Brooks, 'Six Drinks to the End of an Era', *Artforum*, April 1980.

Adams, Jad, *Madder Music, Stronger Wine: The Life of Ernest Dowson*, London, 2000.

Alauzen, André M. and Ripert, Pierre, *Monticelli: Sa vie et son oeuvre*, Paris, 1969.

Albert, Nicole, 'Sappho Mythified, Sappho Mystified or the Metamorphosis of Sappho in Fin de Siècle France', *Journal of Homosexuality*, vol. 25 no 1/2, 1993.

Anderson, E.A. 'Strindberg's Illness', *Psychological Medicine*, vol. 1, 1971.

Anderson, Elizabeth and Kelly, Gerald R., *Miss Elizabeth: A Memoir*, Boston, 1969.

Anet, H., 'The War Against Absinthe on the Continent', *Economic Review*, April 1907.

Applegate, Bergen, *Verlaine: His Absinthe-Tinted Song*, Chicago, 1916.

Arnold, Wilfred Niels, 'Absinthe', *Scientific American*, vol. 260, June 1989.

— *Vincent van Gogh: Chemicals, Crises and Creativity*, Boston, 1992.

Baker, Phil, *The Dedalus Book of Absinthe*, London, 2001.

Balesta, Henri, *Absinthe et Absintheurs*, Paris, 1860.

Barry, Rev. W.F., *Quarterly Review*, July 1890.

Beaumont, Alfred, *Alfred Jarry*, Leicester, 1984.

Beck, J. and T., *Elements of Medical Jurisprudence*, London, 1842.

Bonkovsky, Herbert L. et al., 'Porphyrogenic Properties of the Terpenes Camphor, Pinene and Thujone', *Biochemical Pharmacology*, vol. 43 no 11, 1992.

Bouret, Jean, *Degas*, London, 1965.

— *Toulouse-Lautrec*, London, 1965.

Brake, Laurel, *Print in Transition 1850–1910*, London, 2001.

'Brutal Saxon', *John Bull's Neighbour in Her True Light*, London, 1884.

Buchanan, Robert, *Complete Poetical Works*, London, 1901.

Byrnes, Robert F., *Antisemitism in Modern France*, New York, 1969.

Cabanne, Pierre, *Van Gogh*, London, 1963.

Cavanaugh, Jan, *Out Looking In: Early Modern Polish Art 1890–1918*, Berkeley, 2000.

Charcot, Jean-Martin and Magnan, Valentin, 'Inversion du sens génital', *Archives de neurologie*, vol. 3. 1882.

Choquette, Leslie, 'Homosexuals in the City: Representations of Lesbian and Gay Space in Nineteenth Century Paris', *Journal of Homosexuality*, vol. 41 no 3–4, 2001.

Colson, Percy, *A Story of Christie's*, London, 1950.

Conrad, Barnaby, *Absinthe: History in a Bottle*, San Francisco, 1988.

Cooper, Douglas, *The Courtauld Collection*, London, 1954.

Corelli, Marie, *The Master Christian*, London, 1900.

— *Wormwood*, London, 1913.

Coulon, Marcel, *Poet Under Saturn: The Tragedy of Verlaine*, New York, 1970.

Crackanthorpe, David, *Hubert Crackanthorpe and English Realism in the 1890s*, Columbia, Missouri, 1977.

Crackanthorpe, Hubert, 'Reticence in Literature: Some Roundabout Remarks', *The Yellow Book*, vol. II, July 1894.

Crane, Walter, 'The New Art Criticism', *Westminster Gazette*, 20 March 1893.

Crosby, Harry, *The Journals of Harry Crosby*, ed. Edward Germain, Santa Barbara, 1977.

Crowley, Aleister, *The Confessions of Aleister Crowley*, London, 1969.

— 'The Green Goddess', *The International*, New York, 1918.

Culpeper, N., *The Complete Herbal and English Physician, Enlarged of 1653*, London, 1995.

Daix, Pierre and Boudaille, Georges, *Picasso: The Blue and Rose Periods*, London, 1967.

Danielsson, Bengt, *Gauguin in the South Seas*, London, 1965.

Delahaye, Marie-Claude, *L'Absinthe, son histoire*, Auvers-sur-Oise, 2002.

— *L'Absinthe, histoire de la Fée verte*, Paris, 1983.

— *L'Absinthe, muse des poètes*, Auvers-sur-Oise, 2000.

Delahaye, Marie-Claude and Noël, Benoît, *L'Absinthe, muse des peintres*, Paris, 1999.

Denvir, Bernard, *The Chronicle of Impressionism*, London, 2000.

Dumas, Alexandre, *A Dictionary of Cuisine*, London, 1958.

Dupuy, B., *Absinthe: Ses propriétés et ses dangers*, Brussels, 1875.

Ellmann, Richard, *Oscar Wilde*, London, 1987.

Ensor, R.C.K., *England 1870–1914*, Oxford, 1936.

Fillaut, Thierry, 'Fée verte et poison social: L'absinthe en France au XIXe siècle', *Psychotropes*, vol. 2 no 3, Autumn, 1985.

Flower, Desmond (ed.), *New Letters of Ernest Dowson*, Andoversford, Gloucestershire, 1984.

Flower, Desmond and Maas, Henry (eds), *The Letters of Ernest Dowson*, London, 1967.

Fothergill, John, *My Three Inns*, London, 1949.

Frey, Julia, *Toulouse-Lautrec: A Life*, London, 1994.

Goncourt, Edmond and Jules de, *Pages from the Goncourt Journal*, London, 1980 (Folio Society), 1984 (Penguin).

Goulette, Léon, *L'Absinthe et l'alcool dans la défense nationale*, Paris, 1915.

Guilbert, Yvette, *La Chanson de ma vie: Mes Mémoires*, Paris, 1927.

Hamilton, George Heard, *Manet and His Critics*, New Haven, 1954.

Harris, Frank, *Oscar Wilde*, New York, 1959.

Hartley, Anthony, *Introduction to French Verse III: The Nineteenth Century*, London, 1957.

Harvey, Sir Paul and Heseltine, J.E., *Oxford Companion to French Literature*, Oxford, 1961.

Heilig, Sterling, 'Absinthe Drinking', *Atlanta Constitution*, 19 August 1894.

Heller, Reinhold, *Munch: His Life and Work*, London, 1984.

Hemingway, Ernest, *For Whom the Bell Tolls*, London, 1967.

Hiatt, Charles J., 'The Grafton Gallery', *The Artist and Journal of Home Culture*, 1 March 1893.

Hichens, Robert, *The Green Carnation*, London, 1961.

Hodin, J.P., *Edvard Munch*, London, 1972.

Höld, Karin M. et al., 'Alpha-thujone (the active component of absinthe): Gamma-Aminobutyric acid type A receptor modulation and metabolic detoxification', *Proceedings of the National Academy of Science USA*, vol. 97 issue 8, April 2000.

Hooper, Lucy H., 'Parisian Maniacs and Madhouses', *Lippincott's Magazine*, June 1878.

Huffington, Ariana Stassinopoulos, 'Creater and Destroyer', *The Atlantic*, June, 1988.

Hutton, Ian, 'Myth, Reality and Absinthe', *Current Drug Discovery*, September 2002.

Isnard, Guy, *Monticelli sans sa légende*, Geneva, 1967.

Kay, Arthur, *Treasure Trove in Art*, Edinburgh, 1939.

Kernahan, Coulson, 'Two Absinthe-Minded Beggars', *Chambers Journal*, June 1930.

Kightly, Charles, *The Perpetual Almanack of Folklore*, London, 1987.

Kington, Miles, *The World of Alphonse Allais*, London, 1976.

Laidlay, W.J., *The Origin and First Two Years of the New English Art Club*, London, 1907.

Lang, Andrew, 'Decadence', *The Critic*, August 1900.

Lanier, Doris, *Absinthe: The Cocaine of the Nineteenth Century*, Jefferson, 1994.

Le Gallienne, Richard, *The Romantic '90s*, London, 1993.

Lepelletier, Edmond, *Paul Verlaine: His Life, His Work*, London, 1909.

Littlewood, Ian, *Sultry Climates: Travel and Sex since the Grand Tour*, London, 2001.

Lubin, Alfred J., *Stranger on the Earth*, St Albans, 1975.

Lyndon, Howard, 'The Poet of Absinthe', *The Bookman*, New York, vol. 8, 1898–99.

Magnan, V. and Fillassier, A., 'Alcoholism and Degeneracy', *Problems in Eugenics: Papers Communicated to the First International Eugenics Conference*, London, 1912.

Marrus, Michael R., 'Social Drinking in the Belle Epoque', *Journal of Social History*, vol. 7 no 4, Winter 1974.

Maugham, Somerset, *Of Human Bondage*, vol. 1, 1960.

Max, B. 'This and That', *Trends in the Pharmacological Sciences*, 11, February 1990.

McMullen, Roy, *Degas: His Life, Times and Work*, London, 1985.

Meschler, J.P. et al., 'Thujone Exhibits Low Affinity for Cannabinoid Receptors but Fails to Evoke Cannabimimetic Responses', *Pharmacology, Biochemistry and Behaviour*, vol. 62 no 3, 1999.

Meyer, Michael, *Strindberg: A Biography*, Oxford, 1987.

Miller, Henry, *The Time of the Assassins*, London, 1956.

Moffett, Charles S., *The New Painting: Impressionism 1874–1886*, Oxford, 1986.

Montgomery Hyde, H., *An Introduction to The Romantic Nineties*, London, 1993.

Moore, George, *A Great Poet in Impressions and Opinions*, London, 1913.
— *Confessions of a Young Man*, Montreal, 1972.

More, Julian, *Impressionist Paris*, London, 1998.

Moreau-Nélaton, Etienne, *Manet raconte par lui-même*, Paris, 1926.

Morrow, W.C., 'Over an Absinthe Bottle', in *The Ape, the Idiot and Other People*, Philadelphia, 1897.

Nickell, Joe and Fischer, John F., *The Skeptical Inquirer*, vol. 11, Summer 1987.

Nordau, Max, *Degeneration*, London, 1913.

Norseng, Mary Kay, *Dagny: The Woman and the Myth*, Seattle, 1991.

Ober, William B., 'All the Colours of the Rimbaud', in *Bottoms Up!*, London, 1990.

Olsen, Richard W., 'Absinthe and Gamma-aminobutyric acid receptors', *Proceedings of the National Academy of Science USA*, vol. 97 issue 9, 25 April 2000.

Pagnol, Marcel, *Le Temps des Secrets*, Paris, 1960.

Pater, Walter, *Studies in Art and Poetry*, Berkeley, 1980.

Pearson, Hesketh, *The Life of Oscar Wilde*, London, 1954.

Pickvance, Ronald, 'L'Absinthe in England', *Apollo*, 15 May 1963.

Plarr, Victor, *Ernest Dowson 1888–1897*, New York, 1914.

Plinius Secundus, C., trans. Philomen Holland, *Historia Naturalis*, London, 1601.

Podlech, D., *Herbs and Healing Plants of Britain and Europe*, London, 1996.

'Posteritas', *The Siege of London*, London, 1885.

Prestwich, P.E., 'Temperance in France: The Curious Case of Absinthe', *Historical Reflections* (Canada), vol. 6 no 2, Winter 1979.

Proust, Antonin, *Edouard Manet: Souvenirs*, Paris, 1913.

Quinn, Arthur Hobson, *Edgar Allan Poe: A Critical Biography*, New York, 1998.

Ransom, Teresa, *The Mysterious Miss Marie Corelli*, Gloucester, 1999.

Richardson, Joanna, *Verlaine*, London, 1971.

Richler, Jean, *Paul Verlaine*, Paris, 1975.

Saintsbury, George, *Notes on a Cellar-Book*, London, 1921.

Schneider, Pierre, *The World of Manet*, New York, 1968.

Service, Robert, *Complete Poems*, New York, 1934.

Sherard, R.H., *My Friends the French*, London, 1909.

— *Twenty Years in Paris*, London, 1905.

Sinclair, Harry, *The Port of New Orleans*, New York, 1942.

Sournia, Jean-Charles, *A History of Alcoholism*, Oxford, 1990.

Spender, J.A., *Life, Journalism and Politics*, London, 1927.

Stuckey, Charles F., 'Manet Revised: Whodunnit?', *Art in America*, 71, November 1983.

Sturgis, Matthew, *Passionate Attitudes*, London, 1995.

Sweetman, David, *The Love of Many Things*, 1990.

Thomas, Dwight and Jackson, David K., *The Poe Log: A Documentary Life of Edgar Allen Poe 1809–1849*, Boston, 1987.

Thompson, Vance, *French Portraits*, Boston, 1900.

Thornton, Alfred, *Fifty Years of the New English Art Club 1886–1935*, London 1935.

— *The Diary of an Art Student of the Nineties*, London, 1938.

Trevor, John, *French Art and English Morals*, Liverpool, 1886.

Trevor-Roper, Patrick, *The World Through Blunted Sight*, London, 1988.

Van Gogh, Vincent, *Complete Letters*, London, 1999.

Verlaine, Paul, *Confessions of a Poet*, London, 1950.

Vogt, Donald D., 'Absinthium: a nineteenth-century drug of abuse', *Journal of Ethnopharmacology*, 4, 1981.

Vogt, Donald D. and Montagne, Michael, 'Absinthe: Behind the Emerald Mask', *The International Journal of the Addictions*, vol.17, 1982.

Wallace, Robert, *The World of Van Gogh*, London, 1969.

Waugh, Alec, *In Praise of Wine*, London, 1959.

Wilde, Oscar, *Pen, Pencil and Poison in The Works of Oscar Wilde*, London, 1963.

Wood, Mara-Helen, *Edvard Munch: The Frieze of Life*, London, 1993.

Yeats, W.B., *The Grey Rock in Yeats's Poems*, London, 1989.

— (ed.), *The Oxford Book of Modern Verse*, Oxford, 1936.

Zola, Emile, *Nana*, London, 1962.

Zolotow, Maurice, 'Absinthe', *Playboy*, June 1971.

Newspapers and weekly magazines consulted

Atlanta Constitution
British Medical Journal
Daily Chronicle
Daily Mirror
Guardian
Harper's Weekly
Journal of the American Medical Association

Lancet
Literary Digest
Nature
New England Journal of Medicine
New Orleans Picayune
New York Times
Once a Week
Speaker
Spectator
Stars and Stripes
Sunday Telegraph
Sunday Times
Temps
Times
Westminster Gazette

Websites consulted

www.angelfire.com/tv/absinthe
www.beautyandruin.com
www.eabsinthe.com
www.erowid.org/experiences
www.gumbopages.com/absinthe
www.haut-doubs.org
www.jager.com
www.lechatnoir.free.fr
www.netgoth.org.uk
www.neworleans.travelape.com
www.newspeakdictionary.com
www.pontarlier-anis.com
www.rain.org/~philfear

Index

Abd-el-Kader 19
absinthe
  addiction and 87–88, 141
  alcoholism and 6, 9, 55–57, 117,
    175, 178–79, 181, 209
  use in antiquity 3, 16
  appearance 3
  in art 5–7, 44–45, 87–89, 92,
    108–10, 121–22, 136–37
  cannabis and 63–64, 239
  children and 49–50, 192
  consumption levels of 7, 51,
    123–24, 197, 211
  cost of 48, 51, 124, 198, 203,
    244
  Czech 11, 235–57, 243
  degeneracy and 6, 183–87, 191,
    194, 207
  effects of 27, 60–64, 238, 180–82,
    242, 244
  folklore in 16–17
  forms 18
  madness and 57–61, 180–81,
    209–10, 209, 249
  in medicine 16–20

  military failure and 187–88,
    212–23
  in politics 193–95, 198, 203, 209,
    211–13
  production of 22, 198, 236–37
  prohibition of 9–10, 207–8,
    212–14, 224–5
  role in culture 2–3, 55, 177, 240
  scientific research on 58–61,
    63–64, 175, 181–88, 199–203,
    245–48
  social status and 4, 65–66, 138
  strength of 22, 51, 243–45
  women and 5, 9, 40, 42–43, 49,
    188–90, 192
Absinthe (play) 204
Absinthe and Paranoia 210
Absinthe et Absintheurs 5, 26, 40,
    47–50, 181, 204
absinthe spoons 66–68
Académie de Médecine 183, 190,
    199–200, 203
Adam, Paul 170
Adams, Brooks 215
addiction (theory of) 88

Albert, Nicole 19

alcohol and temperance
movements 178–79, 185,
196–98, 200–2, 207–8, 209–11,
214, 225–26

Alcohol Makes You Mad (L'Absinthe)
211

Aleix, Jacinto 219

Algerian campaign 4, 19–20

Allais, Alphonse 80–81

Anderson, E.W. 120–21

Anderson, Elizabeth 226–27

Anderson, Sherwood 226–27

Andrée, Ellen 54, 162

Angelfire 244

Anti-Saloon League 225

Antisemitism 2, 194–95

d'Ardenne, Jean 41

Argentina 224

Arnold, Wilfred Niels 13, 92,
103–4, 199, 202–3

Artemisia species 15

Arthur, Stanley Clisby 220

Artist and Journal of Home Culture
164

Atlanta Constitution 188

Baker, Phil 14, 244

Balesta, Henri 26, 40, 47–50, 56–58,
132, 181, 204

Balfour, A.J. 186

Balzac, Honoré de 31

Banville, Théodore de 35, 72, 79

Baudelaire, Charles 26, 30, 32–35,
38, 52, 69, 137, 148, 174, 218
Fleurs du Mal, Les 34

Beardsley, Aubrey 8, 148, 152, 167,
169

Beardsley, Mabel 167

Beck, Theodric and John 57

Beerbohm, Max 152

Belgium 35, 41, 208–9, 213, 223, 244

Benasset, Emile, 47

Bernard, Emile 90–91, 94, 98–99,
105, 121–22, 170

Bible 15

Bigelow, Josephine 231

Björk 237

Black Box Recorder 243

Blue Cross 207

Blum, Léon 132

Blyth, Winter 141

Bohème, La 27

Bookman 85

Bourette, Henri 26

Bourgeois, Edmond 30

Brazil 224

British Medical Journal 246–47

Bruant, Aristide 128

Brunschwig, Hieronymus 18

Buchanan, Robert 174–75

Bulgaria 244

Bullier, François 40

Bywater, Michael 239

cafés (Paris):

  Académie 28, 73

  l'Avenir (later du Soleil) 78

  de Bade 38

  Black Piglet 112–13

  Brasserie des Martyrs 31, 32

  Brébant 31, 32

  Closerie des Lilas 120

  de Cluny 136

  Criterion 81

  de la Gare 94

  du Gaz 69

  Guerbois 38, 53, 124

  Hanneton 191

  La Taverne Montmartre 31

  Le Tambourin 91

  Madrid 34

  Momus 27

  Napolitain 66

  Nouvelle Athènes 38–39, 53, 124, 190, 233

  d'Orient 69

  Pigalle ('Rat Mort') 73, 190

  de la Régence 31

  Souris 191

  des Variétés 32

Callias, Nina de 79

Camondo, Count Isaac 166, 194

Canada 224

Carjat, Etienne 72

Carte, Richard D'Oyly 220

Casagemas, Carlos 192

Cazals, F.-A. 82–83

Cazebon, Pierre 227–28

Cézanne, Paul 97, 168

Charenton (asylum) 57, 61

Charlet, Marie 128

Chat Noir 78–81, 128

Christie's 1–2, 160–61

Claudel, Paul 82

Cloisonnisme 98

Cold War 235

Colson, Percy 160–61

Conder, Charles 152, 167, 175

Conrad, Barnaby 13

Contemporary Review 168

Coolus, Romain 127

Cooper, Douglas 165

Coppola, Francis Ford 241

Corelli, Marie 8, 12, 138

  Mighty Atom, The 155, 160

  Romance of Two Worlds, A 155

  Wormwood 8, 147, 155–58, 185

Cormon, Fernand 98, 126, 128

Corsair, Le 27

Couléru, Edmond 210

Courbet, Gustav 31, 33, 52

Courrier Français 136

Couture, Thomas 36–37, 53

Crackanthorpe, Hubert 167

  Wreckage 169

Crane, Walter 165

Cros, Antoine 43, 73

Cros, Charles 43–44, 52, 70, 72–73, 78–79, 85, 156

  'Hareng Saur, Le' ('The Red Herring') 44

  'Journée Verte, La' ('The Green Day') 44

  'Lendemain' ('The Morning After') 43, 251

Cros, Henri 43

Crosby, Harry 228, 230–31, 234

Crowley, Aleister 216–17

  Green Goddess, The 216

  White Stains 217

Culpeper, Nicholas 17

Curdy, Mac 111

Czechoslovakia (and Czech Republic) 235–37

Dadaism 81

Daily Mirror 168

Darwin, Leonard 186

Daudet, Alphonse 49, 73–74, 155, 195

  Sapho 77

Daudet, Léon 195

Daumier, Honoré 30

David, Marie 118

De Quincey, Thomas 28

Debussy, Claude 79, 133

Décadent, Le 7, 82

Degas, Edgar 5, 38–39, 44, 52–55, 88, 124, 129–30, 137, 154, 158, 194, 215, 220

  Absinthe, L' 1–2, 5, 52–55, 159–68

Delacroix, Eugène 30, 33

Delahaye, Marie-Claude 12–13, 96, 165, 210, 240, 243

Delius, Frederick 119

Department of Agriculture (USA) 224–25

Desboutin, Marcellin 53–54, 162

Dickens, Charles 57

Dictionnaire de Médecine 199

Douglas, Lord Alfred 149, 151, 168

Dowson., Ernest 35, 142–47, 155, 167, 169 170–74, 233

  Comedy of Masks, A 146

  Dilemmas 144, 146

  Pierrot of the Minute, The 146

  Verses 144, 171

Dreyfus, Alfred 194

Drumont, Edouard 194–95

Dubied, Daniel-Henri 21–22

Dumas, Alexandre 29, 49

Duparc, Louis 211

Dupuy, D. 61

Durand-Ruel, Paul 37

Duval, Jeanne 33

Ebers Papyrus 15

Ellis, Havelock 169

Emeryk, Wladyslaw 116

England 8–9, 138–76

essential oils 199–203

Eugenics Conference,
    International 185–87

Fénéon, Félix 177

Ferrer, Cayetano 219, 223

Figaro, Le 125

Finland 225

Foley, Charles 204

Food and Drug Administration
    (USA) 234

Forel, Auguste 207

France, Anatole 69

Franco–Prussian War 5, 52, 95, 220
    commune 52, 71, 97

French Art and English Morals 152

Frey, Julia 127

From Christiania's Bohemia 111

Fumistes 78

Gachet, Paul-Ferdinand 104

Galen 16

Gallienne, Richard Le 139–40, 148,
    167

Gauguin, Paul 7, 68, 89, 97–101,
    105–11, 112, 121–22, 125, 170,
    193, 228
    Café de nuit à Arles 99
    *Where do we come from? What are
    we? Where are we going?* 107

Gauguin, Sophie Mette (née Gad)
    97, 109, 110

Gauzi, François 129

Gazette de Paris 32

Germany 208, 212–13, 224

Gide, André 132

Girod, Adolphe 209

Gladstone, W.E. 138

Goluszko, Alex 239, 244

Goncourt, Edmond and Jules de
    24, 29, 32, 41, 62–63, 73–74, 179
    Diary 24
    Manette Salomon 41

Goodhart, Charles 144

Goudeau, Emile 78–79

Goulette, Léon 212

Grafton Gallery 162

Gray, John 148

Green Bohemia 237–38, 243

Green Carnation, The 149–50

Grosvenor Gallery 162

Guilbert, Yvette 129, 132

Guyot, Yves 202, 210

Harland, Henry 166–67, 175

Harper's New Monthly Magazine 148

Harper's Weekly 223

Harris, Frank 172

Harrison (Narcotic) Act 225

Heilig, Sterling 188, 190

Heiple, Fear 242

Hemingway, Ernest 228, 231–33
  Death in the Afternoon 231
  For Whom the Bell Tolls 232
  Sun Also Rises, The 232

Henriod, Henriette (Mère) 20–22

Henry, O. 220

Herbert, Victor 224

heure verte 25–26, 65–66

Hichens, Robert 150

Hill, Henry 159–60

Hill, Radomil 236–37

Hippocrates 16

Hirst, Henry Baker 218

Hirsuites 78

Hodgkinson, Tom 237–38

Höld, Karin M. 245–46

Holland 224

Howarth, George 238

Hugh, H.P. 131

Hughes, Albert and Allen 241

Hugo, Victor 28, 29

Humanité, L' 193

Huss, Magnus 56

Huysmans, Joris-Karl 40, 125, 149

Hutton, Ian 245

Hydropathe (and Hydropathes) 78–79

Iceland 225, 237

Iddon, Brian 238

Idler 237

impressionist exhibitions
  second 55
  fourth 97
  fifth and sixth 124–125
  seventh 125

In Absinthe Country 210

internet 235, 239, 241–42

de l'Isle-Adam, Villiers 39, 69, 79, 85

Italy 214

Jaeger, Hans 111

Jägermeister 247–48

Jarry, Alfred 7, 133–35, 136, 177

Jepson, Edgar 147

Jesus and Mary Chain 237

John Bull's Neighbour in Her True Light 154

Johnson, Lionel 140, 145, 148, 167, 175

Joyce, James 231

Juel, Dagny 112–16, 121

Kay, Arthur 161–62, 166

Kernahan, Coulson 139–40

Kock, Henri de 47

Laborde, Jean-Baptiste Vincent
190, 199, 200, 202

Lair, Pierre-Aime 57

Lalou, S.D. 175

Lancereaux, Etienne 179, 200

Lancet 9, 175–76, 179, 203, 233

Lanfray, Jean 10, 205–7

Lang, Andrew 174

Lanier, Doris 13

Larsen, Tulla 116

Latin Quarter 4, 27, 30, 78

Lawrence, D.H. 231

Ledoux, Eugène 55

Legrain, Paul-Maurice 47, 196

Lepelletier, Edmond 69, 84

lesbians 190–92

Leverson, Ada 64

Levien, D.J., *Wormwood* 241

Libre Parole, La 195

Lidforss, Bengt 113, 115

Lie, Johanas 118

Lindestolophe, Johan 87

Lippincott's Magazine 149

Lombroso, Cesare 186

London, Jack 228–29

Lorrain, Jean 79

Louisiana Purchase 217

Luhrmann, Baz 241

Lys, Georges de 137

MacColl, D.S. 163–64, 167

MacDonough, Glenn 223

Machen, Arthur 149

Maeterlinck, Maurice 83–84

Magazine of Art 153

Magnan, Valentin 59–61, 175–76,
181–87, 200, 202–3, 215, 225
*Principal Clinical Signs of
Absinthism, The* 183

Mahaim, Albert 206

Mallarmé, Stéphane 69, 79, 133

Manet, Edouard 3, 5, 35–40, 44, 46,
52, 88
Absinthe Drinker, The 5, 35–39, 46
Bon Bock, Le 54
Boy With Cherries 36

Marcé, Louis 59

Matisse, Henri 168

Maugham, W.S. 138–39
Moon and Sixpence, The 138
Of Human Bondage 139

Maupassant, Guy de 153

McKay, Charles 155

Meier-Graefe, Julius 113, 115

Mendès, Catulle 69, 151

Mercure de France 134

Meyer, Michael 120

Meynell, Alice 160

Michaud, Guy 86

Michel, Maurice 42

Miller, Henry 72, 75

Millot, Maurice 25

Minogue, Kylie 132, 241

Monde Plaisant, Le 26

Monet, Claude 38, 97, 110

Monge, Jules 95

Monticelli, Adolphe 91, 95–96

Montmartre 4, 127–28

Moore, George 38–39, 83, 142, 159,
    164

Moreau, Gustav 127

Morrow, W.C., *Over an Absinthe
    Bottle* 222

Motet, Auguste 58–59, 200

Moulin Rouge 130–131, 190

Moulin Rouge (film) 131–32, 231, 241

Munch, Edvard 7, 110–13, 116–17,
    119, 121–22

  *Absinthe Drinkers, The (The
    Confession)* 111

  Frieze of Life, The 116

  Hatred 117

  Madonna 113

  Murderess, The 117

  Sick Child, The 110

  Two Music-Making Sisters 112

Murger, Henri 4, 27–29

Musset, Alfred de 28–31

Napoleon, Louis (Napoleon III)
    24, 38, 51

Natanson, Thadée 135

Nation, Carrie 214

National Assembly 198, 209

Nerval, Gérard de 30, 31

New England Journal of Medicine 242

New English Art Club 8, 151–52,
    163

New Orleans 216–20, 226–28, 235

New Orleans Picayune 227

New York Times 220–22

Nilssen, Jappe 111

Nixey, Sarah 243

Noël, Benoît 96, 165

Nordau, Max 186

Notes and Queries 19

Old Absinthe House 216, 219, 223,
    227–28

Olsen, Richard W. 246

Opinions Scientifiques sur l'Absinthe
    204

Ordinaire, Pierre 20–21

Oulman, Alfred 212

ouzo 247–48

Pagnol, Marcel 67–68

Pall Mall Budget 163

Pall Mall Gazette 163, 169

Pan 115

Parnasse contemporain, La 69

Pater, Walter 166

Paul, Adolf 112

Péladan, Joséphin 41

Pêle-Mêle 61

Pelloquet, Théodore 32

Pepys, Samuel 19–20

Pernod Fils 196

Pernod, Henri-Louis 22

Perriam, Wendy 234–35

phylloxera (vine-pest) 50–51

Picasso, Pablo 3, 192–93, 214–15

  Absinthe Drinker 192

  Absinthe Glasses 214–15

  Dozing Absinthe Drinker 193

  Family of Saltimbanques, The 214

Pissarro, Camille 90, 97, 110, 125,
  194

Plarr, Victor 139, 141

Pliny 16

Poe, Edgar Allen 34, 100, 218–19

  Black Cat, The 219

Ponchon, Raoul 1, 32, 136, 201–2

Pontarlier 22, 209, 210, 240

population decline 187–89

Prague 11, 235, 236

Prestwich, Patricia 13, 194

Pretor-Pinney Gavin 237

prohibition (USA) 216, 225–28

Proust, Marcel 133

Przybyszewski, Stanislaw 113–16,
  119

  Overboard 115

  Mass of the Dead, The 114

public houses (London)

  Café Royal 233

  Cheshire Cheese 145

  Cock 145

Punch 169

Pythagoras 16

Quarterly Review 153

Queensberry, Marquis of 168

Quilter, Harry 164, 168

Rachilde (Marguerite Valette)
  134

Raffaëlli, Jean-François 45, 50, 90,
  123–26, 137

  Au Café, l'absinthe pernod 50

  Déclassés, Les (*Les Buveurs
    d'Absinthe*) 124

realism 31, 35

Reid, Alexander 161

Réja, Marcel 119

Renoir, Auguste 53, 90, 97, 124

Rénovation Esthétique, La 105

Revue Blanche, La 115, 132–33,
  135

Revue Socialiste, La 193

Rey, Félix 100–2

Rhymers' Club 145, 146, 147

Ribot, Alexandre 213

Richardson, Joanna 69

Richmond, Sir William Blake 164

Rieu, Marie ('Chien Vert') 73

Rimbaud, Arthur 6–7, 35, 68,
    71–77, 106–7, 137, 218
  Illuminations 75, 98
  Saison en enfer, Une 77, 82
Rollinat, Maurice 42, 79
romanticism 31
Rops, Félicien 35, 40–41
  Buveuse d'Absinthe, La 40
Ross, Robert 172
Rothenstein, William 152
  Men and Memories 169
Roulin, Jean 95, 101
Rude, Maxime 42
Russia 214, 225
Ruy Blas 212
Saintsbury, George 190, 249
Sallis, Rudolphe 128
Salon and Salon des Refusés
    37–38, 42, 55
Saltus, Edgar 77
Sand, George 28
Sarcey, Francisque 80
Sartain, John 218
Satie, Erik 79
Savoy 169, 171
Scènes de la vie de Bohème 27–28
Schleich, Carl 113
Schmidt, Henri 188–89, 209
Schuffenecker, Emile 98
Schwob, Marcel 151

Service, Robert 228–30
  Ballad of a Bohemian 229
Seurat, Georges, 90, 130
Sévigné, Marquise de 18
Sherard, R.H. 46–47, 49, 66, 88,
    155, 172, 174, 180–81, 198, 211
Sickert, Walter 8, 152, 159
Siege of London, The 153–54
Signac, Paul 94, 102, 130
Sivry, Charles de 70, 79, 85
Smithers, Leonard 169, 171
Société française du temperance
    196
Sournia, Jean-Charles 13, 58
Spain 235
Spanish Civil War 232
Spectator 163
Spender, John Alfred 163, 167
  New Fiction, The 168–69
  Stars and Stripes 243
Steer, Philip Wilson 152
Stenbock, Eric 148
Strindberg, August 7, 110, 112–21
  Father, The 113, 119
  Inferno 121
  Miss Julie 113
  Red Room, The 118
  Son of a Servant 117
Strindberg, Siri 118
Sturgis, Matthew 141

Sugar Cubes, The 237

Sullivan Ordinance 225

Swinburne, Algernon 86, 164, 174

Switzerland 10, 20–22, 205–8, 223

symbolism 81, 98

Symons, Arthur 145, 148, 156, 167, 169, 171, 233

Decadent Movement in Literature, The 148, 170

London Nights 148, 169

synthetism 98, 111, 170

Taggart, Chuck 235

temperance movement (British) 56

Tennyson, Alfred 160

tequila 248

Thackeray, W.M. 220

Thaulow, Fritz 110

Théâtre de l'Oeuvre 133

Théâtre des Variétiés 27, 54

Théâtre-Libre 133

Thomas, Dylan 86

Thomas, Frederick W. 218

Thornton, Alfred 152, 164, 165, 166

thujone 63, 211–12, 234, 244–46

Times 141, 162, 176, 203, 208

Toulouse-Lautrec, Henri de 3, 7, 89, 93, 124, 126–37, 155, 170, 177, 191, 192, 233, 243

A Grenelle: Buveuse d'Absinthe 136

Au Moulin Rouge 136

La Buveuse d'Absinthe 136

Monsieur Boileau au Café 136

Portrait de Vincent van Gogh 136

Trevor, John 152, 165

Twain, Mark 220

Uhl, Frida 114, 119

Union française antialcoolique 196

USA 10, 13, 210, 216–35, 240

Vaillant, Edouard 193, 199

Valedon, Suzanne 129–30

Valette, Alfred 134

van Gogh, Joanna 105

van Gogh, Theo 90, 93, 101, 105

van Gogh, Vincent 3, 7, 13, 68, 89–105, 120, 121, 123, 130, 137, 243

All-night Café, The 94

Verlaine, Paul 6–7, 35, 52, 68–78, 82–86, 106, 109, 123, 133, 137, 141, 142, 148, 169, 170, 174, 186, 233, 243

Confessions of a Poet 84

Poèmes Saturniens 69

Romances sans paroles 75

Sagesse 77

Verlaine, Mathilde (neé Maute) 70–73

Vernier, Valéry 29

Victoria, Queen 138

Vie pour Rire, La 61

Vietnam War 234

Virmaître, Charles 191

Vizetelly, Henry 164

Vogue, La 98

Vyver, Bertha 155

Waugh, Alec 233

Weber, Louise ('La Goulue')
128–29, 131, 190

Wedmore, Frederick 159

Weil-Picard, Arthur and Edmond
194

Westminster Gazette 163, 167

Whistler, James 159, 162

Whitman, Walt 220

Wilde, Oscar 64, 145, 149–51, 155,
156, 166, 168, 171–72, 175, 220
Importance of Being Ernest, The 151
Lady Windermere's Fan 151

Picture of Dorian Gray, The 149, 230
Salome 151, 170

wine producers 50–51, 197

Woman's World 156

Women 5, 9, 39–40, 42–43, 49

World War I 2, 10, 212–15, 230, 231

Wormwood 8, 12, 147, 155–58, 173

Yeats W.B. 145, 148, 169, 175

Yellow Book 167

Zacharie, Philippe 211

Zidler, Charles 130–31

Zola, Emile 42, 44, 53, 57, 73, 124,
141, 154, 155, 164, 194
Nana 191
Terre, La 147
Ventre de Paris, Le 124

Zolotow, Maurice 234

Zutistes 44, 78